Oak Tree Farm

Maggi Ansell

Oak Tree Farm

ISBN: 978-0-9940033-4-8

Dedication

To family and far-flung friends,
several of whom have stayed with us on the farm
enriching our lives and experiences.
And in memory of feathered, furry, and four-footed friends
without whom there would be no stories.

MAGGI ANSELL

Contents

Introduction

I always wanted to have a small farm. Many years ago when our children were little we escaped the city to live in South Wales on a couple of acres carved out of a hillside, surrounded by forestry-commission land. We kept a pig, a couple of goats and a few chickens. Our ancient cottage was damp. Water leaked through the cracked kitchen skylight after a goat sprang onto it from the hillside behind, and when it rained heavily water streamed down the 200-year-old chimney on the *inside* of the cottage. It was ours, and it was heaven. Our children in the countryside environment thrived as happy, free spirits. They attended an excellent, old-fashioned village school that paid attention to the three 'R's. After a couple of years, however, Robin's work called for us to move.

From then on we relocated many times and also to different countries as work demanded, but I never forgot dreams of a farm. When working in the Cayman Islands and with the children at university, we bought a confiscated drug boat and set sail across the South Pacific. Many adventures later we were caught in a Coral Sea cyclone and were rescued from the ocean by helicopter as our boat sank. This afforded the perfect opportunity to return to those earlier dreams and find a little farm.

Small-scale farming life I can definitely recommend, just not the particular route we took to get there!

MAGGI ANSELL

1. Holiday on Holiday Road

Man is free the moment he wishes to be ~ Voltaire

Horizontal rain lashes my face as I struggle to see the rescue helicopter in the gathering gloom of the evening. Floating in my yellow survival suit, I'm grateful for an illusion of safety as I catch glimpses of our sinking sailboat rising and falling with the mountainous seas of Cyclone Justin. Our survival dinghy is now upside down, tumbled by the breaking crest of a wave that pitched me into the sea, but I'm still attached to it by my harness. A dot of a man on a wire dangles beneath the helicopter battling to hover in 90 knot winds alternately rising and falling 15 metres with the waves to avoid being tangled in the sailboat's rigging.

My mind blanks, and I drift from reality to a serene place: dreaming of a farm where the sun shines on cows, pigs and chickens—miles and miles away from any ocean.

~~~~~~

Orca, a 50 foot sailboat and our home for seven years, sank off the Australian Great Barrier Reef. Robin and I were winched from the sea by helicopter. In an instant our voyaging dream was over and we returned to British Columbia dispossessed, with a strange sense of surrealism; briefly the subject of TV news and front page stories in newspapers; filming for Discovery Channel; and the focus of radio chat shows, before our story swiftly became insignificant and I was left with a burning desire for the farm, the dream of which had kept me sane and focused during the nautical nightmare.

~~~~~~

Saturday is auction day and prominent on our calendar. We navigate our way through groups of farmers and peer over wooden hurdle pens to see the livestock that is to be auctioned. It's very much a social event in this part of the Comox Valley; mostly elderly farmers joking and sparring with each other, smoking, and laughing; clutching polystyrene cups and scratching their caps on their heads. Some have brought their beasts to be auctioned, others have come hoping to pick up a good deal on additional stock. All are here for an interesting day out and the auction gets under way promptly.

Clustered together, several two-day old calves bawl plaintively for lost mothers; their soft uncomprehending eyes edged with white crescents staring from terrified faces. On our lofty bench above the auction ring we watch them huddle, their bony haunches sticky with carelessly daubed toffee-coloured glue, displaying paper squares with their lot number. The auctioneer's gavel meets his lectern with a splintering crack and the head flies off. If the calves weren't already scared witless, they are now. Nevertheless they have been knocked down to the highest bidder and a brown-coated attendant wielding two long poles hustles them through the exit as a further batch of bewildered calves is prodded into the ring. The auctioneer resorts to a makeshift gavel bearing a remarkable resemblance to a wheel wrench wrapped in rag, causing ill-suppressed mirth among the farmers.

A Swiss chalet style house on Vancouver Island overlooking Baynes Sound is now our temporary home, rented from a university professor. Gradually we adjust to the loss of the boat and our former lifestyle and decide it's time to embrace another challenge and search for that little farm. We become intoxicated with dreaming and planning.

"I think we should have a Jersey cow," I say as we sit on the balcony one morning sipping tea. "I'm sure I could learn to milk it. I remember the yellow salty butter we had from a friend's farm when I was young and oh, those fresh eggs, too.

Robin smiles, "We've got to have pigs. My dad reared them in our back garden during the war, and he still kept a pig when I was little— I used to ride Susie."

A small old-fashioned farm with a milking house cow, a beef cow or two, some pigs, sheep and chickens sounds ideal. About ten to fifteen acres; enough to supply most of our needs, with plenty left over to barter or take to a farmers' market. My heart soars at the thought of having a home again with our roots firmly in the soil. I scoff at the thought that it could be too much for us. We've haven't shirked hard work before and if we don't try, we'll never know.

We plan to view all feasible properties in our chosen geographic area; not too far south where land is overly expensive and not too far north where it's too cold and wet to farm. I feel certain it won't take long to find somewhere suitable so why can't we put the cart before the horse or, more accurately, some animals before the farm? Sounds perfectly sane and reasonable to me. After all, our lease says we can have a dog and a cat, and doesn't stipulate that we *can't* keep farm animals outside, and I'm not about to bother the municipality to see how they feel about the idea.

The local edition of the newspaper, Buy, Sell and Trade, is our best source of livestock information, and also the livestock auction barn in Courtenay. Each week we look forward to Tuesdays for the latest issue of the paper, and to Saturdays for our excursions to watch the animals being auctioned.

On this chilly October morning we drive to the auction barn through low-lying bands of fog drifting across the road, the cattle in the fields on either side appear legless, floating on the mists. We find a parking spot off the road and jump out of our 1973 Series II Land Rover, zip up our coats and pull on toques and gloves. It seems there's always an icy wind here, but at least it will be blowing away the mists today and perhaps allow a little sunshine and meagre warmth.

Watching auctions is not always heartwarming and we realize we'll have to be lucky to find a good sound creature here. Cows, pigs, sheep, chickens, ducks, geese, goats and the odd pony or donkey all pass under the hammer. There's usually a little group of Asian women close to the ringside always willing to pay 'Vun dollah' for spent poultry for the pot.

Following the auctioning of the animals, new owners load their purchases into trucks and trailers and carry them away leaving the barn empty. I give a quick thought to the bawling calves and hope they're going to a happy farm. Bidding now moves outside to the farm machinery which we watch with keen interest. Hundreds of pieces of ancient farm equipment and tools crowd together in seemingly haphazard piles. A bargain can be acquired here as long as we're not competing with a seasoned auction goer. A few of the items—which we feel we just won't be able to live without and must get *right* now—become ours today: a roll of fencing wire (always useful), bolt cutters, a wooden mallet and sundry mystery items in a cardboard box we haven't even looked in. Well, it *is* only $2.00. Must be a bargain. We gaze for a long time at a modern small excavator which hasn't reached reserve price but we know will never belong to us. We leave the auction in progress and head for the food concession where we find a restorative cup of hot chocolate and a deliciously unhealthy hamburger oozing with fried onions, grease and melted cheese. Wiping our fingers on napkins, we join the queue squeezing into a narrow corridor to the office to wait in line to pay for our purchases. With nothing else to do I people-watch and listen in on riveting snippets of conversation as Robin idly inspects the scruffy notices tacked up on the wall. Grubby business cards advertising varied and interesting services; puppies for sale; farm equipment; vehicles, and even boats. As the queue moves, we shuffle along.

"Have you seen this?" Robin points to a neatly lettered card tucked in among the old notices. "There's an ad here for some Buff Orpington chickens."

I raise an eyebrow and give him a sidelong glance. "Aren't they a heritage breed from Orpington in England?" Not wishing to let his thought fade into history I add, "What a great idea, we can call when we get home." Robin scribbles down the telephone number, we pay for our purchases and trundle everything into the Land Rover. Will he really let me have a few creatures soon?

Our phone call about the chickens is answered by Lori in Whiskey Creek only about 50 minutes away from Holiday Road. She's been raising heritage breed birds for some years and has a few surplus young point-of-lay chickens so we make an appointment to visit her on Sunday afternoon. Meanwhile in a state of great anticipation we drive to the local feed store to buy shavings, chicken pellets, feed containers and a water dispenser, then prepare the little shed in the garden to accept the new arrivals.

After lunch on Sunday, in classic fall sunshine we load up large cardboard boxes and set off for Lori's farm. I hop out to open her gate and close it after Robin drives into the farmyard. White Muscovy ducks and Embden geese wander around with broad breasted bronze turkeys. Puffs of woolly sheep graze in the distance and a rich golden coloured Jersey cow in the adjacent field slowly turns her head to cast an eye in our direction while maintaining her rhythmic chewing. I only take my eyes off her when two farm dogs bound up to us; one large old labrador, with a propellor tail, and a young blue heeler pup dividing his time between bouncing up at us and attempting to herd a duck. This little farm is perfect, *exactly* what I would love to own one day.

A petite, vivacious young woman trips out of the cottage licking something off her fingers. She grins, "I've just iced a birthday cake," she says, capturing the last specks of sugary confection with her tongue. Lori has black flashing eyes and burnished chestnut hair cut in a bob. She fairly sparks energy.

The Buff Orpingtons are in a large enclosure, big glossy birds with gold feathers and fluffy skirts. Next to them are equally handsome large chickens with feathers as green/black as a raven's wing contrasting with their blood red combs. "What are they?" I ask Lori, "they're beautiful too."

"Australorpes; developed in Australia from the blood lines of the Buff Orpingtons." We make a mental note of this for future reference. "I keep them separate for breeding purposes," she says, "but most of the time they're all free ranging."

Bodo, Lori's husband and many years her senior, joins us with a curt nod before they enter the Orpington enclosure armed with a large fishing keep-net. This is an operation I need to watch carefully.

Lori points to one chicken and Bodo deftly swoops down on it with the net and the bird is captured. After darting and pouncing for a while they manage to select eight birds for us, plus one young Buff Orpington rooster. "They all have wing tags," she says.

"Wing tags? What are wing tags?" I ask.

"When flocks are tested and are found to be free of pullorum disease, each bird has a tag attached to one wing just where it joins the body. My flocks have all had blood tests and are all clear, so they have wing tags."

"What's pullorum?" We're new to this, so must keep asking questions.

"Salmonella, our flocks are free from salmonella."

We chat about her farm and animals. "We're looking for a small farm," I say, and tell her of our aspirations. It's always good to pick up pointers from experienced people raising obviously happy healthy stock.

"If I can help you with anything or find any other animals for you, you can always give me a call, I've got loads of useful contacts."

Our transaction complete, we tuck the birds in their boxes for the drive home. Before we leave I say, "Can we just see your Jersey cow please? She's gorgeous, what's her name?"

Lori smiles. "Bodo calls her 'Cow'," she says, rolling her eyes.

Cow's coat glows like copper in the sun, complemented by cream undersides and black face and leg markings, and she sports upward curving horns. She's oblivious to her beauty and I could melt, just looking at her.

Our homeward drive seems short, there's so much to think about. "This is exciting Rob, now we have our very first farm creatures and they are Salmonella free. How good is that?"

After a week the chickens have acclimatized to their new surroundings and already started laying attractive pinkish-brown eggs and we've made our first farm sale of one dozen. They're not full-sized eggs yet, but the hens will quickly mature and lay larger ones.

Soon after moving into Holiday Road, Readers Digest calls asking to interview us for a *Drama in Real Life* article about the helicopter rescue from the ocean. I explain that I've written for several magazines and would like the opportunity to write the story myself, and they readily agree. This is the beginning of a painstaking and demanding relationship with the editor to produce for them a minutely-detailed lengthy account involving exhaustive interviewing of the rescue helicopter crews and invoking Australian and US Freedom of Information Acts for the absolute accuracy that Readers Digest demands and checks for veracity. Now I know that if something appears in Readers Digest it is true, and has been checked and rechecked worldwide. If I thought I'd have time on my hands now, I was wrong.

At the beginning of our new life, each morning we wake to the compelling crowing of Bertie the Buff Orpington rooster welcoming the day and proclaiming dominion over his territory—the rallying call to rise at the very heart of traditional farming life. I couldn't be happier.

2. *Finding Perfection*

You are never too old to set another goal or to dream a new dream ~
C.S. Lewis

Autumn at Holiday Road passes swiftly. Gardening when the weather's mild and sunny, or a combination of researching, reading and making plans for our future farm life, when it's wet. Each time another property appears on the market we eagerly view it, thinking *maybe this will be the one.* Alas we look at many unsuitable farms: too big or too small; in a state of disrepair and too costly to return to former glory; in the wrong location—too swampy or too exposed—or simply too expensive. If nothing else, we're gaining a good knowledge of areas of Vancouver Island. I'm impatient, but Robin assures me we'll find the right place sometime. Meanwhile we are fortunate to be in a beautiful location and getting to know several of our neighbours especially the closest, Carol and Bill, directly across the road.

Some afternoons when weather permits, Carol calls from her deck, "Maggi, come on over, it's 5 o'clock," to entice me to visit for a G &T and, not wishing to appear churlish, some afternoons I go. We sit on her deck overlooking the oyster-producing waters discussing our farm-hunting progress. Carol loves all the details. If she spots Robin in the garden too, she calls across the road to inveigle him into joining us, rather like issuing a royal command. On rare occasions he does.

Bill's a retired fire chief from Vancouver and he invites Robin to become a volunteer firefighter for Fanny Bay alongside four of our other neighbours who are part of the crew. Once Robin is trained he's equipped with a pager and waits for a call to action. Callouts are frequent; the bulk to motor vehicle accidents but sometimes a rural house needs assistance, usually with a chimney fire and mostly in the hours of darkness.

Robin explains the procedure. "As the house always seems to be at the end of long, single-track winding driveway," he says, "we always back the fire truck all the way in because there's not enough room to turn round by the house, and the property likely has a propane tank that could blow-up. This way, at least we have a slightly better chance of escaping and driving away forwards, rather than backwards, in the dark." He continues to explain, "The amazing thing is that we even find the houses as most don't have civic house numbers visible on the road, hence the recent push to have everyone use a reflective house number in full view."

Christmas on Holiday Road blows in on the heels of a week of fat white snowflakes whirling and spinning as though a giant feather pillow is spilling its contents from a sulky sky. The chickens are nonplussed at their first white world and are not keen to walk or scratch in the snow. It doesn't prevent Vancouver friends Jan and Donna from joining us and bringing their marmalade kitten for his first encounter with the great outdoors. He's not a country boy and his walks on a new leash are more of a drag with all four paws and claws extended. Thinking he might enjoy things more, they tether him to a tree but in seconds he's run round and round the tree until he's stuck fast. Their week's stay ends with a riotous New Year's Eve party involving the neighbours too and, strangely, no one can remember much about it apart from the fact that someone suggested all meeting for brunch together the following day, but it was a very subdued group who gathered, picking daintily at the food. Next year we'll be more circumspect, or will we?

The beauty of the British Columbian winter is that it isn't a protracted affair and by February snowdrop bulbs melt spots through the January snows, upthrusting their leaves and blossoms, raising drooping spirits and allowing dreams of spring days. The chickens are jubilant to see the re-emergence of a few blades of grass and busy themselves digging for bounty. It's a good time to watch the wildlife too. Before the snow has disappeared a pair of bald eagles start adding chunky branches and boughs as thick as a man's arm to their nest in a veteran Douglas fir tree 15 metres from our fence line. The tree towers over the surrounding forest and is the ideal real estate location with unobstructed flying access to their nest from several directions, and is half a kilometre from the shoreline where there's a plentiful supply of fishy gourmet delights. Their lofty abode is already massive from several previous years' additions and must weigh hundreds of pounds, but they're still keen to re-model and improve their dwelling to add this season's latest fashions and gizmos for the coming eagle confinement and new family. We watch their daily progress through binoculars and follow their path to the shoreline as they fish. Later, we discover it's a double edged sword having nesting eagles as neighbours.

In March the robins are in abundance on the lawn and stand poised with heads cocked, listening for the sounds of worms beneath. They like to start early and raise three broods in a year if possible. On the adjacent small poplar plantation young leaves shimmer silver-green in the sunlight and our flower borders are bright with daffodils. Hyacinths have pushed their snub-nosed points above the earth and break open to reveal coloured stars and share their heady fragrance.

Spring is such a vibrant time. The chickens are forever pecking and scratching, their golden plumage flouncing in the breeze. The result of their varied and ceaseless feeding is that they're laying well and the eggs have rich orange yolks.

As the daylight hours increase one of the hens refuses to leave the nest. "Do you think we have a broody hen?" I ask Robin, feeling a bit cheated because a broody hen stops laying and I need eggs to supply to my rather eager customers. Then I realize this presents a great opportunity. "Hey, Rob, if she'll sit on a few fertile eggs, maybe she'll hatch some new chicks for us."

I select large sized well-shaped eggs and prepare a cardboard box for her with a cosy nest of shavings and hay. She'll need privacy and security in a sheltered area, so I put the box in the studio that is attached to the garage. It makes an ideal location although I'm not sure our wonderful landlord would agree. We erect a wire pen to keep her enclosed and cover her floor with plastic and newspapers, adding a bowl of water and dishes of grain and pellets. In the evening as soon as it's dark we slide the nine perfect eggs under her.

Each morning I give Robin a 'broody' report which usually consists of variations of, "Henny Penny's still on her nest." I refresh the newspapers when necessary and commit the old to the compost heap. Broody hens will produce only an occasional, but nose-wrinklingly, throat-gaggingly awful poop. This is quite normal for them, but rather less than desirable in the studio. Henny Penny is dedicated to her calling and remains in a semi-comatose state staring into the future, from time to time using her beak to rotate the eggs under her breast as they develop.

Halfway through the 21-day incubation period I reach under the hen during the evening and gently take out each egg in turn and 'candle' it by holding it over a bright flashlight to see if there's a dark shadow of a growing embryo inside. I find only one clear unfertilized egg to remove.

I will the time to pass quickly and on day 18, I creep into the studio and sit very close to the nest, listening. Before long I'm rewarded by a few tiny peeps made by the almost-developed chicks communicating through the shell with their mother. Day 19 there's more peeping, but on day 20 all is quiet. I carefully reach under the hen and withdraw one egg. It has a tiny hole in the shell and poking through is the tip of the chick's temporary egg tooth used to create an escape hatch. The chick is now breathing air and will slowly rotate over the coming hours, jabbing its tooth at the shell until it can hinge open the lid and struggle out. It's a massive undertaking. Newly hatched, the chick is wet and appears skinny and ugly but with the heat from its mother's body it rapidly dries to yellow fluffy perfection. It has no need to eat or drink for two days as it has sufficient nutrition from the remains of the egg sac in its body.

Eight bright-eyed yellow chicks are soon running around in the studio while mother hen, fluffed up and with wings held away from her body, stalks around in protective manner. Chicks peck instinctively and soon discover that they can't pick up the newsprint letters, so ignore them in favour of their tiny chick starter granules. They also have the endearing instinctive behaviour of taking two steps forwards then raking their feet backwards and looking to see what they have unearthed. An excellent tool in the barnyard but in the bowls of feed it's not quite so beguiling and broadcasts tiny pellets everywhere.

We've raised our first farm livestock and we have yet to find a farm. As the days progress and the chicks grow, I transfer them from the studio to the hen house outside with a wire chicken run. Every now and again we hear a piercing heart-rending alarm call from a chick that has managed to escape the pen but can never find a way to return. Now we can't wait for them to grow so they become too large to squeeze through the mesh.

The farm hunt continues in earnest. With spring, more properties appear on the market but few are agriculturally suited. "There's a farm in Port Alberni that might be worth looking at, although it's a bit large," says Robin, "it's been empty some time, so let's go tomorrow and have a look."

Port Alberni is at the end of a 60 km Norwegian-style inlet from the Pacific Ocean, bounded on the land side by the snow-capped Beaufort range of Mountains and tucked in a bowl carved out by the ancient Comox glacier, the remnants of which are still visible. It's a breathtaking landscape. We drive round the perimeter of the 55-acre farm that has lain fallow for years. It has a dank dingy one-level farmhouse and two massive barns requiring multiple repairs.

"I don't think this is for us, do you?" Robin says.

I shake my head. "It's a lot more than we want to take on."

On the way out of town driving towards the snowy peaks of Mount Arrowsmith, I suggest calling in at a realtors we haven't visited before. We explain our quest to the husband and wife team on duty and the husband remembers a possibly suitable place listed a couple of years ago and thinks it was removed from the books unsold. They conduct extensive research, rifling through all the old file cabinets, find the phone number and call the owner who says he'd still like to sell. Without delay we jump into the realtors' Lincoln and take a 14 km drive out of town towards the old mountain logging road leading to Comox, the other side of the mountain.

The 13.5 acre property lies beside the Beaufort Mountains, well off the beaten track and with total privacy. Close to the dead end of a 300 metre gravel road a large metal farm gate stands open. We drive in along an impressive curved approach, lined with young garry oak trees on one side and spring bulbs growing in the grass on the other, towards a Dutch barn where the drive forks and we curve to the right to the farmhouse sitting at the edge of the forest. A large oak tree grows from a bank, its branches spreading out to provide shade to a picturesque pond.

My heart thumps. We'd better snap this up quickly, but I daren't say anything to Robin who hates to be pushed into anything. I've already been captivated, but then I've done that before with other properties which haven't really been suitable, such is my desire to find some roots. Robin is much more cautions; there's a lot to find out yet.

The farmhouse is bounded on the south and east sides by Douglas fir and hemlock trees; many are second-growth forest and over 30 metres tall. It is made from cedar milled from the property some years ago. It was built by a Dutchman who had a large family when he started the project but most of his children had left home by the time the house was completed. It is over large with a full unfinished basement half below ground which would make an excellent area for a large workshop for winter, plus room for storing animal feed instead of in the barns, and also an area that could accommodate moveable pens for any newborn or ailing animals. I already have it planned out in my mind. The stairway from the basement rising to the kitchen is beside a huge custom-built wood-burning furnace. The living area on the second floor overlooks the land. From an open plan kitchen and dining room two steps drop down to a sunken lounge with a baronial sized log fireplace. This floor also houses the large laundry room; a half bathroom, and the master bedroom with a 5-piece ensuite that could house a family of four on its own. The upper floor has another bathroom and four more bedrooms, three are 5 metres square, and one is 9 by 4.5 metres. Way too much space for the two of us but a terrific place for visitors and for entertaining.

There are three barns and a workshop, two have upper floors for storage, and there are other smaller outbuildings. The scope and potential is vast as much of the land is underdeveloped. The owner tells us not to expect to be able to grow pasture on the field on the brow of the hill, but he doesn't know we're not afraid of hard work. We expect to have to prepare, plough, rock-pick, enrich, plant and irrigate to create dairy pasture. This whole valley was wooded once but now has large dairy farms. They did it in the old days with sheer back-breaking work, and we can do it too.

After several visits, research and talks with the local Agricultural Office we finally agree on a purchase price with the seller and set a closing date of July 6, some three months away.

It's difficult to grasp the idea that we're driving home today as potential small farmers. I'm wrapped in euphoria, thinking enthusiastic thoughts of the future when Robin says to me, "Remember all those little oak trees lining the driveway and the big oak by the pond?"

"Yes, I do. Oaks make me think of Sherwood Forest and strength."

"Why not call it Oak Tree Farm?"

"That's perfick, Pa," I say, "just perfick."

We've found our farm at last. Now I can throw myself wholeheartedly into the really fun part, finding more animals.

"Champagne?" Robin asks when we arrive home. "Time to celebrate!"

3. Population Explosion

I am fond of pigs. Dogs look up to us. Cats look down on us. Pigs treat us as equals ~ Winston Churchill

Leaning his arms on the gate, Robin looks into the piglet enclosure. "Who'd have thought that they were so sick a few weeks ago?" He smiles as piglets #1, #2 and #3 are busy using their snouts like well-sharpened ploughs, cutting through the sod with devastating ease and turning the clumps, ignoring the spring grasses on top in favour of searching for roots and other tasty morsels beneath. These chubby pink piglets barely survived their traumatic beginning but are now thriving.

Last month we bought the little gilts from the auction barn. We should have known better. "A special consignment," they said, "coming from Alberta," and at a "special price," just for us. It seems we'd been noticed as we watched the movement of livestock, and were singled out since we'd enquired about piglets in the past. It was "a deal," they said, or perhaps more correctly, should have said "a steal."

On piglet delivery day we tuck into a hearty breakfast of eggs, bacon, toast, marmalade and tea. Despite the spring flowers being in full bloom and the trees decking themselves in fresh young green, a late frost lingers on the grass in the shady areas. Rather chilly for young piglets. We stuff the back of the Land Rover with straw and head for our rendezvous with the pig truck. It's sickening to see the terrified youngsters huddling together or skidding around in the cavernous semi-trailer with insufficient bedding to keep them warm. We choose what look to be the most robust of the scrawny creatures and pop them into their straw bed in the Land Rover where they immediately burrow down for warmth and comfort. They remain hidden on the journey home warming up by snuggling together.

At Holiday Road their house is ready, complete with an infrared heat lamp. Although they are very nervous they settle in and will eat and drink as long as we keep our distance. They don't have many reasons to like humans yet. However, within two days the piglets are obviously unwell. Anything they ingest causes immediate profuse and watery projectile diarrhoea.

This couldn't be a worse time to have an emergency family call from England, but I have to fly there immediately, leaving Robin to deal with his three sickly babies, administering electrolytes, warm watered-down milk, and scour mix. After a few days he has an epiphany. "I wonder if I could feed them natural probiotic yogurt to replenish the flora in their guts," he says.

Our neighbour Carol is fascinated watching Robin's dedication and all his endeavours for these poor little beasts. She has a bird's eye view from her deck so when she visits him, Robin sets her a task.

"Could you find me a source of natural probiotic yogurt?" Easy to do today but not so readily available then. Our neighbour rises to the task admirably. In short measure she acquires what is needed from a health food store, and a couple of jugs of milk.

Robin rolls up his sleeves, puts on his apron and gets to work using the original yogurt as a starter to grow copious amounts, liberally feeding it to the babies who now have also succumbed to sticky eyes. He will never give up on them. Several meals of yogurt per day, supplemented with bread from the bakery to line their compromised stomachs, and also frequent eye-bathing with boric acid solution. He continues tirelessly for three weeks and finally they show signs of improvement, stop scouring and begin putting on weight. His efforts have paid off.

On my return from England Robin shows me his three little pigs with great pride, and rightly so. They dig and cavort and jostle each other at the trough and are now the picture of good health. (It was not until a year or so later when we had cause to visit the auction barn again that we had the exquisite pleasure of telling the auctioneer, who remembered us and probably wished he didn't, that not only did the sickly piglets survive with tender care, but the friendliest one who we chose to keep and breed had just given birth to nine beautiful piglets. Oddly, he had nothing to say.)

Back at Holiday road our healthy pigs are fitting seamlessly into the daily routine with much less work for Robin, so we cast our minds to other creatures.

Karen, a young firefighter neighbour and her friend Jacki have a small farm further up the hill with seven or eight goats that they take on daily walks to browse the bushes. Chickens and turkeys wander freely in their yard and they keep a sow and raise piglets from time to time. They also have two North Country Cheviot sheep: Purdy, who has recently given birth to fine twin ram lambs, and Prudence who is due to lamb shortly. Space is at a premium for them and as we have pasture available we offer to let the sheep stay with us for an extended vacation to save us the trouble of mowing the landlord's grass and to give their land a break.

Purdy arrives first with her lambs Rambo and Chop, then two weeks later Prudence joins us with Curly and Shanks. On being reunited the ewes have a bit of a power tussle pushing and shoving each other for supremacy while the four youngsters race off to more fruitful and enjoyable pursuits leaping and springing and totally ignoring their mums as all good young lambs will—until they're hungry. Nothing more readily raises a smile on the face of even the crustiest of persons than watching the antics of lambs gambolling in the spring sunshine, chasing and head-butting each other. They particularly enjoy a tree stump that they spring onto, playing King of the Castle until deposed by a sibling.

The lambs grow fast on their mother's very rich milk. However, our notion that they will just nibble contentedly on lush emerald grass is wishful thinking. We find the mothers teaching them to bark the ornamental trees which means we have to erect temporary electric fences to protect them all.

This is seen as an invitation to the lambs who enjoy the challenge of crawling on their knees under the wires to get at the low branches. Their lanolin rich wool seems to act as insulation making them impervious to the electric charge and they only get a shock if they touch the wire with their noses. When they're not pushing the limits of the fencing, they alternate that activity with pushing on the chicken wire in an attempt to reach the chickens' pellet feeder. "The lambs are really cute though aren't they Rob?" I say, cocking my head and looking at him.

"Well, *you* might think so," he says, "but you're not the one erecting and mending fences. I'm thinking of revising my opinion since we're constantly having to watch to see what they're up to next."

"Yes; well that's because it's someone else's property. On our own farm, we can be a bit more relaxed, and we'll put up permanent fencing."

"I just love your use of the royal 'We'," Robin says.

Spring is certainly a busy time and we're enjoying every minute of it. For some unaccountable reason we haven't yet found the opportunity to tell our landlord that we don't actually have a dog or a cat, but we do have 8 chickens, 1 rooster, 8 chicks, 3 piglets, 2 sheep and 4 lambs. We've decided to operate on the 'need to know' basis.

Along with spring, comes a gardening challenge from Carol. One afternoon we're sitting on her deck for a pre-dinner cocktail. It's been sunny all day and there are balmy breezes riffling through the little paper napkins on the glass picnic table. Carol and I sip our G&Ts, pondering on the beauty of the day and waxing poetical about this charming location on the water; how great it is to have the occasional piercing eagle squawk from our very own eagles, and our general good fortune in being each other's neighbour—a G&T will do this, of course.

"I want to do some gardening and grow a few vegetables instead of just flowers." Carol says. She's been watching our progress reclaiming an old garden area, teasing the weeds from around the strawberry plants in the raised beds, and digging up virgin soil ready to plant potatoes.

"Let's have a gardening challenge," she continues, "we'll grow the same things and I'll bet you anything you can grow, I can grow better."

"Right," I say, "you're on."

Our house stands on the corner of Holiday Road and a track leading to the small poplar plantation. The garden area is highly visible to all who pass by. Carol starts to develop a patch adjacent to the side of her house, also clearly visible to the road and to us. We toil and dig and collect seaweed from the beach. Bill, Robin, Carol and I all go together and fork up heaps into Bill's trailer. Of course, this arduous task necessitates sustenance with a glass of Bill's home-made wine supped as we sit on a driftwood log on the beach. Our gardens become precious and protected and we surreptitiously check each other's efforts.

When Robin and I return from town one day we find a big sign in the middle of our garden proclaiming *'PIT STOP FOR TRUCKS'* angled towards passing traffic. Currently the road is very busy as there are literally dozens of gravel trucks travelling up and down past us every day to supply gravel to the new highway that is being built a few miles up the hill. The trucks must slow down past our garden to stop for a rail crossing. Carol and Bill watch our reactions to the notice and can barely contain themselves, chortling on their deck.

"Right," says Robin, "we'll get them." On our next trip to town we collect supplies and watch and wait for our opportunity. A few days later it arrives when Bill and Carol leave the house together. We drive in stakes to outline Carol's vegetable garden and wind yellow plastic tape around proclaiming, *'TOXIC WASTE AREA—KEEP OUT.'* We add a couple of large universal trefoil hazardous waste signs, for good measure.

As retaliation is the name of the game, we know there will be repercussions, and it will likely take the form of something in our garden again. It is essential, of course, that all of this is highly visible to other neighbours, truck drivers and general passers-by.

Their next attempt to get even must be foiled, and employing our motion-sensor pink plastic pig will be perfect. Anything passing in front of a hole in its snout blocks the light and causes the pig to proclaim loudly, *"OINK OINK....OINK OINK....OINK OINK."*

Now, to enter our fenced garden area it is necessary to pass through a little rustic wooden trellis archway bearing honeysuckle vines. We place the pig on the ground at the base of the archway and cover it with some dead grasses, then switch it on. It works exactly as planned.

Unfortunately we're not there to witness the results because they don't attempt retaliation until we've departed, but Carol tells us that Bill goes through the trellis first, activates the piggy who dutifully OINKs. Bill, who is 6'1" is so startled he leaps up and cracks his head on the top of the trellis.

When we return home we are not surprised to find a camping toilet complete with a toilet roll in the centre of our garden with another *TRUCK—PIT STOP* sign.

The joke concludes later in the evening when we're invited to Carol and Bill's for supper and I think I score the final point. I hand Carol a ziplock sandwich bag, saying, "You won, it worked. I found this." Carol takes the gift, looks at it, shrieks and flings it to the ground. "What on earth's the matter?" I say. After all, the bag only contains two harmless lengths of 3 cm diameter wood which have been dampened then, just moments ago, heated gently in the microwave.

We call a gardening truce and raise a glass to our stirling efforts.

The horticulture work and jollity doesn't bother the eagles one iota. The parents take turns incubating the eggs and hatching occurs at the beginning of May. Initially we think there are two offspring, but later there appears to be only one. Maybe the older one tossed out the younger. Apparently if the older sibling is a female, and therefore always larger, it often happens that she will dispatch her smaller male sibling. Simply charming.

Our solo eagle chick grows rapidly as mum and dad both feed it and there's a great availability of fish so close by. As the chick remains in the nest for 11-12 weeks we will never actually see it fledge although Carol will, I'm sure. She'll give us a blow by blow account with only the merest hint of a smirk on her face because we've missed it. When we do leave Holiday Road in July for our new farm, the chick is at the stage of jumping up and down in the nest, flapping stubby wings and squawking its head off demanding immediate attention as if it's always hungry and never fed. It has no predators, of course, so can draw attention to itself without fear of harm. We hear later from Carol that it fledges successfully and for a long time is seen wheeling around the skies with its parents.

Fortunate has smiled on us once again and we bring a second broody hen into the studio to set her on fertile eggs. I sincerely hope that this is not the time our landlord makes an unscheduled visit. I'm not even sure that we could manage a scheduled visit. Where would we hide the animals? Certainly he could rightly object to the aroma from the mother hen in the studio.

In three weeks the hen hatches more tiny yellow chicks. It coincides with a glorious spell of hot weather and mother is soon in the yard showing the chicks around and fussing when they run in and out of the flower beds beneath the old fashioned crimson peonies, as the scents of summer blossoms waft on the warm air. It's amusing to watch their early attempts at dust bathing. Step 1. Cock head on one side. Step 2. Lower body and flap lower wing stub in dust. Step 3. Rise and flap. Step 4. Repeat process for other side.

All too soon it's time for Karen's lambs to go to the butchers as they are market weight. The wind has changed and the weather turns cloudy with a light drizzle. It's a dismal day, as befits the task at hand. Jacki arrives with her truck and we spend an energetic hour guiding, luring and penning the youngsters, so that Robin can rugby-tackle them to the ground and we can then jointly lift them into the truck. Along with the rugby tackles goes some suitable coarse rugby language. Just when we think we've got one cornered, it bounds on top of the compost heap, leaps over the fence, and races round the field. We have to ask Bill to help and act as gate man while we guide and flush them into the pen yet again. Eventually with lots of encouragement from other bystanders who have magically appeared, but are not keen to soil their hands, we get all four in Jacki's truck and go with her to help unload. Fortunately unloading is a much simpler and less stressful process for humans and lambs alike. I am glad they're unaware of what's going on.

The mums bleat for one day, missing their youngsters as their udders become distended, but they are quiet the next day and their udders shrink down within a week.

When our favourite Buy, Sell and Trade newspaper arrives in the stores on Tuesdays we eagerly pounce upon it and turn to the livestock pages. We've been looking for our Jersey cow so we can have rich Jersey milk and make butter and cheese. We've already contacted a local Jersey dairy farm, but there's no hope of getting a heifer or even an old cow from them.

"Hey, there's a Jersey heifer in calf for sale," Robin says, "in Cedar."

"Really? What's the number?" I immediately phone and the cow hasn't been snatched up yet so we make arrangements to view tomorrow as Cedar is only an hour or so down the road. I find it difficult to apply myself to any task for the rest of the day. All I can see in my mind is a beautiful Jersey cow, I so hope she'll be suitable.

Skip, as she's currently called, is a pale honey and cream coloured purebred three year old Jersey heifer and is in calf.

"She's already had one calf," her owner Marjorie says, "but cows are called heifers until they've had their second calf. I'm still milking her but will dry her off now to give her a break before her next calving." She explains that Skip was bred with a Jersey/Dexter bull whose parentage is Jersey mother, and Dexter father, the Dexter being a miniature Irish breed, usually black, but sometimes red. We decide immediately that Skip must be ours. The owner asks if she can please keep her until August as she has the cow entered in the Vancouver Island Exhibition in Nanaimo. This works perfectly for us, since we won't be taking over our farm until early July and bringing a cow onto the Holiday Road property might just be pushing things a tad too far. Difficult to conceal those cow flops.

We hand over a substantial deposit, absolutely thrilled that we have the start of our herd and amazingly, she'll shortly be calving and giving us milk. Marjorie estimates this will be at the end of September. Things just get better and better and sometimes I wonder why things are working out so well for us.

"Oh Rob," I say as we are heading home, "we're so lucky and we won't have long to wait for a calf and Jersey milk."

Now that we've found our Jersey cow, we offer to buy the two ewes, Purdy and Prudence from Karen and Jaki. While not being the easiest sheep to deal with—the North Country Cheviot breed being renowned for being skittish—we think it's possibly a case of better the devil you know. Happily, our offer is accepted, so we now proudly own two sheep and are contemplating more soon after we move in.

4. We Bought the Farm

There are some days when I think I'm going to die from an overdose of satisfaction ~ Salvador Dali

What a sublime day! Following heavy overnight rain the clouds drift away leaving the sun to steam the moisture from the earth. Possession of the farm is set for noon when the seller will hand us the keys. In bubbling spirits we set off to Port Alberni in a Ford king cab truck towing a borrowed trailer. Both are filled with lumber, electrical cable, chicken wire, fencing wire and tools. We reach Port Alberni a little early so stop for hot chocolate and an oatmeal cookie at the local Tim Hortons, arriving at the farm 14 km outside town on the dot of 12 noon.

The owner meets us at the end of the driveway shaking his head and refuses to give us the keys. "No, you can't have them," he says, shaping his lips in an inverted U and affecting a supercilious smirk.

"But we had a phone call from our lawyer," I say, "telling us that the monies were cashed this morning by your lawyer. As it's past noon the farm is now officially ours."

"*I* haven't had confirmation of that, so you can't have the keys and you can't come in."

I ached to say, "Not much of a lawyer is he? Not exactly up to snuff."

Delays are distinctly unnerving and we want to run power to the animal barn before returning to Fanny Bay. "Do you think you could call your lawyer please?" I ask, "we'll just walk around outside for a while."

Robin says nothing but is looking decidedly stormy. We wander the farm idly inspecting the outbuildings and I become increasingly distressed. Despite his frown, Robin has an outward aura of calm.

It's after 2:00 p.m. when the owner eventually calls us over and gives us the keys.

"So what's the excuse for the hold up?" I can barely contain my irritation.

"My lawyer went out for a long lunch and he's only just got back to his office." he says, and his cheeks puff in and out as he chortles.

"I don't think it's funny. It's pathetic." I tell him.

I can't believe the seller is being so insensitive, especially when we're allowing this man to store his goods and furniture in *our* barns and are even letting him plug in his freezers into *our* power supply until his new house is built on the 50-acre plot between the farm and Mount Hal.

Keys in hand, and out of earshot, I say to Robin, "I so wanted to take a swipe at that odious man." Robin looks at me from under raised brows for a moment but says nothing. Maybe he knows it's wisest not to prod a hornet's nest. Evil thoughts run through my head and I think I'd like to unplug his freezers 'by accident.'

After unloading the truck and trailer we now don't have enough time to run power to the barn so just look around inside the farmhouse, assessing the number of new door locks we must buy as the vendor will not be moving far away and there could be lots of odd keys floating about.

Back at Holiday Road we feed and secure the animals for the night and can now unwind.

"I think a glass is in order," Robin says, popping a cork and we sip pale golden bubbly and relax, lost in exhaustion and our own thoughts. Our dreams are coming to fruition and we're going to develop a farm. To crown it all I've just signed a contract with Readers' Digest to write a Drama in Real Life story about our rescue, and they want to use our picture for the front cover.

Meanwhile we will have much to accomplish in the next few days. Three neighbouring couples plus our daughter and son-in-law have offered to help us with the move to the farm. I think they believe we might be just a bit crazy and want to see the farm and how it will all work out for us. There are just four days left to go to moving day.

Before I slip into bed I look out of the window into the night. It's been lovely staying here. Tonight the sky is perfectly clear; the moon is almost full and illuminates the sheep in their pasture like grey ghosts against the dark trees. They too seem content and will soon have a permanent new home.

Morning arrives swiftly and we get up early. Robin makes omelettes, toast and tea and we plan the events of the coming day. I'd be lost if I couldn't use a pencil and paper to make lists of all the things to do.

Firstly we pen Purdy and Prudence in a small enclosure so we can remove the electric fencing from round the ornamental trees. The sheep are delighted to graze the new vegetation now available to them. Chickens roam the yard as usual and while we're loading the truck and trailer with boxes, a giant pair of wings casts a black shadow across the grass as an eagle descends in a swooping turn and picks up one of our new yellow chicks. The rest of the birds streak for cover then freeze. Our hapless little chick chirps its last as I scream "Noooo!" at the eagle and ineffectually wave my arms as, with open mouth, I follow its soaring path clutching the yellow fluffy bundle in its talons. It was only a couple of metres away but had no fear of me.

Nature is indeed red in tooth and claw and we've now discovered the downside of having free-range chickens with an eagle nesting close by; we're providing an eagle smorgasbord. What is strange is that in place of the chick I find a small fish, obviously released by the eagle which made a choice mid-air to take advantage of a different prey. I imagine the fish would have been the more nutritious of the two, but perhaps a change of diet was demanded by his infant. Who knows what goes through a bird brain? I suppose our chick will now become part of the rapidly growing young eagle. No more free-ranging for the chickens. We hastily usher the flock into their pen, collect the baby chicks and put them together with their mother into the studio. This eagle will have no more free meals.

Although we'd rather the eagles didn't take our livestock, we do admire their tenacious hunting ability and recently witnessed an unusual sight.

Something attracted Robin's attention flapping in the waters of Baynes Sound at low tide. He picked up binoculars to watch. "Look at this, Mags," he said, "an eagle has caught a duck that's too heavy and the eagle can't take off." I joined him at the window and we watched a protracted attempt to land the duck. The eagle repeatedly flapped its wings trying to lift off with the duck in its talons. In between attempts it sank down onto the water to rest. Then we noticed that the eagle was no longer just flapping aimlessly, but dipping his wings in the water like oars and performing a laboured forward rowing motion towards a point of exposed beach way out from the shoreline. He had more than 100 metres to go to reach the point.

"Why isn't the eagle bringing the duck ashore in this direction?" I asked, "It's a much shorter distance."

Robin moved the binoculars towards the eagle's intended destination. "There's another eagle crouched on the beach at the water's edge. I think the bird's moving towards its mate." The onshore eagle was watching the proceedings calmly, possibly with the stones in its crop grating in anticipation of a ducky feast. We had to attend to some chores, but returned somewhat later when the bird had almost reached the shore and the second eagle was very agitated; hopping up and down, stretching its neck and wing-flapping. The hunter touched bottom and dragged the bird ashore aided by the considerable tugging and snatching of its mate. The soaked bird was exhausted and sat with outstretched wings for a while, to recover. Later we saw the duck has been dragged higher up the beach and the birds were feasting. The hunter had no apparent ill effects and was well rewarded for his efforts.

For three days the hot sunny spell continues as we tackle the tasks that must be accomplished before we move at the weekend. Robin and a fellow firefighter collect an old Massey Ferguson Pacer tractor he's bought and transport it to Port Alberni while I continue with the mindless chore of packing belongings into boxes; something I've done many, many times.

It gives me an opportunity to review the past few months when we've been so enjoyably busy. As well as our little animal band of chickens, sheep and pigs we've also had our daughter's young Newfoundland dog, Kurri, to recuperate for a few weeks with a cast on his foot because of a broken toe. When he went home we exchanged him for Kano, his glossy long-haired German Shepherd brother. Each had its own agenda. Kurri, bumbled around in a cone for the first while to prevent him chewing his cast, but was still quite able to clean up the odd chicken manure. He managed to spring a catch and burst through the little gate into the sheep pasture to engage in the timeless doggy pastime of sheep chasing. He was only interested in lumbering and chasing, though, not killing.

Of the two dogs Kano had the greater potential to be deadly. He wandered around nonchalantly on the correct side of the fence but always with one eye on the animals. He could leap any fence with ease so had to be watched carefully. Even so on one occasion we had to pry a wayward chicken from his jaws. I somehow don't feel a household or farm is complete without a dog or two, though, and we'll have to give careful consideration to the breed we choose to ensure that it's compatible with farm animals.

We've owned the farm in Port Alberni for a few days now; have completed some pre-move electrical work in the barns, and have organized to move our belongings and creatures there tomorrow. However, old friends Jim and Kathie, from our days in Brega, Libya, are visiting Canada from the UK and their travel schedule brings them close to the area today, so we can host our first visitors to the farm. We pack a picnic and collect them from Nanaimo airport. As the farmhouse is unfurnished, we spread a tablecloth on the carpet in front of a picture window and dine on meats, cheeses, crusty bread and fruit, catching up on news of the past few years. It's a perfect day for showing off our new domain beside the Beaufort Mountains. We relax on the grass outside, the scent of honeysuckle carried on a riffling breeze as we watch cumulus clouds morph into mystical shapes, drifting across the summer sky. The flower garden is bursting with colour, Swallowtail butterflies flit on the deep blue delphiniums and our visitors are enthralled to see their first humming bird as it hovers, visiting the lilies that thrust orange stamens from their white trumpets.

We savour every peaceful moment. From tomorrow onwards, days off will be the fabric of dreams.

5. Choreographing Creatures

Never look back unless you are planning to go that way ~ Henry David Thoreau

Too excited to sleep, we've already been busy for a few hours when our moving volunteers arrive promptly at 8:00 a.m. Lisa and Pete have a Budget rental truck, Carol and Bill, Ray and Wendy, Vic and Barb all have pick-up trucks. They are super-efficient and immediately start work. We must resemble leaf-cutter ants moving in an orderly line into the house empty handed and out with boxes in a constant, if staggering, stream.

Everything is loaded in two hours and we drive in procession to Port Alberni under increasingly leaden skies. Our helpers opt to get straight to unloading and everything is completed by 1:00 p.m., just as it starts to rain. Carol and Barb stopped in Coombs to pick up lunch—pizzas, salads, fruit and sticky buns, beer and juice, and we are all famished.

The move has proceeded smoothly, how good it is to have friends! Ray and Wendy leave but Bill and Vic helped Robin in the rain to finish running the power for the electric fencer at the barn. Carol, Barb and I unpack plates, cutlery, utensils and kitchen equipment and Carol chooses the most sensible places for the items for an efficiently run establishment. Her choice of which cupboard is suitable for which items is perfect and remains in use for all the years we stay at the farm.

Back at Fanny Bay, after evening feeding we put the chickens and babies to bed for the last time, then go to Carol's for supper. My offering is a rhubarb crumble and cream, made with our own rhubarb from the farm. Carol, a superlative cook, provides a delicious prime rib roast then we sleep for the last night in our chalet home, on borrowed camping mattresses on the floor.

The night has passed all too fast when the alarm jangles. A quick cup of tea first then Robin drives the Land Rover into the field and backs up to the pig gate so we can load up #1 and #3 pigs to take to the meat processors. He must go carefully to avoid marking the grass as the ground is still soggy from yesterday's rain. First we try to lure the pigs up a ramp into the Land Rover using bread and cake treats, but they are suspicious and won't budge outside the safety of their pen so we have to manhandle them. Robin clutches one and hangs on tight pulling it up the ramp as I work from behind, putting my shoulder to the reluctant hindquarters. Getting the second one in is rather trickier than the first because when we edge it to the top of the ramp, the first one wants to jump out. Once secured, the pigs settle down in their straw bed for the journey, separated from our front seats by a temporary piece of paige wire, their snouts and beady eyes occasionally surfacing above the straw.

Immediately we are back at Holiday Road we must load Purdy and Prudence for the journey to the farm. I'm glad to see they're still in their temporary enclosure. A fine persistent rain has returned plastering the hair to our heads and trickling in our eyes and down our necks.

Robin drives the Land Rover down a slight incline to the triangle where we've corralled the ewes overnight. They too refuse to be lured up the ramp, preferring to gallop helter-skelter round the pen. They are big sheep with heavy thick coats as they've not been shorn yet and you'd think we could get a good hold on their fleeces. Not a bit of it. After a while Robin just throws himself on one and hangs on, arms round her neck, and together we maneuver her struggling and bleating into the Land Rover and shut the door. That's Prudence captured. Well, that wasn't *so* bad was it? Now for Purdy. But the already skittish ewe is almost demented, huffing and puffing in her wool jacket, flecks of saliva flying from her lips.

"I hope she doesn't have a heart attack, Robin."

"Never mind her, I hope I don't have one," he says.

We slowly edge towards her, arms outstretched, but in an instant she has dived right underneath the Land Rover and crawled commando-style to the freedom of the hitherto pristine front lawn and flower gardens. Oops! We have to drive away to unblock the gap in the fence, so we can round her up and usher her back into the corral. Although we're trying to approach her calmly, we seem to be transmitting negative energy and end up running her round and round the gardens which are now pockmarked with hoof prints and strewn with broken flowers. By this time neither of us is in the best of humour. Robin yells, "she's coming your way, grab her."

There's no need for Robin to shout, I *can* see her. I lunge and thrust my fingers deep into the wool of her back. She leaps forward and I can't hold on and am left with a few tufts of lanolin-impregnated wool in my hands.

"You had her," Robin says, "why did you let her go?" I glower at him through the drizzle.

Not surprisingly the local tom-toms have been busy and we now have the benefit of Bill and Carol, and Jacki and Karen all giving superb advice to these idiots who can't manage the simple task of catching a supposedly simpler sheep. Carol can't disguise that she's finding this superb entertainment, and is chortling and snorting with glee, barely able to catch her breath.

"Right, don't just stand there, you lot, we need your help," I say, and arm them with plywood boards.

With all of us advancing holding the boards in front of us, we encourage Purdy forwards and guide her into the pen once more and reposition the Land Rover to close the hole. Now we're back where we started an hour ago. Robin blocks off the bottom of the Land Rover this time so we're not caught out the same way twice. We're all feeling like wet noodles when we've finally secured her with her sister.

Robin sets off for the farm in Port Alberni to deliver his cargo to the barn. Good luck Robin! At least the clouds have thinned and we're now treated to occasional flashes of sunshine. I remain in charge of #2 pig and the chickens and start the final house-cleaning.

You'd think we'd have enough to occupy us at the moment, but no, we've offered to look after our landlord's elderly golden retriever for six weeks, while he and his wife are visiting his homeland, Ireland. Most of the housecleaning is finished when Kevin, the landlord's son, arrives with Connor around 3:00 p.m. He's an absolute sweetheart. Connor, that is. I don't know about Kevin yet, who doesn't seem to realize that I'm trying to complete the cleaning and last minute packing and insists on trailing me round the house and yard like a puppy. I give him the royal tour of the premises to prove to his satisfaction that it's in pristine condition. He checks everything in minute detail and takes multiple pictures to send back to his father including one of me with #2 pig. I feed Kevin tea and biscuits and after two hours he leaves Connor and me in peace.

Connor is 12 years old, has a special diet and comes with medication and a very helpful list of instructions from his mum. We're thrilled we can have him with us at the farm. He has the typically placid Retriever nature and loves everyone and his toys. He definitely recognizes his annual holiday home here at Fanny Bay and bounces round with glee, glad to be away from the city sidewalks. Just after Kevin leaves Robin returns from the farm having put the ewes in the lean-to of the barn and connected an electric fence so they have an inside and outside area.

It's raining again and time is passing all too swiftly. It is *not* a good time for a chick to go missing. "If it doesn't show up soon," says Rob, "we'll be leaving a meal for the eagle." After an extensive search he calls, "look up there." Following his line of direction I see the chick, sitting in an apple tree. It's quickly apprehended and returned to its family in a crate on the front seat of the Land Rover. Our 'future breeding sow' who is a Large White breed is loaded in the back of the Land Rover for Robin to chauffeur. Now she can have a name, Mrs. White, of Clue game fame, or Whitey for short. The other chickens are boxed and placed in the bed of the king cab truck, along with cartons of kitchen gear, while Conner rides shotgun on a blanket in the cab with me.

We arrive in Port Alberni at 9:15 p.m. pleased that it's not raining here and is a fine summer evening. Connor happily accepts being on a running line so he doesn't get lost in an unfamiliar place, and settles down to watch activities.

First we take the Land Rover to the barn to unload Mrs. White into her stall.

What do you know? One sheep has already escaped. It seems she's pushed aside a vertical barn board which has slipped back into place after she exited and she can't return. She's now on the wrong side of the electric fence looking in at her sister. Both ewes are bleating pathetically. They can be really exasperating, but I guess they *are* feeling rather strange. After unhooking two sections of electric fence wire we try to lure her back, but no luck. I think she's had enough pushing around for one day and with her sister captive she won't go far. We continue with our plan and the unloading of Mrs. White goes without incident and she happily chomps a late supper snack. Then to the hen house with the truck to install the chickens and they immediately start investigating, stretching their legs and scratching around in what little is left of the daylight.

Through the gathering dusk we can see that Purdy has decided to return near to her sister and is standing inside the electric fence line, so we run out to the barn, replace the fence wire and reactivate it. Connor is waiting patiently and we're all in the house at 10:30 p.m. Food and water for Connor, and a beer for us before we crash for the first night in our own home.

6. Summer Nirvana

*A good farmer is nothing more nor less than a handy man with a
sense of humus* ~ E. B. White

Bertie Rooster starts crowing at 4:30 a.m. Is he as pleased to be here
as we are? It's certainly no chore to get up early to feed the animals
before breakfast. Chickens first, then to Mrs. White who is trying to
knock the stall door down because she thinks she's starving, and
finally the sheep. It seems prudent to run a fourth electric fence wire
low down around the temporary animal enclosure in front of the
barn, shared now by the sheep and Whitey, before letting her out.
When we've finished we open her stall door and out she trots, runs
to the fence and investigates it with her snout, gets zapped and
squeals. She tries it twice more with the same result.

"Pigs are smart," says Robin, "she won't do that again intentionally."

On our second day at the farm, after seeing to the stock and eating breakfast, I notice someone in the vegetable garden, digging potatoes. A petite woman with wavy black hair looks up as I saunter along towards her with an enquiring look on my face. She introduces herself.

"I planted these so I figured I could scratch around the surface of the plants and take a few new potatoes." She's the wife of the former owner and she mostly lives on Saltspring Island where she can involve herself in a more interesting artisnal community. She finds rural farmers and the local community a bit dull. When it suits her she visits her husband. It's going to be difficult to explain to her that since we bought the property, I was under the perhaps erroneous belief that everything on it now belongs to us, so I ponder the prickly subject.

"I wonder if you could you please phone to let us know if you would like something. We rather chose this location because we favour our privacy. If you call ahead, I won't refuse you."

As the days go by I notice gaps appearing in the flower borders where chunks of perennials have been divided off but I never do receive a phone call. Maintaining privacy seems to be a bit of an issue in these parts, although I totally understand the urge to be inquisitive and see just what the new people are doing, but it's becoming a rural pastime. One neighbour wanders in and brings us a gift of a knitted dish cloth and we show her around. Then elderly twins, Jean and Joan who, legend tells us, hold the distinction of being the first twins born without aid on Vancouver Island and to both survive, drop by with a bunch of hedgerow flowers. They are simple folk in the best sense of the word, but we never quite understand what they are talking about as they assume we have the same prior knowledge of their ancestry as they do. Their family squatted and homesteaded in this area and, according to them, owned vast tracts of land hereabouts and in fact that very creek there, and here one of them points, is really called 'Uncle Ben's Creek.' They do have some fascinating history if only one can tease it apart and put it in some kind of order.

I discover that our neighbour's wife is not the only one who's fond of our produce. When I'm in the garden with Connor I notice my pile of freshly dug small potatoes has been disturbed. I take a break and watch for a few moments. Connor saunters over to the pile, noses through them, selects a likely candidate and walks off, drops to the grass and chomps his prize.

Meanwhile Whitey has adapted well to her new surroundings but it's become a high priority to complete a dedicated pig house for her with a small yard, and a gate leading to an extensive back 40 including her own section of swamp. One length of fencing is completed, and we're now building the pig house. Sweat's running in our eyes and I have a strange pricking sensation at my neck hairline. I turn slowly, ever wary that there are wild animals hereabouts, but it's a little man, arms folded on the fence, and smiling. "We've got company," I tell Robin from the side of my mouth.

"Hello, can I help you?" I say.

The man introduces himself and he lives down the road and has just brought us some chard from his garden. "Next time, could please phone to let us know if you're coming, or at least call out when you're here?" We chat for a while and he says, "I was enjoying watching you work." I'm sure he was but there are labels for that sort of conduct. He's a kindly but bored man, and over the years we can never break him of this habit of quietly creeping up on us and I must confess to sometimes hiding in an outbuilding until he's gone away, which can talk half an hour until he's certain he can't locate us.

The animals have learned their territories and routines and seem to be quite at home. Textbook July weather continues with day following day of brilliant sunshine, endless blue skies, and an occasional cooling breeze. The green grass has crisped to brown. At the end of the month the temperature reaches 39°C in the shade and like us, the plants and livestock are wilting.

This is the weather that welcomes our son Bill and his wife Laurie arriving from Nova Scotia with a unique gift. A magnificent 7-year-old long-haired black cat called Pepper. Lisa and Pete collect them from the airport in Comox and bring them to the farm. Connor isn't used to living with a cat, and such a self-possessed one at that, so avoids any contact with Pepper. In Nova Scotia, neighbours of Bill and Laurie had complained because Pepper stared at their indoor cat through the window which intimidated the prisoner causing it to pace the windowsill, knocking over the pot plants. So Pepper will spend her days in freedom on the farm because, like us, she's an outdoor lover.

Next day Lisa and Pete must return to work and Bill and Laurie throw themselves into farm life. "Look at the colour of all the animals," says Bill, "the chickens and the cows you're planning on getting. Aren't you going to call this place Buff Acres?" I look at him and roll my eyes but don't comment.

Whitey insists on sunbathing and gets sunburned despite our best efforts to prevent her from becoming pork crackling. Being pink she lacks protective pigmentation but loves the attention it brings as Laurie administers copious amounts of calamine lotion to her back while Bill bends and ties branches down to create more shade, but as soon as it's secured, Whitey's had enough of that location and moves on.

As electric fencing will be really important until we have all permanent fences, I've decided to follow a regular fence-testing programme and, wearing rubber boots and leather gloves, I simply hold the wire and can feel a slight pulsing tingle. This morning Billy's with me and says, "Does that pack much of a punch?"

"It's not something you'd want to do voluntarily. I'm wearing boots and gloves but your dad won't do it even dressed like this. I think it's quite a deterrent for a pig's snout."

Bill sees this as a challenge and wearing trainers, steps up to the wire. "Can't be that bad," and gently takes hold. "That's not much." He steps back, kicks off his trainers saying, "I'll try it without these." This time he takes a firmer grasp. Next second he's lying flat on his back on the grass a couple of metres away.

Suppressing a giggle I say, "Are you OK, Bill?"

"Oh... My... God!" he gasps, "those poor creatures." He doesn't offer to test the fence again. Once the hand tremors subside he's able to help Laurie with a less galvanizing task, trimming Connor's over-long claws after she's groomed him. Laurie loves working with animals; she only has to whistle and Pepper will come running to her. I'm not quite sure how the separation will go.

On Friday night Lisa and Pete arrive for a working weekend, Lisa on the highway with the dogs and Pete drives straight from work via the logging road over the mountain from Comox. A rough road but much shorter distance. Saturday morning, armed with boxes of nails, screws and bolts; wire, tools and lumber, Robin, who will fabricate anything, makes a new gate for the pig enclosure while Bill and Pete collect a two-man gas powered hand auger from the rental outlet and together dig many large deep holes for setting the remainder of the pig posts. When Robin did the first fencing he laboriously dug the post holes by hand and really appreciates two very strong helpers. It's no mean task considering that every few moments they must stop to hack through the network of forest roots with an axe and it's very hot work necessitating copious amounts of water and the occasional beer. The girls spend all day driving the truck and Land Rover into the back 40 to collect several cords of logs, cut and split last year, to stack in our wood store.

We have a fair amount of juggling to do to keep the three dogs, the cat and the young chicks apart, but it works. Pete promises to make a pen for the dogs under the deck next trip. In the evening we eat, drink beer and wine, tell stories and laugh. Lisa and I take the dogs for a late evening stroll round the farm in the dark. Kurri is in the lead and we follow, using flashlights, along a little trail through the forest. Suddenly he springs backwards. Scanning with the light we spot the source of his anxiety, a fresh pile of bear scat. Funny how a discovery like that can make you lose all interest in your walk.

Having everyone together has been a bit of a dream and we've accomplished so much work. If only family and farm life could always be like this. First thing in the morning they all depart and now it's far too quiet, so I'm glad to be busy with the animals. Connor nuzzles my hand, telling me that he understands and he's still here. Robin and I throw ourselves into work, and leave Pepper shut in our bedroom for safety. When we return she's gone. She's pushed out the screen in the bathroom window and escaped. I can't believe I've lost Laurie's cat already, whatever will I tell her? We have to be away from the farm for the rest of the day and when we return there's still no sign of her.

For the next ten days we search everywhere and whistle and call. There's evidence that she's somewhere around and we leave food and water in the workshop for her but it's not touched, although Robin finds a trail of fresh little rodent bodies and assumes she's responsible. I have no idea what to tell Laurie, and when she phones for a Pepper check I skirt around the question, saying, "I think Pepper's fine, loving roaming round the farm and she seems to be eating well."

After two weeks, as we're going outside Connor starts bouncing up and down by the door. When I open it, there's Pepper, tail like a bottle brush held upright, and she haughtily strides past us into the house. She's moved in and intends to take over. No more subterfuge needed with Laurie.

Long summer days means we can accomplish many things and become contentedly tired. At the end of our work day at twilight we sit on the deck with a glass of wine as a bat begins its own day, swooping and diving in the endless task of locating insects, then after dark we hear an owl's mournful hoot as it ghosts through the trees hunting its prey. It is beyond beautiful: and with the total absence of artificial light it seems we could merely reach out to touch the myriad stars.

Pete has now constructed a sturdy pen under the deck, working like a Trojan to finish it in two days. It is wood-framed, has wire sides, a dividing partition, locking doors and kennels inside. This serves us very well for any visiting dogs and will for our own dogs in the future. Robin has finished straining the wire round Whitey's new area and the house is ready for occupation and becomes known as Farrow 1. He makes a new sturdy ramp for loading her into the Land Rover which, of course, she steadfastly eschews.

The transfer is effected with muscle power as usual, and once she's installed, we wander around her new domain with her for an hour or so to make her feel at home. We celebrate with a glass of wine; Whitey preferring milk, cookies and apples.

We have only a few more days left with Connor, our adorable senior golden retriever. He has thoroughly embraced the spirit of being the farm dog and been a champion all through our move from Holiday Road and the first several weeks of settling in. Soon his owners will return from Ireland and we'll have to say goodbye. He'll be sorely missed. He accompanies us everywhere, initially riding in the back of the Land Rover, where we lifted him onto a thick blanket, and then at our destinations he lay in the warm sunshine or in the shade, watching us tackling our land clearing and fencing tasks. Over the weeks he became increasingly active so that he preferred to bound along the tracks with me and catch the scents on the bushes rather than ride in the Land Rover.

"It's been good having Connor here," Robin says.

"Yes, I wish we could keep him it'll be such a wrench when he has to go home."

All too soon Connor's owners have arrived and we're giving them the 'Royal Tour' of our new farm and animals and now we must give Connor one last hug. His family are ecstatic to have him back and to see their young farm boy looking so hale and hearty. Their reunion is sweet, but bitter sweet for us. My eyes seem to prick as they all drive away—must be some blowing dust about.

7. The Novice and the Cow

All is not butter that comes from the cow ~ Proverb

Days race by in busy mode. Besides fencing and housing we've cut down truck-loads of bracken to dry to use for bedding in stalls. It needs to be eradicated before we can create pasture and we aim to employ the pigs to do that work, hence the necessity first for strong fencing.

We've been waiting patiently for the middle of August when we have to see a woman about a cow. At last it's time to hitch up a horse trailer we've borrowed and drive to Beban Park in Nanaimo to the Vancouver Island Exhibition. After parking we walk from the bright

August sunshine into the shady Agriplex Building and allow our eyes to adjust.

"Look a rhinoceros!"

A little boy yanks on his mother's arm and stabs a finger in the direction of a large Black Angus steer. His mother giggles nervously, pushes his arm down, and hisses, "It's a cow."

It's hot and the air moves sluggishly in this building where the bovines are displayed, and the boy's mother brushes strands of damp hair from her brow, then darts a glance at her neighbours. They are all beaming indulgently. Does TV perhaps place too much emphasis on exotic wildlife at the expense of informing us about domestic animals that provide our daily sustenance? Would the boy be horrified, I muse idly, if he knew that his breakfast milk doesn't originate in a carton sitting on the supermarket shelf but from that hairy pink, heavily veined fleshy bag with teats like stubby fingers hanging beneath the cow's bottom?

I turn back to the stall I'd been scrutinizing. There before me in shades of gold, cream and brown my vision lies on a bed of straw. Skip, the three-year-old Jersey house cow, languorously doubles her neck back along her wedge-shaped body and lowers fan-sized eyelashes, blinks and gives me a bored myopic gaze. An egg-sized lump rumbles up her throat to her moist waiting mouth and dexterous purple tongue. She chews rhythmically. Beautiful. Snuggled beside her on the straw lies a minute brown heifer calf, the Jersey/Dexter cross, her coal-black nose glistening and filmy blue doe-eyes focusing on nothing. At one day old, she's unaware of her outstanding beauty and the attention she's commanding from the onlookers. Most amazing of all, from the end of this afternoon, both mother and calf are ours. I inhale deeply, enjoying the comforting cow smell rising from mother's warm coat.

Three months ago, when we negotiated her purchase in Cedar we arranged to collect her after the exhibition today. We were told she'd been 'running with the bull' and would calve in September but apparently dates were confused. Much to the enlightenment and total delight of all those in the Agriplex Building she demonstrated a text-book calving right there in her pen. The exhibition's on-call vet checked mother and daughter and gave the 'thumbs-up.' They are in perfect health.

"She's a very quiet cow," Marjorie says as we stand before the pen, which I interpret to mean that she's mild mannered, gentle and easily handled. Robin hands her an envelope and now it's time to take home our cow and calf, who we'll call Buttercup and Blossom. I hand a new head collar to her former owner, who stealthily approaches Buttercup's head holding the item clutched on her off side, shielded from the cow's view. She springs forward to the recumbent beast, throws the halter over her head, buckles it deftly and retreats before Buttercup realizes what is happening. Robin picks up the calf, backs out of the stall and heads outside. Mother instantly jerks to her feet, rear end first, smartly pirouettes and follows apace, dragging her erstwhile owner on the end of the line. The waiting horse-trailer is a Rolls Royce double-barrelled affair with a groom's compartment.

Buttercup charges up the steep ramp behind Robin the Calf-Abductor, menacingly swishing her head from side to side. The gravity of the situation has occasioned her to loosen her bowels and with lashing tail she liberally splatters cow flop as she goes. The trailer walls and floor are generously decorated, as are our clothes together with those of several innocent inquisitive bystanders. The door is safely slammed behind her and we bed down Blossom in deep straw in the groom's compartment, so the distressed mother can't turn the trailer into a calf-blender as we journey.

A couple of hours later we reach home without mishap, unload them into the prepared stall and offer food and water to Buttercup, which she accepts graciously. I turn my attention to the trailer where the flop has set up like cement in the heat and steadfastly refuses to be hosed off , so must be painstakingly scraped away, blob by limpet-like blob. Now I understand why manure was used in days of yore to bind the straw for wattle and daub houses. Once the trailer is returned to its pristine condition, more or less, I no longer have an excuse to linger near the stall and after one more look drag myself away to allow them a quiet night. Blossom is sucking lustily as I leave.

Next morning our own vet visits to check over the new arrivals and confirms that mother and baby are in rude health. Won't it be lovely, I think to myself, to see them strolling around in the sunshine instead of being penned in. So when the vet leaves I open the half door and invite Buttercup and Blossom to step out. They waste no time escaping the stall and look magnificent in the pasture as I joyfully skip back to the farmhouse. When I check half an hour later, to my dismay they have vanished. My heart raps a tattoo. Robin's gone to town and I'm alone. His final words are replaying in my head. "Now don't do anything silly while I'm away."

I know our peripheral fences are a bit 'slack' in places and feel convinced that she's marched straight off the property. What will I tell Robin? My heart rate increases further as I run to the workshop for my mountain bike, regretting bitterly that I've not kept the tires pumped up. I set off along the perimeter track, with the pancake tires dragging along the gravel. In frustration I fling down the bike and start to run. But what will I do if I find them? I double back to the barn grab a rope and set off again at a gallop or, to be more precise, a laboured trot. My chest heaves, my lungs burn, and I sweat profusely in the hot August afternoon sun.

An initial check reveals that they have not taken the easy route along the driveway. My unfit state forces me to temper my pace and I'm now really concerned about the swamp. Our year-round creeks bring sparkling clear water straight from the Beaufort Mountains not only for the house and farm but also supply the generous bands of swampy land bordering the farm. The ground stays wet in patches, even in the driest of summers.

Earlier, when I told the neighbour that we were having a cow, he gleefully regaled me with horror stories of a previous owner who'd invested in 20 feeder calves that took off, disappearing into the swamp and dropped dead one by one, until none was left. He also said that a huge Charolais cow wandered into the swamp, foundered, and her carcass had to be lifted out using a crane. It is the same smug neighbour who formerly owned our farm and I really shouldn't listen to him. He has a mean streak and seems to delight in the discomfort of others.

Beset by these mental images I rush on. I can't spot anywhere a large beast may have pushed its way through the seemingly impenetrable bush bordering the track so retrace my steps. Where to search now? Back at the barn I cut across the field at a tangent to the road towards more swamp, and squelch my way into rich peat bog, pushing between scrub alder, fir saplings, huckleberries, and brambles that mass together. I force my protesting body through the scratching jungle and pungent waist high skunk cabbage, calling Buttercup by name which, of course, she doesn't recognize. I revert to her former name, calling in panicked overtones as I quarter the underbrush.

At last I am rewarded. A shaft of sunlight pierces through the tall trees as if through a cathedral window and I glimpse cream and golden buttocks, then a bovine head swings round, ears alert, challenging my intrusion. I can't get near enough to fling my rope around her neck to lead her out. I recall that at the exhibition she was reluctant to be led by the head collar—the same head collar that I'd so cleverly removed for fear it might be uncomfortable. But where is Blossom? Brown calf, brown trees, brown swamp—not a chance of spotting her if she remains still. Buttercup is behaving like the perfect cow and has hidden her newborn. She stands, idly flicking flies away with her long black-tipped tail, waiting for me to make a move.

For the moment I'm beaten. One point to the cow, nil to me. I push my way back to the field and tie my rope to a tree to give myself a fighting chance of rediscovering the spot. Back in the cool of the farmhouse I pour a glass of mountain water to revive my flagging spirit and review my strategy. At least she's still on our property. I'll wait for a good while, perhaps till evening when she'll be hungry for grain.

My resolve is weak and twenty minutes later I'm back on the trail and locate the rope but not the cow who has wisely moved on. I scrabble my way forward, parting branches and making what I think are friendly noises, until there under a cedar is the picture of tranquility, Buttercup with her calf sucking contentedly. Boosted by an adrenalin rush I erupt from my hiding place, yank the calf off her feet and carelessly crash my way through the swampy undergrowth back towards the pasture hugging my prize. If I can't have the cow, at least I'll have the calf.

My arms ache with the weight of my uncomfortable 40 lb. burden but I start to run when I hit the open field. Even above my rasping breaths I can hear the crashing of one thousand pounds of cow flesh a little way behind. Just as I gain the safety of the barn she rushes up snorting, udder swaying and sides heaving like bellows. Obviously yet another abductor is trying to steal her calf. She's not amused. I drop Blossom onto the deep hay bedding, catapult through the stall's back exit, sprint round the barn and slam shut the wooden half-door on the front of the stall while mother is still checking her offspring for damage.

In the shade of a big maple tree I lean on the barn wall, panting, trying to recover my composure as flies buzz round my sweat streaked face. It's not so bad, I reflect, Robin need never know of my foolishness. Now it seems like an excellent proposition to keep Buttercup in for a few days, feed her molasses-rich grain and best hay, while she gains visual cues from her surroundings and recognizes that she and her calf will be safe and comfortable with us.

Of course I immediately blurt out my stupidity to Robin on his return, which serves to reinforce his opinion of my blundering farming abilities.

It's a week later, for it takes that long to get a head collar back on her (perhaps in no small measure because of the clanging cowbell I've now appended to it), that we think we'll tether her outside to graze the tasty grass adjacent to the barn. We wrestle to attach the line to her collar avoiding getting our arms broken by her flailing head. I ease the barn door open and Buttercup spies the great outdoors and freedom. We all explode from the stall like fireworks, Buttercup in the lead. Robin runs to clip the free end of the 100 ft line to a swivel on an auger he's screwed into the ground. Blossom trots out with fawn-like daintiness to join mother whose nostrils are flaring ominously.

Perfect. They can have a little more freedom yet not escape. I just wish she'd stop swinging her head from side to side in the gesture that is becoming all too familiar. Now I understand why dairy cows are dehorned as calves. To allow them some peace we retreat to the house.

"She's off!" We gape from the farmhouse window in disbelief as Buttercup walks backwards trying to rid herself of the long line she's dragging. She's bent open the clip attached to the auger swivel and also bent the auger into a singular shape and she's only been attached for ten minutes. It's becoming obvious that our 'quiet' cow does not appreciate restraint. Out we rush, pounce on the free end of the line and lean backwards clawing our way towards her head in a real tug o' war. Suffering only a few minor contusions and a bruised arm and shoulder from her battering-ram head, Robin succeeds in freeing her from the line. "Right," he says, "If she walks off now, too bloody bad." He's at his most erudite at times like these.

But she doesn't leave. In the evening when I rattle grain in a bucket, she walks calmly into the milking parlour and I close the restraining stanchion around her neck. Time to try my milking technique. I wash and dry her udder, squat on my new 3-legged stool that Robin's fashioned from a slice of tree trunk, and balance the bucket between my knees.

I grasp two of the plump, warm teats. Her reaction is not totally unexpected. A rear hoof whips out and sends my polished stainless steel bucket ringing across the milking parlour floor. Try again. I start higher up on the udder, massage it gently and talk soothingly to her as I slowly slide my fingers into place on the teats and give a slight squeeze. The nipples feel like water-filled balloons beneath my gentle pressure, but nothing comes out. I close off the top of the teat more firmly with finger and thumb and squeeze again. A couple of drips form on the teat ends, wobble, then plop into the bucket. As Buttercup frequently shifts her weight I have to release the teats adjust my stool and re-steady the bucket between my knees. This may take a while.

"All right," I say in an authoritative voice, "stand still and let's get this done." One-two-one-two; squeeze release, squeeze release. OK I'm getting it, I think, as I catch another few splashes. By this time Buttercup has finished all her grain and is banging her head against the sides of the stanchion and stamping up and down. "Shall we give her some hay?" I suggest to Robin, who is standing behind me, head tilted, trying to fathom my technique. He throws some hay into the manger and Buttercup buries her muzzle in it. I replace my hands quickly and start squeezing. A warm sticky flow, the most promising so far, squirts directly up my cuff and sluices my non-waterproof watch. I've inadvertently bent the teat as I squeezed. By the time I've finish working on all four teats, I have at least half a cup of milk running round the bottom of my bucket, together with sundry bits of hair and dust.

After first thanking Buttercup profusely, I triumphantly show Robin my prize. Her udder has not appreciably reduced in size following my withdrawal but feeling sure I've got all that there is, I let her out of the stanchion. She cautiously backs from the parlour, rotates and strides off to rejoin her calf. Blossom heads straight under the udder and sucks lustily, long hard pulls and we watch her throat flex as she swallows the milk. When satisfied, she turns to look at me with her liquid eyes, white bubbles of creamy milk popping around her soft black lips. "That's the way to do it," her gaze seems to imply.

"Just what I intended," I say to Robin, "I wanted to make sure I'd left enough for the calf. You'll see, it will be fine now Buttercup knows who's boss."

8. On the Sheep Trail

The farmer has to be an optimist or he wouldn't still be a farmer ~
Will Rogers

The glorious August weather continues into September. Grapes are
ready for harvesting and blackberries hang in abundance on the
briars, their glistening purple globes crammed with the sweetness of
summer ripening and just waiting for someone to brave their
backward-facing thorns to retrieve the bounty. Well worth the effort,
especially if it's Robin or our visitors picking them instead of me.

The days are shortening and as the sun moves further South
towards the equator, it rises slightly lower over Mount Hal, yet the
sloping profile of the mountain means that for a while we see it rise
at the same time each day.

We've just completed the cows' morning feeding and milking before dawn and fed the other animals earlier too as we're going to spend the day at Port Alberni's Fall Fair. As we turn down the driveway I catch a glimpse of 3-week-old Blossom amusing herself once again, chasing Purdy and Prudence round the barn. The sheep just won't stand their ground so the calf is definitely the boss. I secretly think we should get a couple more young calves to rear as we have so much milk from Buttercup and it would be company for Blossom, but for now I hold my counsel. We're hoping to finish some more fencing soon, and then the sheep can be separated into their own field.

This first weekend of September is the traditional time for our Fall Fair. Locals vie with each other for ribbons and accolades for everything from produce to photography, and livestock to logging sports. Many blue ribbons are given out in each category in the produce and crafts sections, there's not just one First, one Second and one Third place. It's an interesting concept to me that everyone who reaches an acceptable level will receive a ribbon, so everyone's a winner. Perhaps it's prudent to appease all opposing factions.

Hunting for more sheep to join Purdy and Prudence has become an ernest endeavour and the Fall Fair is a good place to talk to breeders. We've arranged to meet Peter and Maureen Lenihan who raise Hampshire sheep in Cherry Creek. Hopefully we can breed ewes this fall and have lambs next spring. There's something inherently visceral about newborn lambs.

My favourite area of the whole fair is the livestock barn where sheep, cows, pigs, and goats lounge in their stalls until it's time to enter the show ring. 4-H children are busy outside the barns with their charges: hosing down, shampooing, brushing, snipping, and polishing, until the prized animal they've been working with for months is groomed to perfection. 4-H is a club for young people to develop skills, social behaviours and leadership qualities. The members here today are from the region's agricultural branches of 4-H. I notice that in the livestock section of the Fall Fair the First, Second and Third place rule still holds true so the young folk entering their animals and gaining ribbons can feel justly proud of their accomplishments.

"Look over there, Mags," Robin says pointing. "young pigs in the ring." We can't resist and hurry over for a closer look. Judging by the size of the crowd this is a popular event. These sparklingly clean pigs are as close to tame as can be achieved, having been nurtured, frequently bathed and handled daily by their owners since infancy. In the show ring the young handlers employ only two aids; a long stick used to guide the snouts in the right direction, and a small scrubbing brush with a handle.

"I wonder what the brush is for," I muse. We laugh to see it used to administer a pig favourite, a belly-scratch, to keep the pig in a sweet and gentle mood. "And what do you suppose those people are doing?" I ask rhetorically as I nod towards the inside edge of the ring. Half a dozen sturdy men and women stand watching the pigs parading round before the judge. Each is holding a board about 60 cm high by 1 metre long with two slots near the top edge so they can put their fingers through to maintain a firm grip.

We don't need to contemplate for long because suddenly there's action in the ring. Pigs are not known for their social nature when meeting strange pigs, and feel the need to assert their individuality and dominance. Nothing is more enjoyable to them than a bit of a scuffle with lots of pushing, shoving and side swipes with their burgeoning tusks.

"BOARDS!" The alert is shouted and some brave helpers rush forward to insert their boards between two scrappers. These encounters can escalate rapidly into all-out war. The young handlers try to soothe the combatants with extra belly massages and calm talking as the board holders stand firm making sure they have none of their own body parts near the pigs' powerful heads and jaws. Usually within a few moments the situation is defused, the pigs each feel they've vanquished the foe and turn their attentions elsewhere, while the board bearers retreat to the edge of the ring as the pig parade continues. It's a real challenge for the handlers and unlike the other halter or collar-wearing animals pigs can't be lined up side by side in a neat row for final appraisal, using just a stick and a brush. The pig judge, therefore, must do his inspection and summing up on the trot.

"I really admire those kids, aren't they amazing?"

"Absolutely," says Rob, "they've worked really hard, it's impressive." The pigs receive their placings and the owners, the rosettes. Robin checks his watch. "It's about time to meet the sheep people at the sheep section."

Pat and Maeve are sitting on camping chairs in a sheep stall, sipping mugs of coffee. Their immaculate young sheep are bathed, groomed and lying down in the deep straw beside them, chewing the cud or snoozing. The Lenihans are showing several sheep in the ring today, entered in various classes. Their breed-of-choice, Hampshires, is rather more docile than our North Country Cheviots. They are certainly pretty with their sooty black legs, faces and ears; white woolly topknots and fluffy cheeks.

We chat for a while, admiring the sheep and make arrangements to view three 4-year-old ewes and a ram lamb. Though I try to remain outwardly cool, I can't help grinning with the anticipation of our increasing stockholding.

I make an early lunch on the day of our visit and everything is cleared away. I'm ready. "Come on Rob, isn't it time to go?" I try to encourage him to leave a bit early but hustling him never really works. I should know by now that it only serves to make him drag his feet a little, to balance my impetuousness. One day I'll learn to slow down—or perhaps not.

Along Beaver Creek Road we branch off through a picturesque rural area to the agricultural portion of Cherry Creek and the Lenihans' farm. It is evident that we are leaving summer behind. An occasional majestic horse chestnut tree stands proudly beside evergreen neighbours, its large palmate leaves already brown, presaging the coming winter. The grassy verges beneath are dotted with polished mahogany conkers, their split porcupine cases, once bright green, now the colour of rust. It brings back fond memories. "Remember the days when we used to pick them and soak them in vinegar overnight to use for conker games in the playground at school?" I ask.

Robin laughs, "I had a really good one once, it was a 'fivesy'—I broke five other conkers with it!"

At the farm we climb out of the Rover in the mellow sunshine to greet Peter and Maureen.

"I thought you'd like to see the ram lamb's sire first," says Peter, "he's over there in the orchard." We wander across the yard and rest our arms on the wooden fence railing and watch a very large ram leaping high into a tree. Peter grins. "This guy just loves pears."

Ripe fruit still dangle among the yellowing leaves, and the ram gives us another exhibition of his skill. "If the ram lamb turns out like his sire, he'll be just fine," Robin says.

The ram lamb's mother, G.I. Jane, is shy and rather smaller than the sire, so we hope their son will grow into a fine beast and inherit the amenable personality of his father.

Now we get to see the three ewes and the lamb himself. We check the conformation of each, having recently studied what characteristics to look for. Their wool is very tightly curled with the classic wiry, slightly greasy texture. One of the ewes has two supernumerary, or 'extra' teats. They are not milk-producing and haven't affected her breeding ability so won't be a problem as long as her offspring are not used for the show ring or breeding, but just reared for meat. They are definitely not cheap at $150 for each ewe and $250 for the pedigree lamb, but on the basis of the teats, we offer $650 for the lot. Robin and Peter shake hands on the deal and I rub my lanolin-enriched hands together reflecting that it makes a wonderful additive to cosmetics and salves, waterproofing and insulating the sheep's wool so well.

"The ewes haven't been handled much, but if you work with them every day, they'll soon start coming up to you," explains Peter.

"I hope so," I say," we certainly can't get very close to our Cheviots."

"No, that's a common trait of the north of England hill breeds."

The ram lamb looks beautifully sound and seems quite friendly. Peter is keeping his brother for his own future breeding plan, as he considers it to be a slightly better animal. He'll transfer the pedigree documents to us and we'll receive our own papers in due course. "The bureaucracy of these things," he warns, "can take quite a while."

We're very happy with our purchases and will call our little ram Charlie.

Waiting two whole days until delivery of our Hampshire sheep gives us plenty of time to finalize arrangements for their living quarters. On the appointed day after supper Pat's truck growls its way along our drive and we guide him to the barn where we unload our new 'flock' into the large cow stall. Ariadne, Bertha, Chloe and Charlie waste no time finding their fresh sweet hay and doing what they do best, chewing. We leave them to settle in for the evening.

In the morning they seem well content. They no longer have to compete with so many others in their old home barn. Charlie is very happy to receive hands-on treatment so we have no trouble putting on his head collar and walking him around before turning our attention to the girls. They make no secret of the fact that they don't want any part of this game. With difficulty, in turn we back each one into a corner and put new collars on them. Ariadne is Red, Bertha Purple and Chloe Green. Then we can identify them at a distance using binoculars.

The next day we take things a step further. Once more Charlie basks in attention as we clip a line on his halter and take him for a walk around the barn, ending up at a bowl of sheep text—a mixture of barley, corn, wheat, distillers' grains, molasses, vitamins and nutrients, like a high class muesli, and a definite sheep favourite. He behaves beautifully on his walk. "We're so lucky we've got a good tempered ram," I say, "Catherine's neighbour along Beaver Creek Road has a ram he can't get near, let alone walk him. Every time the man goes into the field, the ram charges him."

The girls, however, are not so keen on a daily constitutional. Ariadne then Bertha just barely suffer the indignity of being led or perhaps *dragged* around the barn but they remain on all fours and enjoy their food reward. Then it's Chloe's turn. She's beside herself with fear, showing the whites of her eyes and breathing heavily. Immediately the stall door is opened she senses freedom and bolts, or tries to. But she's attached to a line. When it comes up short she leaps in the air and throws herself on the ground rolling her eyes and looking as though she's in her last death agonies. Then she springs up and tries to run before collapsing again, but we refuse let her get away with these histrionics. "Just a little more halter training necessary don't you think, Rob?"

"Hmmmm, I guess so."

Breeding season is fast approaching and we'd like to know when each sheep is served. As we don't have the expensive custom-made nylon harness that carries a large red chalk marker block and is strapped to the ram's chest, we resort to the poor man's method, mixing Vaseline with red chalk dust to plaster on his brisket then when he mounts a ewe his chest will leave a red mark on her rump and we'll have some indication of when each sheep is bred. After three weeks we'll change the colour of the chalk.

"Robin, Robin," I call the very next morning when I look over the half gate into their stall. "Chloe has some red on her rump." Next day there's more red on her, so we're hopeful that one ewe has already been served. We enter the date into the farm log and compute approximately 147 days ahead. If all's well we may have our first birth in early February.

Now that Charlie and his ewes are becoming familiar with their surroundings on their walks, we let them out of the stall. They are getting more approachable and can free range in the field and woods, alongside Buttercup and Blossom. The calf is growing well but still sees it as her mission in life to play with the sheep. Sometimes when she takes off at a sprint in chase mode, Buttercup bellows and lumbers along behind her, milky udder swinging, and I can just imagine rich yellow cream churning to butter inside the heavy appendage.

Soon we take Charlie for a walk to introduce him to Purdy and Prudence across the drive. He spies them and immediately chortles and snorts, huffs and growls in his throat. He's very keen to join them but instead we return him to his own girls for their evening feed in the barn. Allowing the ram to visit is supposed to encourage the ewes to come into season. In a couple of days Purdy and Prudence join the Hampshire flock without any visible compatibility problems. Charlie is here to maintain order among the ranks.

The morning following the sheep integration there's a keen sharpness to the air as we walk towards the barn to milk and feed the cows and I can see my breath as I sweep the beam of my flashlight across the field. What a relief to see six pairs of orange lights seemingly suspended above the brow of the hill as their eyes reflect my light. "Thank goodness," I say, "they're all here; no one's run off."

As the days shorten, Charlie keeps a close watch over his flock. His concern is amusing to see as he's still considerably smaller than his ewes. Not for long though: he's fast maturing into a handsome adult. Robin now feeds them all in individual bowls in a large semicircle among the russet-tinged leaves fallen from the spreading maple tree.

Blossom's bossiness over the sheep has been terminated. If she tries to intimidate or chase, Charlie now advances upon her with a stiff-legged gait, head thrust forward and runs her off. Amazingly he hasn't actually attacked her, preferring dummy charges. She's finally learned to read his body language and is getting the message that her attentions are definitely unwanted and will surely not go unpunished.

9. Piglets, Pups and Poultry

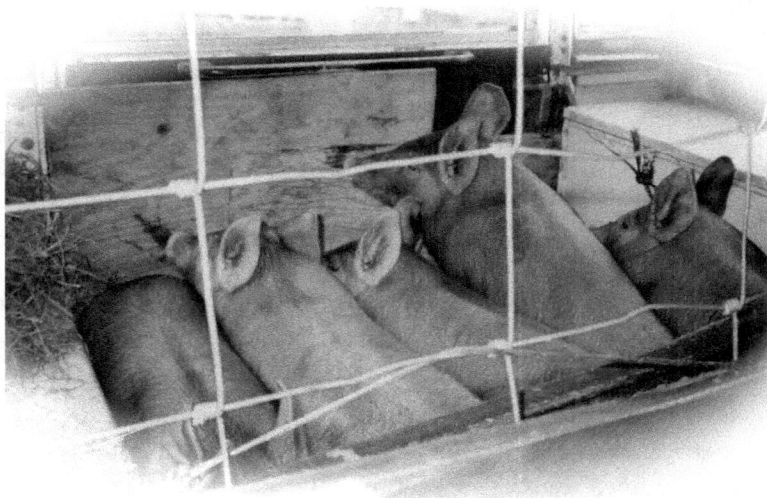

Happiness is a warm puppy ~ Charles M. Schulz

The serenity of September gives way to a damp, blustery start to October. The maple at the farm gate is dropping its dinner-plate red and gold leaves, which now cover the driveway and gravel road. On a crisp dry day I'll rake them into piles and pick them up between boards, pack them into the Land Rover and use them for mulch and weed control.

Charlie continues with his sterling work and within a few weeks the ewes are all sporting coloured marks on their rumps. "He's a bit like an LA policeman," I say to Robin.

"What on earth are you talking about now?"

"Well, like them, his motto is obviously *"To Protect and Serve."*"

"Ah, yes, and maybe we'll have five to ten lambs in spring."

"Well newborn lambs will certainly bring an increase in our farm guests."

For the past three months we've had a constant stream of visitors admiring our little corner of rural BC. Carol and Bill are first bringing Jaki and Karen, former owners of Purdy and Prudence. They have a litter of piglets ready for sale and wonder if we'd be interested in a couple. They're Tamworths, an English heritage breed from Staffordshire, with dark red skin and hair.

"We'd love some," Robin tells them, "we'd like five." I can almost hear the cogs of Robin's mind working on the expansion of his pig herd.

"Sorry, you can't have that many, we already have some possible orders and wanted to keep a couple ourselves."

I figure the best thing is to withdraw the offer, so one moment they have a confirmed purchase of five and the next, zero. We'd really like these piglets and I'm working on the premise that it's difficult to resist a confirmed cash sale now in favour of *possible* future sales.

"Never mind," I say, "we'll watch the Buy, Sell and Trade and find some, we're not in a hurry." When have I ever *not* been in a hurry to buy livestock?

Jacki and Karen wander off ostensibly to admire something and chat together for a few moments then return, and Jacki says, "OK, you can have five." I glance at Robin and grin.

Not wanting them to change their minds, we go to Fanny Bay the next day in time for coffee and a tour before we collect our new stock. What a tussle it is to capture them. They're larger than 6-week-old weaners: solid, feisty, and heavy. It takes all four of us leaping into the skirmish to eventually corner them and pick them up kicking and protesting with their ear-piercing squeals. Good job their mother can't get to us; she'll be frantic and would do serious damage to us to protect her offspring. Eventually all five are loaded into the back of the Land Rover on a hay bed and resemble nothing so much as a pound of well-cooked English bangers.

They travel calmly without stress and are much easier to unload. The 'Scarlet Pimpernels' as we call them, take up residence in the half of the duplex, next to Whitey. Initially they're terrified and won't enter their sleeping quarters preferring to dig a den under an old-growth cedar stump overhung with brush. At first we can't find them they're so well hidden and think they've escaped. Gradually they become bolder and jostle each other to reach their food, liberally laced with milk or whey left from cheese making. They grow quickly and soon realize it's much warmer to take themselves into their sty to sleep and keep snug. In time we chose to keep the friendly male, who we call Colonel Mustard, and he takes up residence with Whitey and will be the sire of our first litter of piglets. It takes time for her to accept him in her domain and initially she insists that he sleeps just outside the sty under their lean-to shelter but then relents and allows him inside where they burrow together under the straw.

With a distinct nip in the fall air, dew drops sometimes form on our noses when working outside. Overnight field mushrooms pop up like giant pearls in the pastures and dewy cobwebs spangle the tussocky grass. After morning milking I quarter the meadow to pick new mushrooms before they're trampled by the beasts. We've also discovered quite a good bed of chanterelle mushrooms which make delicious eating.

Although Buttercup and Blossom range freely on Sunset meadow with the sheep, Blossom is still young and vulnerable so we put them in a stall overnight. This is cougar and bear territory but so far we've only seen an occasional pile of bear scat. Another bonus to the stall is that we don't have to hunt for cows in the morning. It is easy to lead Buttercup straight into the milking parlour and clamp her in the stanchion where she stands, her tongue nimbly collecting the molasses-rich dairy grain from her tub. When every scrap has been cleaned up she starts on the fresh hay that keeps her busy until I've finished hand milking.

As I sit on my stool, my head against her warm flank, my mind can wander. We've been thinking a lot about dogs recently and both miss Connor. We'd love a canine companion who can also act as an early warning system if predators are around.

"Do you think we could go to the SPCA to find a dog?" I ask Robin a few days later, "There are so many needing homes."

Robin nods, "Yes, that's a good idea."

We lose no time in visiting. After wandering along the wire enclosures greeting the dogs in the pens we choose a handsome one-year-old Rottweiler, Ben. We'll have him on trial for two weeks to see if he'll be happy with us. He seems to have a beautiful nature and comes for a walk on a leash to meet the animals. He's excited by the new sights and smells and watches intently while Robin feeds Whitey and the Scarlet Pimpernels, but as cows are notorious for their dislike of some dogs we decide to leave him in the pen under the deck when it's time for milking.

Ben easily slips into our lives and hearts. He knows basic commands, doesn't yap, or whine, doesn't jump up, and is non-aggressive. For several days we play ball with him alongside the field where the sheep are grazing and he pays them no attention. After a week of taking him everywhere with us on a leash it's time to let him off while we play our ball games. Robin throws the ball but Ben totally ignores it and instantly bounds over the fence trying to latch onto the back of Purdy.

"BEN!" I scream and scissor-jump over the fence. Robin vaults clear over it and we grab the dog/sheep duo, leash Ben and check Purdy who is unharmed but terrified. Ben is smiling, big mouth open, sides heaving and tongue lolling. "That's the best fun I've had since coming here," he's telling us, "this is more like it."

With heavy hearts at our failure we return him to the SPCA and Robin tells them, "He's a lovely dog but he can't be trusted with sheep." I'm sobbing and can't speak as we hand him over: magnificent Ben who will never become a farm dog. The manager assures us that they'll have no trouble finding a suitable home for him and agrees that adopting a puppy might be our best idea so it can grow up with the animals and she assures us that we shouldn't have too long to wait.

A few days later she calls. "We've just got a litter of lab mix pups if you're interested but they're only four weeks old at present."

"Oh, yes we're definitely interested, thanks." Once chores are finished we drive into town to visit the litter. Mum is very gentle with five energetic little bundles romping and rolling together. We pick up pups, revelling in the reminiscent puppy smell. Each one is adorable and it's impossible to make a choice just yet. Several times we visit to familiarize them with our scent and eventually settle on one engaging little chap we call 'Acorn' of Oak Tree Farm.

When it's mid-October and Acorn is seven weeks old we drive to collect him as the cold rain eases off and a weak sun briefly emerges through the clouds. We're well equipped at home with new puppy paraphernalia, everything from a crate to a ticking clock and a couple of gel heat pads to act as sibling substitutes.

At the shelter Acorn sits in Robin's arms, alert but relaxed. We complete the paperwork and the pup snuggles down in a blanket on my lap without a whimper or a shiver for the 20-minute journey to the farm.

He's so tiny, but manfully struts along beside Robin as we walk him around outside the house and up to the fences to see some chickens and the pigs where, sensibly, he stays between Robin's feet. Whitey and the Scarlet Pimpernels are fascinated and inquisitive, pushing and shoving and poking their snouts through the fence to assess the newcomer. He shows no desire to reciprocate, but is not submissive or terrified, just watchful.

It's time to introduce Acorn to our living area. As he's rather too small to manage the stairs we carry him indoors to show him his bed in the kitchen in a crate next to the old range. He investigates the area for a few moments then chooses to curl up like a little comma, on a sheepskin rug in front of the log fire. At evening milking we take him to the barn to introduce him to the comforting smell of warm cows and sweet hay although we don't present him to Buttercup and Blossom yet.

The next day we're continuing with some fencing work; replacing barbed wire with strained paige wire and are making our way across a swampy area behind the house. I've been busy hammering in staples when I say, "Where's Acorn, Rob? He was here a minute ago, is he with you?"

"No, I can't see him."

I put down my hammer and splash up and down the swampy undergrowth, the mud sucking at my gumboots, calling Acorn's name but there's no sign of him. I have visions of him dropping into a swampy hole and not being able to climb out. How could I have lost the poor little chap? After quartering the area I go into the farmhouse to look around and finally find his little black form sleeping soundly, curled up on a sweater on Robin's side of the bed. I smile to think of this scrap of a new puppy plodding his way out of the swampy area and into the house, scrambling up the stairs and finally dropping down dead tired onto something with a familiar scent. Now at least we know he's quite capable of getting upstairs.

Acorn is bolder the following morning, casts caution aside and trots behind me into Buttercup's stall and sniffs her hocks. In a flash Buttercup whips round, lunges and flips him, then picks him up on her muzzle and slams him against the wooden staging on one side of the stall. "NO, NO, BUTTERCUP!" I scream, hammering my fists on her rump. She steps back and tries a second time but Acorn manages to crawl through a gap underneath the staging. It all happens so fast. Buttercup wheels round, snorting, and bolts out of the barn to check for Blossom whom she's just defended. Acorn shrieks constantly as I gently lift him from his hiding place. Gradually he quietens down and I carry him to the house. We rush to the vet but although badly bruised he has no broken bones thanks to being young and supple. "Little chap's going to be pretty sore for a while, though," the vet says as he gets his hand thoroughly licked.

Acorn doesn't much care for the comforting smell of warm cows any more but there are many other fascinating things in nature to engage him, particularly raindrops sitting on the tops of mushrooms conveniently growing at chest height to his diminutive form and perfectly positioned for licking. It becomes something of a hobby as he makes his daily beeline for the mushroom patch behind the house and we start wondering about the properties of these fungi; are they perhaps the BC Magic Mushroom variety?

Walks round the farm and in the woods are high on the list of Things Puppies Love To Do. Today he doesn't want to come back indoors. As we pass by Whitey's field he greets her through the fence, but one flick of her head and he shrieks and runs away, no doubt a safety tactic reinforced by his trauma with Buttercup. He's soon running around again tail in the air as we walk on. In the sheep's field he bounces and trots thoroughly enjoying himself until three sheep saunter towards us. He shrieks again although they are still several feet away and have no interest in him. At the moment everything seems so huge and threatening to him but in time, as he gets bigger, things will shrink into proportion. Luckily other canines don't fall into the category of intimidating, strange-smelling, monster farm animals. He loves his German Shepherd and Newfoundland friends and the visiting neighbouring farmers' dogs. He's also learning to bark: a first teeny tiny 'wuff' escapes from him while playing with his reflection in a glass door one evening, but he uses his new skill sparingly.

Days, though, are for running carefree and he accompanies us everywhere. We're locating and marking out our east and south boundaries that run across woodland and scrub threaded with gravel berms and braided streams from the mountain. As we work he leaps little rivulets and splashes through larger ones; stalks frogs and paws bubbles in ponds; digs for small rodents and steals our work gloves, racing away with them. Life is just too good for a puppy. He's growing up and instead of indoors, he now prefers to take refuge in his insulated outdoor kennel under the deck, with its unobstructed view of the driveway and fields, to conduct important undertakings like gnawing a bone. Occasionally at the end of a work day we'll have a bonfire. There's something elemental about fire, powerful and all-consuming. Acorn lies near the embers chewing sticks while we sit on camp chairs, sipping wine and reflecting on the direction of our traditional farming enterprise.

The farm creatures have all settled in successfully and it's hard to imagine life without them. Now it's time to increase our chicken stock. In the Buy, Sell and Trade there's an advert for point-of-lay chickens; the commercial Isa Brown variety that are prolific egg layers. The Buff Orpingtons are beautiful, but rather too expensive for a large flock, and it will be good to see more birds ranging on the farm. Robin builds a secure removable back for the truck covered with netting and a roof for protection from the elements and we drive to Nanaimo to pick up our order of 80 birds and unload them into their new premises. They have lots of roosting perches in their airy chicken house, 16 nesting boxes filled with hay, and shavings on the floor.

To acclimatize them to their new surroundings we leave them inside the house for a couple of days but as they've been raised on the floor of a barn, they haven't yet learned to fly up onto perches to roost. At dusk we pick up each bird from where it's squatting and pop it onto a perch. A few nights of this and they've learned to roost on their own. As they've not encountered the great outdoors either we have to launch each one out through the small chicken door into their yard. After a couple of days they realize that investigating, eating grasses and scratching for grubs is chicken heaven and go outside unprompted in the mornings. Soon they reward us with their first eggs, most in the nesting boxes, a few on the litter underneath the boxes and before long we're in full egg production. It's time to join the local Farmers' Market to sell our bounty.

10. Winter and Sheep Concerns

I am intoxicated by animals ~ David Attenborough

The advent of November brings a mix of weather. A flaming sunrise in oranges, reds and golds makes a glorious backdrop to the dark mass of the fir forest standing out in stark relief. Then flawlessly clear skies and a plummeting temperature brings a night of iron frost, and heavens bright with sparkling constellations. The ground remains frozen for several days and patches of grass stand stiff with hoarfrost and the freezing of the drinking water produces curious ice sculptures that must be broken with an axe and pulled from the troughs so we can add hot water three times a day. Then a rise in temperature is accompanied by rain and a stiff breeze sending dead leaves scudding across the ground.

In such inclement weather Spot and Sox, two very young calves, join the herd to be raised on Jersey milk. Having the misfortune to be born male they are surplus to requirements in a dairy herd and if we buy them we can save them from going to auction in Vancouver. Being herd animals they happily stay with the other cows in the barns out of the harsh weather.

Rain in November means it's time for the coho salmon to return upriver to spawn in the shallow gravel streams between the farm and the mountain. Already the sockeye salmon have passed through Stamp Falls in the provincial park on their way to their spawning grounds. With the extra rain streams are now swollen, the swamps are flooded and battered coho salmon forge their way, some coming through our pond and Little Hal creek that leads to their destination. They struggle so hard on their marathon journey and so many die before they reach the end.

The new chickens, however, have not been deterred by the harsh weather and have been laying well and we also have a batch of fertile Buff Orpington eggs incubating in a brooder indoors and eagerly await their hatching. Boxes and heat lamps are prepared in the basement and there's only a day or two to go when we have a power failure. It doesn't return promptly so there's probably a tree down on the line.

"Oh dear, Rob, what can we do now?"

"If I light the kitchen range perhaps we can put the eggs in the oven to keep them at the right temperature. It's worth a try."

Robin takes the oven door off, and once the oven is warm we carefully transfer the eggs from the incubator into an egg box and place it on a shelf in the oven; adding a thermometer and some little pots of water to keep the atmosphere slightly humid. We constantly feed small pieces of wood to the firebox to maintain the heat, but with this old range the temperature can quickly rise too far so we rotate the 22 eggs by employing a 'surrogate mother' hen to share the chore. We make a nest in a cat carrier placed on the kitchen counter and introduce the hen; she's not a broody hen but by putting her in a limited space it's more comfortable for her to sit on the eggs than stand.

For 11 hours we take turns to stay beside the range feeding it fuel and changing the egg positions and are rewarded when some chicks start to chip holes in their shells. Out of the 22 possibilities, 14 hatch successfully. Quite an achievement, given the difficult circumstances. Robin vows to install a generator for such emergencies in the future.

The ewes are settling into potential motherhood with gradually expanding waistlines. On milder days they lie down in the pasture, sides resting on the ground like pannier bags. I'm not sure if they're all carrying twins, or if they're just fat. They're definitely fat. Charlie seems to be the contented prospective father and is still friendly with us and easily handled.

The week before Christmas we have our first snow. The animal barn is outlined in twinkling white lights and looks bewitching as befits the nativity theme. Just after New Year the temperature rises to 0°C, and the snow gives way to a thick all-enveloping fog. We're treated to only glimpses of the livestock when the fog thins. This is a good time to be indoors making a list of jobs to be tackled in the coming months. There's so much we'd like to do but fencing always seems to top our list.

One afternoon in late January, after returning from Parksville collecting more fencing supplies, Robin's just made a cup of tea and we're sipping it and looking out of the window when we see Charlie jumping up and down in the pasture in great agitation.

"What's going on out there?" I say. We dash outside and through the gate. Charlie is being menacing; prancing along sideway and feinting mock charges. Robin immediately grabs him and rolls him to the ground to prevent him attacking, then lets him get up. I look around quickly for the reason for his behaviour and realize we're one Hampshire sheep short. There's no one with a green collar so Chloe's missing.

"Do you think she's gone off to give birth?" I say, "Although it's way too early." We frantically hunt around and find her lying on her back in a hollow beneath a cedar tree, her feet sticking out to the side. She's not moving and her rear is greatly distended. Charlie gallops towards us, jumping up and down and making mock attacks on Robin interspersed with pawing the ground and pushing Chloe with his head.

"Get off, you stupid bugger," yells Robin and thrusts his fingers through Charlie's head collar and marches the bouncing ram away and puts him through the nearest gate into the cows' field.

I take hold of the ewe's head and she grunts, her breathing ragged and rasping. Her eyes are open now, bulging and showing white crescent moons of terror.

"It's OK, we'll help you," I croon to her as we try to roll her onto her knees to right her. "It's OK, it's OK; let's not give birth here." She's so fat with babies that whatever we do she keeps rolling back into the depression. She's tired and can't get any purchase with her feet.

"I'll get the handcart. Perhaps we can lift her in and wheel her to the barn." I'm already off and running as I say it, leaving Robin to care for Chloe. It takes me several minutes to collect the cart and I race back, pulling it behind me as it bumps up and down over the ruts.

"You take the head and shoulders and I'll grab her by the rump," Robin says, "and on the count of three we'll lift her in." We try to steady the rickety handcart with our legs as we heave and grunt and struggle with the poor creature but end up laying the cart on its side to roll her in. She doesn't fit and her head and sides overflow.

"If you can hold her and keep her in, I'll wheel," I wheeze.

We strike off towards the multi-purpose barn across an undeveloped wild area on the edge of the forest, pock marked with holes, small hillocks and rocks and the cart lurches along. Poor Chloe is terrified and pees and poops to show her distress. My arms are getting longer and longer as I hang onto the handle of the cart with our casualty; my lungs scream for air, my muscles beg me to let go. The barn is a hundred metres away and somehow we make it, tip the barrow and gently roll out our cargo onto the straw in the birthing pen. Now we're on solid ground we can get her upright and onto her feet, and in doing so her distended rear end miraculously retracts. The resilience of animals is amazing. She immediately undertakes some nesting activities, rearranging the straw bedding as if nothing untoward has taken place. I straighten up with difficulty. My arms have been stretched so much that my knuckles are down around my calves—or it feels like it. We offer Chloe water, but she's not interested. Perhaps we are the ones who need a reviving drink.

Next morning the sky is grey with cloud and an ominous stillness hangs everywhere, as though we're awaiting something menacing. Nervously I go to check on Chloe and am thrilled to find that she's fine with no signs of imminent birthing. It was obviously a false alarm; she must have lain down and just rolled into the hollow. We'll keep her here in the little paddock by the birthing pens. She seems well content and now has no competition from the others.

The rest of the animals are fine. Spot and Sox have settled in and are thriving on their calf feed and milk and go about their daily business with Buttercup and Blossom. We hope after a recent visit from the 'Bull in the Bowler Hat' to artificially inseminate Buttercup, that she's in calf again. Whitey has been served by Colonel Mustard and is due to farrow in March.

Chloe's lambing date is very close and it's been snowing on and off all day. She's mainly stayed in the barn and I notice she's developed a firm bag, so in the evening we put her into the lambing stall, trim off some bits of matted wool around her tail and wash her udder.

"Look," I murmur to Robin, "I can express milk from both teats. It shouldn't be too long now."

I'm excited but a little anxious as it's our first sheep birth. We check in several times until bedtime, but no labour yet. She's still calm when we visit her early in the morning. The temperature is now -1°C, thin crunchy snow covers the ground and the water hoses have frozen again. This means hauling more warm water to fill drinking troughs.

We let her outside for some pale sunshine. She hasn't eaten her grain and wanders over towards the hay manger but just stands around uncertainly. She goes back into the stall by herself at 11:30 a.m.

"I reckon this is it, Rob." He picks up my maternity kit containing long polyethylene gloves, mineral oil and kitchen roll; iodine for dunking navels, reference books and many other accoutrements and takes it to the barn. We settle down quietly to watch for a while. Chloe sits down, gets up, and circles round several times. By 12:30 p.m. a purplish bag the size of a walnut is hanging from her vulva. "This must be the water bag," says Robin.

"Yes, looks like it. I'll just pop back to the farmhouse," I say, "and bring back some sandwiches." I return in ten minutes.

"I can see the tips of two tiny hooves just protruding," Robin says. "They're front hooves and are pointing downwards so hopefully it's a normal presentation." The ewe strains and a little nose appears above the hooves. In a couple of minutes she delivers the head and the rest of the body rushes out, plopping down onto the straw, stretching and snapping the umbilical cord in the process. Chloe starts making soft grunting sounds to the lamb as she licks it vigorously to remove the semi-transparent birth membrane. Just 25 minutes after the appearance of the fluid filled water bag, the little lamb is on its feet and wobbling around gaining strength by the second. Shortly, another purple sac is hanging down and a second lamb is born very quickly. Mum gives it the licking treatment and it too staggers to its feet. They are making little bleating sounds but neither has found a teat yet.

We give the lambs a brisk rub down with towels and an iodine dip for the umbilical cords to reduce chance of infection or disease. In turn we put each in a cloth sling and hang it from a spring balance. They are both rams weighing 9.5 lb. Robin holds Chloe still while I offer each lamb to the udder so it can take hold of a teat and have its first slug of colostrum, so essential for immunity. Now it's all over, we offer the new mother a molasses and warm water mix. She sucks it down greedily and it will provide a blood sugar boost and keep her hydrated; she also eats a little grain.

When Chloe has delivered the afterbirth we remove it and leave her with hay to eat and her babies snuggled by her side. At 4:00 p.m. before the evening feeding and milking routine Robin again steadies the ewe's head while I gave each lamb another turn at the udder. This does more for our peace of mind than it does for the youngsters, I'm sure, because these two are capable of feeding themselves. I check their mouths and both feel warm inside, so the lambs are not chilled. We leave them basking in the heat of the infrared lamp while outside snow is softly falling. On the way back to the farmhouse we check them again and Chloe is lying comfortably with her family. Fortunately she's suffered no ill effects from her uncomfortable ride in the hand cart.

By morning there is an accumulation of 10 cm of snow. Chloe is eating and drinking well and has a good supply of milk. She's a docile mother and not concerned when we move them to an adjacent pen so we can clean and sterilize the birthing pen ready for the next confinement.

The lambs look adorable wearing tiny tight grey-tipped curls and by the time they're three days old the snow has thawed, the sun's shining and it's time to let the family back into the pasture. Robin and I each carry a lamb holding them close to the ground so their mother can follow the scent. They obligingly bleat plaintively now and again as we lead Chloe into the new sheep house in the south west pasture, where we feed her grain and give her hay. Later she emerges and sits outside, the lambs springing and gambolling nearby. Our first sheep birth has come to a very happy conclusion.

In the next few days we should have more sheep births and also Whitey's much anticipated first farrowing; she's blossomed throughout her pregnancy and Robin is so looking forward to her piglets.

11. The Midwife's Tale

It was the best of times, it was the worst of times ~ Charles Dickens

It's a raw evening and the temperature hovers around zero but has a degree or two still to fall. Already in places the grass is crispy underfoot. A cold March wind swoops down from Mount Hal and I'm hoping the old adage, 'the North wind doth blow, and we shall have snow' is not going to hold true just now. There's no moon tonight so when I've switched off the barn lights, I use my head lamp to light my way to the house, carefully carrying the frothy milk in my pail. Acorn trots along beside me keen to have his supper and take a spell in front of the wood stove back in the farmhouse. He's learned well that he must keep clear of the cows now, and is a joy to have as a companion.

My evening barn ritual is complete. Chickens, pigs, sheep and calves are all fed and, where necessary, shut up for the night. Buttercup's a contented mother in calf again and the cows have settled down to munch their way through their evening hay in the stalls. Once I have the milk safely stowed and cooling at the farm, I return to the sheep barn to check on Bertha. She's due to lamb so for the past few days I've been re-reading the animal books and swatting up again on sheep births; my mind a jumble of regular and breech presentations, backward pointing heads, multiple births, mixed up legs and heads, and other nightmare scenarios.

Robin has been called away to England and the farm animals are left in my tender care. I dread doing this on my own with several births imminent, especially Whitey's as she's been 'special' since he saved her from near death as a youngster.

Speaking softly to Bertha as I approach, I swing the barn door open and switch on the lamp. My pulse races. Looking into the pen I see a familiar liquid-filled purplish balloon, like an oversized teardrop, hanging from her vulva.

OK, keep calm… this is it.

I settle down quietly on a stool, glad that I've already checked and rechecked my maternity kit including extra flash lamp batteries, a book and refreshments for me, and have it stowed beside me in a cool box. Her water bag has broken and she's panting, getting up and down and straining. I spend an hour with her watching while she tries to deliver the lamb. I can see the hooves and nose in the accepted position but she's not getting anywhere. The books say not to intervene too early. Is this too early?

My heart hammers when I realize I really am going to have to help. She may have more than one lamb and further delay could be fatal. I swallow a mouthful of wine to give me Dutch courage then take a long deep breath. "You can do this, Maggi," I say out loud as I stretch long surgical gloves over my unsteady hands and lubricate them with mineral oil. Gingerly I slip my fingers just inside feeling carefully around the snug rim of the vulva, like a tight elastic band. Very gently I stretch it, working with Bertha's contractions, until I have eased it over a lamb's big head and expect the rest of the lamb to follow. Nothing happens. The tiny nostrils twitch in an attempt to draw in breath, but its chest is compressed in the birth canal and Bertha still doesn't deliver the rest. "Oh no! What now?"

Mentally flicking through the pages of the sheep book, I wonder if I can pull on one foreleg to angle the shoulders so they both don't try to emerge at the same time. I insert my hand and take hold of one leg just above the knee and pull gently but firmly. Round and round the pen goes Bertha with me following behind trying to keep hold of the leg of the slippery lamb and pulling each time Prudence stops to strain. Just when I think this isn't going to work the lamb suddenly drops in a heap on the floor with a liquid swoosh, and severing the umbilical cord.

It seems lifeless after its ordeal. "Please, please be all right," I say as I clear mucous from its nostrils and mouth and rub it briskly with towels to stimulate its shallow breathing and help it dry off. Bertha is lying down, exhausted so I bring the lamb to her head. She sniffs it thoroughly, locking the lamb's unique scent into her brain, and starts talking to it, a low huffing, snuffling sound as she licks it vigorously and bonds. "Wonderful," I say, "so far so good."

When Bertha stands up to continue her ministrations, I milk some colostrum from her bulging udder into a small sterile jar and feed it to the lamb with an eye dropper. The books say that the first colostrum is so important and gives the lamb not only antibodies but the strength to continue sucking. The rich sticky liquid trickles in his mouth and around his lips.

Twenty minutes later, at 8:30 p.m. the lamb is standing and I'm grinning like a clown. Mum continues chuntering and licking her baby. 9:00 p.m. comes and goes and there's no sign of another birth. I feed more colostrum to the lamb and he gets up and gives a plaintive little bleat. He hasn't suckled on his own yet and mum devotedly works on him. She breaks off to accept a few litres of warm water and molasses to drink.

It's time to leave them alone and I retreat to the farmhouse, drawing my jacket close. Looking up I can see a billion stars twinkling and marvel, as generations have before me, on the wonder of birth that is always enthralling and never grows stale.

Now Bertha has settled, my thoughts turn to the next maternity case, Robin's pig. "Please, Whitey," I implore, "don't decide to give birth now. I'm *really* tired."

Indoors I greet young Acorn and throw more logs in the furnace. He raises his head, grins and thwacks his tail on his blanket. "I've been looking after the fire for you, mum."

At midnight I check back in the barn. Bertha has delivered the placenta which I pop into a bag for incineration. Byron, her lamb, now feels warm and dry to the touch, bleats loudly and nuzzles mom's udder to suckle.

"Hey, I think we won that battle," I say to Robin, thousands of miles away, "and now I'm going to bed. Goodnight." But not before I slip quietly to the farrowing pen. I find Whitey is inside and shut her in. The last thing I need is for her to give birth in the back 40 overnight.

A peaceful night, however, is *not* in my destiny. I'm slipping into a gentle slumber... visions of sunny days. Puffy cumulous clouds lazily float across an azure sky. Little lambs frolic in the sunshine on luscious green grass and I'm pointing out Byron to Robin, saying proudly, "That's the little lad I pulled from Bertha......"

A loud bang brings me instantly awake.

"Oh no! Please, please, no. Not now."

The baby monitor I've installed in Whitey's pen is relaying roaring, crashing, and splintering wood. The clock says 3:00 a.m. I throw on pants, sweater, thick socks, toque and coat. Hopping into my boots in the basement I grab my headlamp and with much trepidation run to see her.

Whitey is in a black rage and wants OUT. My fear that she'll do real damage to herself and her house takes precedence over my worry that she'll farrow in some godforsaken spot in the forest. She stomps off into the bush huffing and in a fine old snitch. I follow her around by the light of my headlamp. A full moon would be really helpful at this point. The low temperature hasn't been enough to freeze all the water and mud in the forest and she's getting filthy as she rips down low-hanging branches and drags them around. She's on a mission and nothing is going to stop her. A natural pig farrowing in a swampy area is probably an awesome event indeed but I certainly don't want to experience it.

I stay with her until 5:00 a.m., my eyes scratchy with fatigue, then take a break and dash to the farmhouse to collect my maternity tote and put it in the pen adjoining Whitey's while she's still stomping around rearranging the undergrowth. Her stamina is incredible.

It's close to her breakfast time and I manage to tempt her back to the sty from her rest in the forest by offering a slice of melon and ginger nut cookies and shut her in once more while I hurry to do the morning chores. Happily Bertha and Byron are fine.

Some early morning cloud has raised the temperature a little and the wind has dropped. We've been spared the freeze and later a weak sun breaks through, glinting on what's left of the frost in the shady hollows.

When I return to Whitey she's stripping bits of wood off her door as if it's scotch tape. In the interests of safety I let her out again and she parades up and down in the mud. I hoped she'd be clean and dry for the farrowing, but that's not going to happen. Snorting, she grabs the rim of her water bucket in her teeth and deliberately flips it. Oh good, that means more mess. Whatever can I do with a very cross, very pregnant sow? If only there was someone here to help me, or talk to me.

Whitey enters her den at 9:00 a.m. and I hope she's close to farrowing but instead of lying down she decides this is the perfect time to make extensive remodelling changes to the house and the piglet creep, the area cordoned off where the piglets can escape under the bars and sleep beneath a heat lamp to avoid being squashed by a blimp of a mother.

From my stool in the pen next door I can hear the shattering of wood as she crunches on the creep bars, the 2 x 4s treated like matchwood. To Whitey they are simply surplus to requirements. Next she drags big sticks and large branches into the house for bedding. So maybe that means she'll give birth inside after all. When this is organized to her liking she decides her gravel drive needs to be ripped up and re-laid. Is this is her demented 'transition period' between first and second stages of labour? Now she's decided she isn't happy with Robin's new door and attacks it viciously, leaving it crooked and loose on its hinges; far more satisfactory. Unbelievably, this pattern continues for another three hours and I think longingly of one of Rob's cooked breakfasts and a warm bed.

At 1:00 p.m. she lies down for the final time. As she strains and grunts I feel her discomfort. The first piglet is born at 1:30 p.m., a pink boar, but it's stillborn. I have to bite my trembling lip while I try everything to revive it: massaging with a towel, cupping my hand round its snout and giving little puffs of air. No response. I expect it's been in the birth canal too long and the edges of its little tongue are crenelated like skin following a prolonged soaking. Tears escape and slip down my face.

Half an hour later the next piglet arrives. This time it's a large gilt with a big spot on her back, a black tail, and she's alive. I rub off the remains of the membrane and dunk her long navel cord in 7% iodine, before popping her into a box under the heat lamp. Piglets are born with blue eyes already open and are able to walk. The pig, unlike many other mammals, cannot mother her offspring from birth. She can't bend her neck round and doesn't lick the membrane from the piglet so plays no part. Once expelled from the birth canal it's up to the piglet to shrug off its thin overcoat and scrabble by instinct to find mother's teats. So Whitey isn't worried that I take the babies and put them in a box so long as they don't squeal.

Number three takes another 40 minutes to put in an appearance, a large white gilt, then 10 minutes more and number four pops out, a small spotted gilt with a white tail. This is more how I'd imagined a farrowing would be. They weigh only a pound or so and are so tiny compared to Whitey who is a massive 500 pounds, and yes, she's maybe a smidgeon on the fat side which is probably why she's taking such a long time to deliver them. After a while I take out the first few piglets from the box and put them by Whitey's teats where they squirm and scrabble with their tiny trotters, seeking a teat and latching on for a drink of antibody-rich colostrum.

It's not until 5:30 p.m. that Whitey delivers placental material and I assume the birth process is over. She's delivered 11 piglets: two stillborn white males but she has nine alive of various hues from spotted through red to pale pink: six gilts and three boars each with a fine covering of short shiny bristly hair.

Whitey is absolutely exhausted and I feel that way too. "Well done, old girl," I tell her as I give her a drink of warm molasses and water. She barely raises her head to slurp it down. I place all the babies with her and remove the box and my maternity tote. A huge weight has been lifted from my shoulders now that we have piglets. I feel quite lightheaded, but then I've not slept much nor eaten anything for a long time. Still, Robin will be so happy that Whitey's a mum.

Ariadne, the third of our Hampshire sheep, is also due to lamb today. How grateful I am that she's waited until Whitey finished. At least she's safe in her birthing stall in the sheep barn, not crashing around in the cold forest.

12. The Midwife's Tale Part II

You are never strong enough that you don't need help ~ Cesar Chavez

Just as I'm packing up my maternity chest I hear a Jeep pull into the drive. Lisa and Pete have arrived and hop out to join me at Whitey's stall. After a quick look to admire the new family Pete picks up the chest and we walk to the farmhouse for a cup of tea. It'll be a relief to have help with the barn chores and company for the evening as they'll be staying overnight. They unload the dogs, Kurri and Kano, and put them into a pen. Acorn is delighted to see them again; he's been a bit lonely.

I've slept so little in the past two days I feel rather disconnected as we complete the evening feeding and milking together. Pete checks Ariadne for me at 7:00 p.m. and returns to say she's started labour and the water bag is showing. We all rush out and already one lamb has been born. We towel it and dunk its navel and show it to the ewe. She talks to it but nothing more. Agitated, she turns circles in the stall and we can see another pair of hooves appearing. We watch her straining for a while but as she doesn't seem to be progressing I dive in and deliver the head. No waiting around this time. The rest of the body follows in a rush and after rubbing it down and treating the navel, we weigh the ram twins and each is a healthy 10 lb. We leave them on their feet and suckling as Ariadne continues to do what's necessary in the cleaning up department. Back at the house I can finally strip off my filthy clothes and stand in a hot shower. Bliss! I'm still hankering for breakfast so Pete cooks cheese omelettes, bacon and toast for us, heavenly comfort food.

The baby monitor is still active to alert us to any problems with Whitey who is my last check of the evening before bedtime. She's still lying in the same place and the piglets aren't under the lamp but huddled beside her. I have an uneasy feeling but I'm new to this so maybe it's normal. The books don't give me an answer.

Saturday brings another cool but dry day. After a cup of tea I'm at Whitey's pen by 6:00 a.m., just as it's getting light. My uneasiness solidifies into a leaden feeling in my stomach. Something's wrong. Whitey is still prostrate in exactly the same position and won't get up. She isn't interested in food or drink. By 9:00 a.m. the rest of the farm has been seen to and I'm really worried. It's fully light now so I take her temperature and it is over 40°C, a bit high. Her vulva is very puffy and fluid-filled. I discover a 12th piglet behind her, a large dead gilt, dry and wrapped in its papery membrane. I'm thinking that Whitey must have an infection and needs antibiotics. Her nine piglets occasionally shiver violently and I figure she hasn't produced enough milk to feed them.

I call the vets and as it's Saturday the answering service tells me the vet will call back. When he does I pour out my troubles to him and beg him to come and see Robin's favourite pig but he can't fit me into his rounds today. He diagnoses metritis, and purulent infections require immediate antibiotics.

Poor old Whitey, this is dreadful, what am I going to do? What if she dies and I have a litter of orphan piglets? Would they survive in my care?

Lisa drives the 15 km to the surgery to collect the penicillin and we give Whitey her first large shot in a big syringe with a long sharp needle. She doesn't even register that I've done anything to her. A very bad sign as pigs don't take kindly to being stuck with needles. She won't raise her head to drink or eat so I use a turkey baster to squirt some water and electrolytes into her mouth. It trickles out the side of her crenelated lips, but she does attempt a swallow. I try her with slices of sweet apple but she won't countenance food. She's really sick.

Sadly, Lisa and Pete have to return to their home on Quadra Island before it's time to do evening barn so I hug them tight and thank them for coming to help. It was heartening to have someone here. As soon as their vehicle disappears down the drive I burst into tears. "I can't do this," I wail, full of self-pity, but I know that I'm solely responsible for the welfare of all the stock. They depend on me so I must just keep going. It's hard enough when they're healthy, but now?

I check Whitey again; no change. When I gently squeeze her teats I can release no milk, not a drop so I'm terrified the little piglets aren't feeding. "Whitey," I cry, "what can I do for you?"

The vet himself answers my second call and I'm unable to stop sobbing as I tell him the sorry tale. He still can't make a call to see Whitey and chirpily tells me he'll put out some oxytocin for her and I can collect it from his mailbox. This hormone should cause her to let down her milk within 10 minutes of administration.

Somehow I manage to fit in the other feeding and milking, running from one job to the next. What I omit to do is feed myself. There's just no time. I jump in the old Land Rover and make the 15 km dash to the vets for the hormone, taking the back roads so I can exceed the speed limit. This is definitely a life or death situation.

I stab the long hypodermic needle into Whitey's rump and depress the plunger. After ten minutes I try to express milk but nothing happens. I move the little ones close to her belly and they try to suckle. The smallest one, a little spotted gilt, doesn't have the energy to wrestle with her siblings for a teat. She seems so pathetic I can't bear it and I tuck her into my jacket and put her in the kitchen in a box under a heat lamp. Then I warm a little milk and feed her some with an eye dropper.

At 9:00 p.m. I manage to get some water with electrolytes into Whitey's mouth but I'm so worried about the piglets starving and not surviving the night that I take them out four at a time in a box and bring them into the kitchen and feed them with a turkey baster. What a messy business. When they're all back with their mum I give her another hormone shot. I repeat this process with the piglets at 1:00 a.m., carrying boxes of piglets across the field to the farmhouse and back, then again at 3:00 a.m., this time giving Whitey another dose of penicillin. Pus is dripping from her vulva and her temperature is now 41.5°C. The spotted kitchen piglet seems fine and after each feed snuggles down in the warmth. She now has a name, Gloucester, after the Gloucester Old Spot breed.

Following a couple of hours of sleep I'm back with Whitey. The piglets are still alive and she's still lying in the same position. I put the baster in the side of her mouth and squirt in some warm electrolyte water and she swallows. Then I give a hormone shot before I attend to morning barn. The piglets huddle beside her, not under the lamp. I desperately hope she'll let down milk and they'll feed.

At 9.30 a.m. I take her more drink and check her temperature. Hallelujah! It's down to 40°C. The penicillin must be working and I am beyond overjoyed. She struggles to her feet, first hauling herself up so she's sitting like a dog then lurching into standing position. I run to get her a small warm bran mash meal and a four litres of warm Jersey milk. I stay with her and she eats it all so I fetch more but she's had enough. She goes outside to urinate and defecate then returns to her den and flops down.

Dare I hope we're over the worst? I call the vet and report the progress and he thinks she may be improving but warns me not to be overly optimistic, there's a long way to go yet. My previously rising spirits plummet to the ground. He tells me to keep giving penicillin twice a day for 3-4 days, or as long a she'll let me. In my innocence I ask, "How will I know when it's time to stop?"

Judging by the tone of his voice he's smiling as he says, "Oh, you'll know all right, you'll know." It's at this time he thinks to tell me that the oxytocin should be injected into the pig's neck 10 cm behind the ear and at a 45° angle, not into the rump. A quicker route to the pituitary gland rather than through the fat of the rump. Thanks for that, I think, but it's a wee bit late.

When I look in again all the piglets are lined up attached to spigots, so I run to the house to get Gloucester and remove the biggest piglet and replace him with Gloucester to make sure she can get some colostrum if Whitey's still producing any. Gloucester has a feed then goes from one teat to another as the piglets, now replete, make their way under the heat lamp and lie down. I'm so happy I could do a jig as I carry Gloucester back into the house.

I spend a large amount of time in Whitey's pen the next day. Penicillin a.m. and p.m. and trying to entice her with tasty small meals and treats. She always enjoys her four litres of Jersey milk, but only eats very little. I can see the piglets at the teats but I'm not convinced they're getting enough. The vet tells me to increase the dose of the hormone.

Over the intercom I can hear her honking and piglets squealing and when I check they are all huddled near her and some are shivering again. Once more I collect them in batches and take them to the house to supplement their milk intake. Now mother is a little better and more mobile I have to be cautious as she becomes very anxious if one squeals.

Gloucester's doing very well with accepting the milk feeds I give her, as are some of the others; sucking the baster. A few buck and gurgle, but I hope they're getting something and I'm not just covering everything with milk.

Completely exhausted, I perform my other farm chores mechanically. All the animals appear in fine health for which I'm hugely grateful. My brain is so befuddled, though, I can't imagine why I ever wanted a farm and animals.

At 9:00 p.m. before I go to bed I feed all the piglets again then take Whitey her penicillin. As she's recumbent I jab my syringe into her rump as usual. It needs to be a quick forceful jab because the skin is very tough. The needle has only penetrated 2 cm when, with a deafening roar, Whitey rears up and spins round on the spot. Could this possibly be what the vet was alluding to regarding her letting me know when she'd had enough? I'm ecstatic to see her so active but now she's glaring at me with her beady black eyes blazing, the syringe still sticking in her rump. She's positioned between me and the piglets, grinding her teeth and frankly, I'm scared. I can't possible leave the hypodermic to fall out on its own into the bedding with the babies running around and I'd never find it again in the straw. I have a dilemma: I daren't try to pass behind her for the syringe because she'll think I'm advancing on her piglets.

"OK, Whitey, I'm sorry, I won't do it again, I promise." I speak in what I hope is a low soothing voice and not the terrified shriek I hear inside my head. I thrust my hand into a pocket and bring out a couple of chocolate chip cookies. (Never be without treats.)

"Hey, Whitey, would you like a cookie?" She takes one from me and it disappears with a mighty crunch. I'm glad to see her appetite's returning and that I still have fingers. The second cookie, though, I throw onto the floor half a metre away. She has a very good snout for cookies and, as anticipated, she steps forward and picks it up. I have just enough time to whip behind her and pull the syringe from her ample rear.

"That's definitely the last time for any injections I swear," I tell her as I bolt from the sty.

I'm not attempting a 3:00 a.m. visit and intend to sleep through the night. Robin will be home tomorrow afternoon then he can take charge of his pig and do what's necessary. She likes him; he hasn't tortured her as I have.

I sleep very well and wake refreshed. It's a splendid spring-like day with a sky the colour of a robin's egg. I take time to look around me, a luxury I've been denied lately. The breaking leaves of the alders are changing from a pinkish haze to a full young green, and there's a flurry of nesting activity with the robins. Spears of bluebell leaves are well advanced among the crocuses, and dandelions and daisies spangle the fields. The air smells fresh and scented with spring bulbs. I make a mental note that it's time to put up our hummingbird feeders as the males arrive during the fourth week of March.

After Gloucester is fed I struggle to hold her eight unwilling siblings once again to supplement their milk. They have moved from baster to bottle and have caught on to the bottle technique. They are much stronger and I'm hoping they're now getting more milk than I first thought. Whitey is accepting small meals and I've seen her basking outside in the sunshine. The little ones have become very engaging, popping in and out of their house, racing around outdoors, doing 360°s on the spot and having a rough and tumble. Nothing much wrong with them now and their satiny coats bear a translucent gleam in the sunlight. At four days old they've had their last force-feed from me, but I do bring in the smallest of them, a pink boar, to help relieve the pressure on Whitey and as company for Gloucester. I complete my morning chores in good time to collect Robin from the airport in Nanaimo.

"Grand little chaps." he says, as we check out Whitey's offspring, "absolutely super. Well done Mags!" Robin's very happy to be home again and Whitey strolls over to the fence to receive an apple and a belly-rub from him. She's glad to have him home too. He's the one who usually feeds her and she doesn't associate him with painful injections from oversized hypodermics.

As we continue round the farm, five robust comical lambs gambol in the field in front of the sheep barn, hopping up onto hillocks, playing King of the Castle; all of them ram lambs. I smile and point to Byron, the oldest. "There's the little lad I pulled from Bertha."

Purdy and Prudence have yet to lamb this week so Robin hasn't missed all the fun.

He offers to feed the indoor piglets for me and I watch without comment as milk from the bottle squirts and dribbles all over the piglets and Robin too.

"It's not so easy feeding these, is it?"

I smile and nod, thinking of the recent drama: he doesn't know the half of it. "Yes, it can be a bit challenging sometimes."

The intercom is ceremoniously switched off and Robin pours me a large duty-free G&T as I sink into the couch, more than ready for a relaxing evening. It's great to be able to share burdens.

Two weeks later when the vet is visiting to dehorn a calf, I proudly show him our piglets and ask why he could never manage to come to see Whitey.

"I make it a rule never to get into a pen with a sow and her litter. Even if they're pets they can be extremely dangerous and unpredictable." He smiles wryly, "actually we rarely ever *attend* full-grown pigs. Strictly phone advice only." He picks up his kit, gives an exaggerated wink, and saunters off.

13. Storms and Spring

The talent for being happy is appreciating and liking what you have,
instead of what you don't have ~ Woody Allen

It's so much more enjoyable when two people are farming together.
With Robin home from England things return to normal, if *normal* is
a word one can use to describe any part of traditional farming. The
sun bravely finds holes in skies laden with rain, providing us with a
glimpse of one of nature's wonders, the double rainbow.

Acorn is in seventh heaven and loving farm life, especially contact
with the livestock. We find him cavorting in the field playing chase

with the baby rams who are practicing their head-butting techniques on him. However, remembering Rottweiler Ben's episode with Prudence the sheep, it's something we'd rather not encourage. One day we see him playing in the cow's field with something we can't identify. It's giving him a great deal of enjoyment as he tosses it high in the air, leaping and pouncing on it, doing a 360° turn and throwing it again. Robin investigates and finds that he has found a withered lamb's tail. When the ewe lambs are tiny we position a special elastic band 6-7 cm from the root of the tail. This cuts off the blood supply and within a few weeks the surplus tail withers and drops off. We do it for the lambs' ultimate health and comfort. With only a stub of tail left there's little likelihood of dung being trapped on the fleece to attracts flies that will lay eggs, and so eliminates the risk of emerging maggots eating into the lamb's flesh. The ram lambs who will be market weight in a few months, don't need to have their tails done, only those kept for breeding.

Anything sheep related is a favourite of Acorn and if the opportunity arises he'll sneak a few mouthfuls of the lambs' pellets from their bowls as they're feeding. What a delightful life it is for a puppy on a farm.

The weatherman is forecasting a big March storm, so we spend a couple of hours making sure everything round the farm is secure with nothing left lying about to act as a flying missile. The winds howl all night with hurricane strength gusts flinging rain, small gravel and broken tree bits at the farmhouse. We hardly sleep and lose electricity at 11:17 p.m. In the early hours we hear a powerful roar ending with a mighty crack, but don't venture out. When it's time to start our day the power is still off so using flashlights we survey the land outside.

"Oh no," I say, "one of our Douglas fir trees is down."

It was one of the 25-metre tall trees growing only three metres from our main entrance on the side of the house.

"Thank goodness it fell away from the house," Robin says, "and didn't bed itself in our roof."

"Yes, and thankfully we don't sleep on the upper floor."

The wind's still blowing, but with reduced strength. After a soggy tramp round the farm to inspect for damage we find all the animal houses intact, but we've lost 13 really big trees and some trunks and branches are pinning down fences, so Robin will have a few days of chainsawing and fence repairing to do and it's not made easier by the drop in temperature accompanied by a snowfall.

Just what he needs: more fencing work. Still, we can always make use of the wood in the furnace next year.

Fortunately in nature there's always a balance and soon the natural order of things prevails. Winter and its storms makes way for a magnificent British Columbian spring. The skunk cabbages, whose mustard coloured blooms in February pierced through the snows and populated the swamp with their signature scent of garlic and promise of better weather to come, will soon send up their massive leaves that will grow four feet tall and are useful for standing on when traversing the swamp—like using snow shoes.

We find a couple of piles of scat in the woods, so the bears have emerged from hibernation. Best of all, spring is proclaimed by Pacific Rim tree frogs providing us with night after night of endless frog symphonies. A wonderfully relaxing sound to lull us to sleep and to serve as a useful early warning system. If we approach the ponds they instantly fall silent, so we know if they're chirping there are no predators close by.

April brings an occasional cool breeze and showers, but also glorious sunshine. The early snowdrops and crocuses, lenten roses and hyacinths have given way to daffodils, narcissi and bluebells jostling to display their beauty. Skies are as blue as the robins' egg shells we find deliberately jettisoned a long way from their nests, and the air is bustling with all the birds driven to rear a new generation. Spring grasses are growing fast so the sheep and cows are very contented now after their winter diet of hay. We have to strip graze the cows initially to allow them access to a small portion at a time, otherwise unlimited fresh young grasses coupled with the keen appetite of a milker will result in 'Jersey squirts.'

The valley tom-toms have been beating and we hear news that the sheep shearer is coming to a neighbour's farm in Beaver Creek in a few days' time, so we think we'll get Charlie sheared professionally. It's probably a good idea not to ruin our hitherto good relationship by subjecting him to our novice shearing techniques. We bought brand new electric sheep shearing equipment and got as far as upending Charlie when he was smaller, before deciding it wasn't a good idea, but we will do the girls ourselves after they've given birth.

Charlie jumps into the Land Rover with ease and we fasten off his halter. He seems to quite enjoy his rides. At our destination we let down the tail gate, Charlie hops down, and Rob leads him like a dog on a leash. As I follow behind them I notice the faces of the other sheep owners watching Charlie walk in.

"How do you manage to lead him like that?"

"We've done it since we got him as a lamb," I say, "so he's used to it."

"Huh, I can't even go into the field with my ram, he just charges at me, and knocks me down."

Oblivious to the astonishment of the onlookers, Charlie waits patiently for his turn with the shearer, Joanne, a tall strikingly attractive girl wearing a sturdy leather apron, her long black hair tied out of the way into a complicated knot. Taking Charlie's halter she immediately flips him onto his rump so he's in a sitting position, and then deftly manoeuvres the electric shears round his face and up and down his body. How skilled she is. In less than five minutes I'm holding a naked ram wearing only his halter and Robin is rolling up the one-piece fleece. It all looks so simple.

Charlie is quite interested in the other sheep around and makes a few chuffing sounds, then his attention is focused on three burley men fighting with a big woolly body: legs, hoofs and heads, sheep and human, flying in all directions. We spectators flatten to the side of the driveway to allow them passage with their charge which they drag into a holding pen and bolt the door.

"Hmmm," I say to Rob, "I guess another willing ram has just arrived for shearing."

With that, we pay the fee, say thanks to the shearer, and I walk Charlie away towards our truck. "Good Lord," says one of the men, still florid of face and out of breath, "I wish mine was like that." Then with a twinkle in his eye he adds, "you wanna have a go with him? You must be a sheep whisperer."

I smile, and shrug my shoulders. "Not today, thanks, no time. C'mon Charlie, let's go."

Robin is always looking for new projects with moneymaking potential to increase our income and one day has a bright idea. Noticing that wild mushrooms do so well on the property in our damp rain-forest climate, he's been researching the growing of mushrooms. There's always time to squeeze in one more task.

"Why don't we grow shiitake mushrooms on logs?" he says. "They're well known for their superior taste and medicinal properties."

Off he goes for a weekend course with a 'mad professor' on the BC mainland to learn all about it while I hold the fort. He's very keen when he returns with his new knowledge so we enrol in a day course on a shiitake mushroom farm on Denman Island. Growing the mushrooms entails cutting metre lengths of 15 cm diameter hardwood logs and drilling them with countless evenly spaced 1 cm x 4 cm deep holes. Fortunately we have lots of Alder trees. Robin orders fresh mushroom spawn from the mad professor that arrives in a big growing clump the size of a pumpkin. He crumbles it up and rams it into the holes using a sterilized acrylic rod. I then paint the holes with a tree sealant before we take them into the forest; hanging some and laying others out on racks.

"What happens now?" I say.

"It can take up to a year for the spawn to grow and colonize the logs before they'll start to fruit, so we'll just check them from time to time."

Our lambs have now been separated and weaned from their mothers and we decide we'll sell the ewes, preferring to concentrate on pigs, cows and chickens. The five ewes are quickly snapped up after we place an advertisement in the Buy, Sell and Trade Agriculture section. The separation from their mothers doesn't improve the behaviour of the lambs who become increasingly good at escaping to the neighbouring properties, to explore and race around. Having to stop work several times to help me retrieve them sometimes makes Robin hopping mad. Their antics are tiring us out.

As they are now they're approaching market weight I say, "Shall I take the three largest lambs to the auction barn, to see whether they'll sell?"

"Won't hurt to try. It'll save us the heartache of taking them to the processor and then having to sell the meat, when we're so busy."

I load up the Land Rover and take the trio to the auction where they are bought pre-auction by the local butcher who's in need of good quality lamb. He doesn't usually like to buy at auction, he says, because he never really knows what he's getting. I explain that my lambs are well muscled from ranging over the farm and the neighbours' land and they've had the best quality lamb feed too. He examines them minutely, checking their body fat, the depth of loin, their mouths, gently probing the flesh, and we agree a price on the spot and transfer them into the back of his SUV. Perfect. I don't have to wait for them to go under the hammer.

A few days later the butcher calls me. "D'you have any more lambs? Those one I bought were excellent." So a deal is struck and he'll take all of our lambs, and prepare one for us. That was easy—well, not so much the rearing part, although without them now we'll have to cut the grass around the house again—they surely did make good lawnmowers.

Despite the many interruptions to Robin's work in order to retrieve wayward lambs, he manages to dig out some old growth stumps from a new pasture he's preparing. It is a really big job for the small John Deere 450 bulldozer, especially when he has to dig down eight or ten feet to be able to break out the roots of stumps nearly as big as the dozer. Days of warm early summer sunshine help and the lack of rain means he doesn't get bogged down when he drags the stumps away.

He intersperses this work with the continuing chore of replacing the old barbed wire fencing with paige wire, impossible to accomplish on the difficult terrain without two of Robin's toys, the old dozer and his trusty Land Rover.

Then there's rock-picking, always rock-picking. What looks like a beautiful expanse of brown earth one day appears peppered with rocks after a light shower washes the soil off them. It's an endless task we carry out with buckets which we fill with rocks and lug to the tractor to be finally deposited near the swamp, thus forming our own private mountain. Who knows, we might need them again. In the old days the hauling was accomplished by a horse dragging a *stone boat* like a sled, back and forth across the land as the rock pickers picked and threw the stones onto the boat. For us, though, it's man hours, buckets and a tractor. Little by little it gets done, and the rocks we're picking are smaller and smaller each time until we call a truce. Several of the visitors we have to the farm happily pitch in for a couple of hours in the sunshine in exchange for a hearty farmhouse meal. At this rate the field will be ready for muck spreading and seeding in the fall. We intend to create a productive pasture and will prove to our neighbour that hard work *can* produce good results.

In the kitchen garden all those little seeds we merrily planted in spring have grown and now there's an abundance of produce to be harvested daily. Peas and broad beans must be picked and blanched for the freezer and there are already some early runner beans. It's time to search the Buy, Sell and Trade publication for another chest freezer so we can enjoy the produce over the cold wet winter months that seem so very far off.

14. Dog Days and Hog Hijinks

*When we have a construction job to do, we want an uncommon
engineer ~ Herbert Hoover*

The early days of May follow one another with increasing warmth
and fragrance. A Swainson's thrush sits on her nest in the contorted
hazelnut tree, cleverly hidden at the junction of the trunk and a
branch a metre and a half from the ground. The nest lining is smooth
and as beautifully rounded as the speckled breast of the bird that sits
so patiently on her four brown-flecked, pale blue eggs. The male
thrush is not far away and waiting to pitch in with the feeding of his
offspring, for when they hatch the pair will be working nonstop.

We feel we're already working nonstop on the farm using all the hours of daylight, so if there's a feasible way to reduce our workload, yet achieve our objectives, we try to employ it. Our free range pigs fall into this category. They devote themselves wholeheartedly to the delights of rooting in the fields and while doing so, completely eradicate noxious plants like brambles and bracken from areas that are to be cultivated with crops for animal fodder. A favourite treat is the ubiquitous prehistoric-looking horsetails that feel remarkably like a doll's plastic hair. One wouldn't imagine it was palatable but Whitey is convinced otherwise.

The pigs become an invaluable tool for preparing the ground. They get into areas we can't and as they turn over the sod they eat all the bugs, beetles, leatherjackets and every single root in sight. This nourishment, along with pig pellets plus surplus milk and whey, results in the tastiest pork while their by-product fertilizes the pasture too. It is an ingenious concept and really can't be faulted as a circular system.

Sows roam the topography with their large families and even the tiny piglets copy their mothers executing their own miniature version of ploughing furrows with their mobile button-sized cartilage-tipped snouts. They play a great deal too: jumping and spinning, pushing and chasing showing remarkable agility and speed, especially if you want to apprehend them. The piglets quickly learn to steer clear of mum's nose if she's found a particular delicacy, for if it pokes its little snout where it's not wanted then mother has no compunction in lifting it, and with a flick of her powerful neck and shoulders sending it spinning into space before it bounces back to earth and trots off, quite unfazed. They keep us endlessly amused.

Whitey is indifferent to the fact that her offspring are too adventurous and regularly escape their field to explore wider horizons. Acorn, though, is always watchful and acts as nursemaid on diaper duty, trailing them around the farm. If they tire and briefly flop down onto the grass, Acorn will lie down too and let them walk all over him and push him around.

This litter is particularly friendly and will approach us if we're nearby and chew our boots. Sometimes we can crouch down and give the occasional belly-rub with the recipient arranging its body to allow greater access to its tummy and becoming almost comatose with ecstasy. They are especially engaging because of their variations in colour: red, pink, ginger, large spots and small polkadots, all the result of genes inherited from their red-skinned Tamworth father.

One day I find the marauding troupe of little hooligans sprinting up the driveway to the cows' barn and nudging a feed sack to make it dispense treats, and have to bring pressure to bear to get them back to their mother who, incidentally, hasn't minded their absence at all. She's supremely content in a wallow, rolling in cooling mud as the temperature climbs into the high 20s.

Unrepentant, the piglets are soon off again running amok in the kale patch we're nurturing for the cows. Then they race like a little band of desperadoes with Bossy in the lead, through the gate into the farmyard to check out the chickens and then on to the grape vines. It's not unusual to hear one of us cry, "Quick, they're in the vegetable garden," and we drop everything to chase them out. It's all jolly good fun if you're a young porker. Next they burst through the fence and set off down the drive towards the road but Acorn heads them off. Whitey, showing slight concern at last, gives a coded call, a loud woof and they all race home. It's obviously time for a restorative snack and the milk bar is open and all that can be seen are curly tails and colourful chubby hindquarters.

"Well," says Robin sighing heavily, "I guess I'll have to put paige wire all round Whitey's field too if we're to save the farm from total destruction."

"Ah yes, the price we have to pay to have happy animals, but we couldn't do it any other way."

I smile indulgently; it's easy for me to say because *I* won't be the one doing the fencing.

The catching of piglets, however, is a specialized skill and we must devise a foolproof plan so they are ready for their new owners. The first time we had a litter, three of us raced round and round a small enclosure chasing them with fishing keep nets, but when a piglet was trapped it just ran straight through the netting. Not at all satisfactory, so on the morning before the weaners are to leave we keep them in their house with their half-door closed. The Land Rover is parked outside the pen and I climb over the half-door in with the piglets. I lunge at one, grabbing a rear leg. Then I try to get hold of the other leg and stand up with the creature, its hocks pumping up and down like pistons as it kicks. Before it slips from my grasp I heave the piglet up and over the door to Robin and he carries it snugly in his arms and pops it into the Land Rover. Sounds simple, but at this tender age of 6 weeks the piglets already weigh around 40lb.

The first ones are relatively easy to catch since the piglet house is full and I'm not exhausted. The last ones, however, will run circles round me in an attempt to escape as I repeatedly lunge and miss. When they're finally all caught we drive them to the multi-purpose barn to spend the night in a new pen. We must go through the chase and capture process again in the barn when their purchasers arrive and actively encourage owner participation, if only to act as a barricade. To raise pigs, you can't be afraid of getting in there with them.

"Feisty little buggers," says a hefty red-faced chap, giggling as one slips right through his hands, "and don't they weigh a lot?" Eventually all have been captured and gone to their new homes and the barn is quiet.

The next day, the couple from Lantzville who had collected five weaners, calls us. "We absolutely love the piglets and couldn't be happier with them. When you have your next litter can we have some more please? Seven, if possible. And when you're down this way please call in and have coffee and come and see them." It's so encouraging to hear from satisfied customers.

For Acorn, though, life is empty and he has much free time so he mooches around looking for something interesting to occupy him. "Look what Acorn's found," I say to Robin one day, "a hen's egg." The egg is intact and Acorn has carried it onto the grass and is gently licking it. "I hope he doesn't accidentally break it and find out how good it is to eat," I add, "or he'll be squeezing though the chicken house door and helping himself." I thank Acorn for the egg and he wanders off. Later he brings back a second egg, then a third, followed by a fourth in the evening, carrying each one gently and placing it onto the grass to wash. I praise him each time and determine to keep an eye on him to see where the eggs are coming from. When he saunters off nonchalantly down the drive towards the workshop barn I trail him. He has no guile and guides me inside to a hen's nest on the floor hidden behind a big wooden box. It has another nine eggs in it. This chicken, part of our commercial flock that is not supposed to go broody, obviously hasn't read the right instruction manual and has decided she wants to be a mother.

A few days later I'm weeding the garden when I hear Acorn barking excitedly. It's unusual to hear him so I stand up to see where the sound's coming from. A brown bear is ambling down the driveway past the cows' field. Acorn tears after it chasing the startled creature back up the drive towards the mountain and into the forest, before returning, tongue lolling, and feeling pretty pleased with himself. He has certainly earned his *Fearless Protector of Oak Tree Farm* badge. "It looked like a juvenile bear," Robin said, "and as long as it doesn't interfere with us or the livestock, that's fine. This is his territory too."

Soon after, the neighbour who lives closer to the mountain phones to alert us that his dog, Sam, has disappeared and that he can see the prints of wolf and cougar. Sadly, Sam never returns. We've got to watch out for Acorn. Perhaps it's time for us to think about getting another puppy soon, maybe there *is* safety in numbers. Acorn would love a friend, he gets on well with visiting dogs and we certainly have room on the farm. Robin has always had a hankering for a bull mastiff, but is disinclined to part with the very high price the breeder is asking, so I think we should get another rescue a dog.

The warm weather that ushered in June is continuing with glorious hot sunshine. Our big oak tree is nobly decked out in its new leaves creating welcome shade for the birds as well as land based creatures. Acorn, though, lies panting in the sun and Whitey foolishly sunbathes. Everyone loves the sunshine. On the lawn, a mother robin, followed by four babies larger than herself, hops along snatching up any morsels available and returns to thrust them down gaping throats. She never stops and this is probably her second or third brood this year. Meanwhile Robin and a friend have been busy scything down the 60 cm high orchard grass we planted in one of the chicken fields. The amazing growth shows how high in nitrogen and fertile the ground is after the chickens have been running on it.

Early summer heat means Farmer John is taking advantage of the weather and completing his first cut of hay. We buy a wagon load of bales for the cows for the coming winter and later we'll have two more loads of fine, second-cut dairy hay to see us through till next spring. Last year we tried to be superhuman and made several trips to pick up bales direct from his fields, loaded them on the back of the truck, and Robin pitch-forked the bales from the truck into the upper storey of the cow barn, where I stacked them. We saved 60 cents a bale on two hundred bales, but never again. Sometimes we forget we're not in the first flush of youth. It nearly killed us and we did it in the scorching heat.

This year Farmer John will deliver the hay to us on his hay wagon direct from the field and lend us his electric elevator to load the bales into the barn. A far more sophisticated and satisfactory method.

The day after hay storage is complete I'm walking along through the south pasture and spot something moving in the neighbour's field. Oh no! Surely not the Colonel. I check his pen but he's not there; our boar has gone AWOL. He's grown from a cute little 'English banger' into a formidable 600-pound beast with lower tusks that curve up from his crenelated lips into very effective 7 cm slashing tools. A few days ago he went walkabouts taking with him our new gilt, Miss Plum, but Robin and I were able to retrieve them from the swamp area without too much trouble. He forces his way through the stranded barbed wire fence we inherited and, typically for a pig, if the snout can get through then the wedge-shaped body will follow. Today he's gone solo, and he's made his way through the swamp area into the neighbour's field. I run back to the house for food, my heart thumping in my ears.

Standing on the two old lower wires of the boundary fence to stretch them, I heave up the upper ones hoping to make enough room for him to get through. Then I lay a trail of delicacies and rattling the food bucket, I call him. He saunters over, noses the goodies and starts picking them up, making his way towards the fence. After a slight hesitation he pushes through and I scatter more edibles to lure him in the direction of his house. Then the unthinkable happens. I run out of food. I've miscalculated and we have 15 metres yet to go. He's not fooled by the rattling bucket and the Colonel loses his temper and swings at me with his snout. Throwing the bucket at him, I start to run but slip on the grass and fall to my hands and knees. Facing certain death and fuelled by a large adrenaline shot, I leap up and run behind the closest tree, edging round to keep it between us.

Mesmerized by what is unfolding, Robin roars up on the tractor and smacks into the pig's gatepost with a crack. He leaps down and runs to my aid, diverting the Colonel's attack towards himself. Retrieving the bucket, I throw in a handful of earth and rocks and vigorously start rattling. I gain his attention and we lure him into his pen and secure the gate with chains, leaving Robin the task of resetting the offset gatepost and tightening fence wires. The only positive thing is that at least the neighbour wasn't aware of his unwanted guest, and didn't encounter the Colonel.

"Robin," I say later after thinking over the day's events, "I *never* want to deal with that pig again."

I have a pleasant diversion from farm chores for a while as my father's visiting from England to celebrate his 83rd birthday. He loves the countryside and is in his element helping with chores around the farm, digging, planting and weeding in the vegetable garden, and coming with me to the Farmers' Market to sell eggs and meet customers. Oh to have such a willing helper all year round. He's a mechanical engineering draughtsman by profession and has designed some amazing things: the jib of the W1400 that was the largest walking dragline in the world in 1951; the rotating base for London UK's first revolving restaurant on the 34th floor of the Post Office Tower in the 1960s; and several massive lock-gates for dams in Australia. He was invited to use his skills on the NASA programme but being such a self-effacing man and close to retirement, he declined. He's the ideal candidate to design and build us a mobile hay manger that we can place in different areas of the field to relieve the muddiness from bovine foot traffic in the winter.

He draws a detailed design to Robin's specifications and makes a list of the lumber and other requirements. However, he's unfamiliar with the North American lumber dimentional terminology. Being a precision engineer and used to working to thousandths of an inch tolerance, he erroneously believes that a 2 x 4 measures 2-inches by 4-inches, when in fact it measures rather less. When starting to assemble the manger, something isn't right, and he goes over his figures again. Oh dear! Robin has to gently explain that 2 x 4 is the measurement of the rough lumber, which is then milled. I didn't help matters by saying, "Oh Dad, don't fuss, just jam your hip against it to hold it in place and bang a nail in." We do end up with a perfect manger which, of course, he isn't really happy with, but it works faultlessly for all our years on the farm and is much admired and coveted by my farmer friends.

Tomorrow is his birthday and we're busy preparing for a garden birthday party when we have a surprise call from the manager of the SPCA. "Could you possibly accept seven Muscovy ducklings and one

Canada goose gosling?" She's affecting her cheery, hopeful voice. "They're just a few weeks old and they're in need of a farm home and you came straight to mind. They're mine actually and over the past few days we've lost ten ducklings to a pair of eagles, and we can't bear to sit by as the rest are taken one by one."

"We'd love to have them; we have a pen ready under our grape arbour where they can settle in before being given freedom. It's right next to a pond."

"Oh that's great," she says, "I'll come myself tomorrow morning and deliver them on the way to work. I've been wanting to see the farm."

Robin happily continues with the baking for the party while Dad and I spend the rest of the afternoon adding chicken wire to the underside of the grape arbour frame, so the ducklings and gosling will be secure from above as well as all sides as raccoons and mink are particularly partial to ducks.

So now we've increased our numbers by seven Muscovy ducks and one Canada goose and Acorn can watch the flock. Next month we're expecting more piglets, then he can once again take up his role as nanny.

15. Season of Fruitfulness

Black bears rarely attack. But here's the thing. Sometimes they do. All bears are agile, cunning and immensely strong, and they are always hungry. If they want to kill you and eat you, they can, and pretty much whenever they want. That doesn't happen often, but,— and here is the absolutely salient point—once would be enough ~ Bill Bryson

The soft-fruit season is upon us and we have much harvesting to do. Red currants for making jelly and black currants for jellies and pies. There are raspberries and strawberries and soon there will be plums, then pears and apples, too. The lawn by the house is crispy now and scorched brown by so much sun with no rain, the only real green in it belonging to the deep tap rooted plants like plantain. We snatch a rare moment to sit in the sunshine on the grassy bank outside the house with a mug of tea, wallowing in the scent of the warm earth and lavender flowers, surrounded by the sounds of bees and insects busily pollinating and collecting comical orange pollen sacs on their rear legs.

"It *is* lovely here," I say, "I could breathe in so deeply it just pops the buttons right off my shirt."

"Yes," replies Robin, letting his gaze wander slowly around, "and it looks like we'll be able to make some wine this year, there are so many grapes. That's if we don't lose them all before they're fully ripe."

Quite brazenly the Steller's Jays are harvesting the unripe grapes from the upper vines while the chickens jump up and pluck all the lower grapes within range, it's quite comical. Despite this help from the wildlife we manage to pick 25 lb. although the resulting wine turns out to be not the *greatest* product we've made on the farm, in fact it's downright disgusting. Next year the birds are welcome to the grapes.

We're not the only ones who love the bountiful fruit harvest. Robin drives home from town one day and tells me that Elsie, our elderly neighbour, has a live bear trap in her front yard by the gnarled old apple tree. Then later in the afternoon he calls to me from outside. "There's a bear by Whitey's pen!" By the time I get out of the house, of course, the bear has evaporated into the forest. The next day Elsie calls us to say a bear has been caught in her trap, so if we want to see it we'd better go now before the wildlife people come and take it for relocation in the back woods of BC.

The bear is sitting in a wire enclosure surrounded by, and occasionally swiping at, a cloud of wasps as it eats the honey bait. It is unharmed and not fully grown, perhaps just an adolescent. Without getting *too* close, I bravely lean forward with my camera, but for some reason the resulting picture comes out blurred. Nothing to do with a shaking hand, surely? Must be the camera.

Only a few days later when I'm churning butter in the kitchen, Robin's standing and looking outside when he says, "I can see a bear."

"A bear? Another one? Where is it?" I rush to the window. To be truthful, I'd rather not have a bear at such close quarters.

"No, no, no, not a *bear*. A *pair*. A pair of mallards on the pond! They're happily swimming around and our ducks are taking absolutely no notice of them."

It wasn't long after this that I recounted the bear sightings to our daughter on the phone. She has a very healthy respect for bears since she's a marine biologist and often visits fish farm sites which, not surprisingly, are quite heavily populated with black bears and therefore she's always on high alert. She said that she was recently at a barbecue party where she saw a three-legged bear climb over the back fence into the yard. Because the beer was flowing freely no one would believe her '3-legged bear in the yard' warning, and lots of bear jokes were cracked until someone else spotted the creature. All previous bravado vanished, the back deck emptied immediately and the house filled until the conservation officers arrived to take control of the situation. Indeed, the bear was missing a foreleg from the elbow down but tracks showed that it had long since departed the area.

One of the delightful things about a small mixed livestock farm is that we're always having babies. Whitey delivers another delightfully colourful array of 13 piglets exactly on time. We have none of her earlier problems with lack of milk, but decide to rear the three smallest by hand to give them a better chance and reduce the stress on their mum. She only has 12 teats, two of which are rather small, and after the first day or so each piglet has its own specific spigot, so the larger piglets muscle their way to the most productive teats and the very small piglets would have a rough time of it and wouldn't thrive. Why lose babies when we can step in and help them survive?

Fortunately we've discovered that the indoor piglets can learn to drink from a small bowl by the time they are two to three days old. No more of the messy turkey basters and having to sterilize bottles. Whenever the weather's good they enjoy an outing in a little pen on the grass outside, but when the weather's inclement we bring them upstairs into the living room where they're a constant source of delight for Acorn who monitors their every escapade.

The piglets are quite happy running around and exploring as long as their tiny hooves are planted firmly on the floor. If you pick one up, it immediately releases an ear-piercing squeal, and continues shrieking until it is returned to the floor.

"I wonder why they do that?" I say.

"Well," says Robin, "I have a theory." (He often does.) "Piglets are born with little pressure sensors in their feet. As soon as we pick them up, their sensors tell them that they are no longer in touch with the ground, so that means they're flying, and that's scary, so they squeal. The minute we put them down, they have landed safely, equilibrium is restored, they stop squealing and continue about their business as though they've never been airborne. Like the old saying indicates, pigs aren't meant to fly."

"Hmmm, well I guess that's as interesting and inventive an explanation as any."

I know for a certainty that at some time in the future Robin will recount his new theory to some poor gullible person who will believe his every word.

September arrives as mellow as a late, ripe golden pear. It's time again for Port Alberni's biggest annual event, the Fall Fair. Each year it's blessed with incredible weather and this year we decide to enter a few categories. Robin shows Charlie the ram in a yearling and ram class. There are eight rams in his group including his sire, and the judge studies them all in detail, returning to Charlie a couple of times. He tells Robin, "he's got good width between his hips, very strong loins and a good deep body." He checks Charlie's hooves and teeth and adds, "is he old? His teeth are small and is this a broken tooth?"

"No," Robin says, they're baby teeth and that is a new one just coming in, he's only a yearling."

"Well, he's massive," says the judge, "wouldn't anyone just love to have their ewes served by him?"

We couldn't be more surprised and thrilled when Charlie takes first place, and beats his father. Not only that, he's awarded the Grand Champion rosette. It is a great honour for us. Charlie, as usual, is unconcerned, and has behaved impeccably while surreptitiously checking out all the lovely ewes around. It is a good day for prize money for us as we also claim second place for our Buff Orpington trio (two hens and a rooster), and two firsts and a second place for captioned photographs. One of the blue ribbons was for 'Bringing Home the Bacon,' a picture of Whitey returning to her pen with some of her colourful young piglets.

Peter Lenihan, owner of Charlie's sire, talks to Robin after the awards, "I wish I'd kept him now," he says wistfully, and proceeds to question Robin about what we feed him to keep him in tip top condition allowing him to realize his full potential.

A few days later Charlie becomes rather pushy. He's just seen lots of sheep, it's breeding season and we have no ewes this year. We're especially concerned with his boisterous tactics because Buttercup is close to calving.

"I've had a thought, Rob, why don't we call Peter and see if he would like to use Charlie to breed some of his unrelated ewes this season? He could board him for a few weeks and then Buttercup and her new calf will be in peace."

"Good idea," he says, "give him a call."

Peter is thrilled with the suggestion so we put Charlie straight into the Land Rover and drive over to their farm.

Two days later we have a dreadful call from a very distressed Peter. The Lenihans have two other rams, and they put Charlie in a field with them. The rams saw Charlie as the rival he was, galloped at him from opposite sides of the field and rammed him between them, snapping his neck. We are stunned. We all made a big mistake and have a lot to learn. Hopefully death was instantaneous. Our colourful character, Charlie, will be missed.

Shorter days and a few shrivelling leaves denote the end to the Indian summer and the changing of the season. We discover a huge bear scat at the front gate, full of fruit pits and berries and our neighbour Elsie phones to say she's seen a real *big bugger* in her fruit tree again. She tells us that another neighbour has lost several branches off her plum tree from the bear gorging on the unpicked fruit. The black bears are busy storing as much fat as possible for their coming hibernation. Several have recently been at Stamp Falls, the provincial park lower down the hill, feasting on salmon returning upstream to their traditional spawning grounds at the head of Little Hal creek that runs along the north edge of our farm. The bears are gradually migrating towards the forest and the mountain to hibernate, and they sometimes call in on their way to take advantage of an easy fruit harvest.

"We'd better pick all our crab apples, Robin. They're the only thing to attract the bear too close to our house." This big bear is an annual visitor and has probably been caught in a live trap before and is no doubt too canny to be caught again. Despite being relocated a great distance away, they seem to easily to find their way back to their old territory.

Our September sunshine gives way to a brooding dampness wrapping the countryside in still greyness. Mists envelop Mount Hal, hiding it from sight; water droplets bead the bushes and the pasture is spongy underfoot.

Things are quietening down. Harvesting is over, fruit and the last of the vegetables frozen and preserves have been made, although there are still multiple field chores to accomplish before winter; harrowing, tining and finally sowing with fall rye. Despite its well documented beauty, so loved by poets and writers, I find fall to be rather melancholy, preferring the joy of springtime and new birth, rather than death and recycling.

I am much cheered up when Bill arrives to stay with us for a couple of days following a week's course in Victoria. As he's stationed in Nova Scotia with the air force we don't often see him so we have a lot of news to exchange. We tour the farm to see all our animals and current work projects before completing evening barn chores, retreating to the cosiness of the farmhouse for supper and glasses of wine around the roaring log fire in the hearth that amply combats the chill of the evening air.

The next morning dawns with a rare beauty. Fluffy pink clouds reflect the rising sun, bathing all in rosy light. I go to my usual venue at the Farmers' Market while Billy helps Robin feed the creatures and then does some autumn harrowing.

I arrive home in time to share a late lunch then Robin and Bill capitalize on the good weather and tackle some tricky fencing across a swamp requiring two people, the Land Rover, and the bulldozer. I also take advantage of the day, spending a few hours cleaning out all the chicken houses, installing new litter on the floors and nesting material in the boxes. A task that always makes me feel virtuous.

Buttercup still has a week to go to calving and we're keeping a close eye on her. This afternoon as I work, I can see her slowly ambling towards the forest so I call the others and we gently head her off and lead her into the calving stall. She might as well be in there for a few days so she doesn't give birth when we're not there and hide the calf in the bush again like last year. As with all our imminent births, we have the baby intercom installed in the barn and can listen in on the receiver in the farmhouse.

The last of the evening sunshine is gilding the roofs of the barns. Robin and Billy stand at the picture window, beers in hand, looking out towards the mountain and discussing important topics while I assemble supper.

"Listen," I say, "what's that?" I increase the volume of the intercom and can make out what sounds like a little gentle lowing, as if Buttercup is humming through her muzzle. Armed with towels, iodine and a warm drink just in case, we approach the barn quietly and peep over the half-door. Standing in the bedding is a dark red/brown bull calf 'Betelgeuse.' He's still wet and nosing around under his mother's belly instinctively seeking, but not yet finding, her teats. Soon his orientation skills will be perfect.

I gently pat Buttercup's neck then run my hands along her back as Robin gives the calf a brisk rub down with the towels, then we treat his navel with the 7% iodine to avoid any infections. "Good girl, Buttercup," I say, "you've done well." She moos and licks her calf again. I offer her the warm water and molasses drink and she thirstily sucks it down.

How glad we are that we put her in the stall this evening. When we check them once more before bedtime I can remove the remains of the afterbirth. Buttercup is resting and the calf is curled up nearby, comfortable in his new world. All is well.

"I'm glad I didn't miss this," says Billy, "now I understand a bit more why you like farming."

We wake to a foggy Sunday morning and at 6:00 a.m. we go quietly to the barn. Mother and baby are lying down and we encourage her to stand up and offer her some grain. Robin cleans the stall while I milk some colostrum from each of the four quarters to relieve the pressure in her distended udder. "We'll freeze this in ice cube trays," I tell Billy, "then we can use it for any young animals born here; sheep, calves or piglets as the colostrum has the antibodies to give the young immunity to organisms in this particular area." Buttercup hasn't drunk any water yet but just before Billy and Robin leave for Victoria airport, we visit again and she's drunk a whole pail and Betel is contentedly suckling. Poor yearling Blossom, our last year's calf born at the exhibition, is mooing mournfully to herself in the next stall because she's lonely and can hear Buttercup making baby sounds to Betel. Blossom will have her nose put out of joint for a while but she'll soon recover and then she'll have a playmate.

September often bathes us in balmy sunshine, but much cooler, wetter weather isn't far off. "How about taking a couple of hours off?" I say to Robin.

"That sounds like a good idea."

The fir and pine trees reach into the cobalt sky dotted with cumulus clouds and we unpack our picnic hamper in a favourite glen in the back forty. Relaxing, we chink crystal glasses and raise a toast, "to us; the farm and the future." Robin slices into a fresh crusty baguette as I unwrap the farmhouse pate and cheeses; grapes, sliced apples, and melon. Sipping our wine we reflect on how far we've come and where we hope to be going. All our hopes and aspirations are laid out along with our picnic. Mellow with wine and food, we recline, letting the sun caress our bodies as we slowly entwine in love.

16. The Milkmaid's Tale

Cows are among the gentlest of breathing creatures ~ Thomas de Quincey

Rain is in the forecast but the morning is bathed with glorious autumnal sunshine and for a few hours we revel in a spell of brightness highlighting the fall colours. Later, clouds gather and there's a brisk heavy rainfall and we're treated to a dazzling double rainbow. The clouds swiftly depart and then the sunset is as spectacular as was the dawn, with added tones of amethyst. This is an enchanting time for the new calf to find his way in the world, exploring, yet staying close to mum.

As we can't use Buttercup's early milk for human consumption for a few days because it contains colostrum, Betel is allowed to suckle as much as he wants but there's no way he can consume it all. On his second day it's noticeable that he has one favourite teat and is only drinking from the left rear quarter so I milk more than two quarts from each of the three other quarters by hand. By mid-morning Buttercup's udder is again very large, so I will have to milk her out completely this evening. Mum and son are in the field but I bring them back in at 4:30 p.m. after we see her tramping once more over the bramble hump towards the woods. Catching up to Buttercup we clip a line to her head collar and lead her back to the stall. It's some time before Betel decides to follow and mum is getting frantic, but all is well when he finally trots along to her side. In the morning it will be time to start Buttercup's proper milking routine and I'm not looking forward to it.

Buttercup is lying down in the stall with Betel when we arrive, so I grasp her head collar as she gets up, and lead her into the milking parlour next door and clamp her head into the stanchion. She's a little reluctant after her months of freedom. As I endeavour to milk her she shows her displeasure; she flops, and pees and flops and flops again, trying to jerk her head back out of the stanchion; I didn't know she could produce so much waste in such a short time. Perhaps it's because she can't see her calf. I eventually get just four litres of colostrum milk. Robin tries feeding some of this to Betel in a calf bucket but he just blows bubbles in it—the calf, that is, not Robin. He carries Betel to another barn to separate mum and son for a few days, hopefully out of earshot, where Betel quickly latches on to the idea of bottle feeding rather than the bucket. We can try the bucket again in a couple of days.

By the afternoon mum's udder is again huge. I must take some of this milk so instead of using the milking parlour, we tie her in the large stall so she can munch hay and be more relaxed. I milk one handed into the fore-cup working my way round the teats. I stop after ten litres when my stainless steel bucket is brimming.

"It would be great if we could use the milking machine," I say to Robin, "Buttercup has so much milk and this is really hard on my hands."

We had this thought in mind when during the summer we located an electrically powered vacuum pump and also some stainless steel milking equipment. We knew that milking two or three cows by hand would be tough. If we'd been brought up on a farm hand-milking from an early age we might have developed the right muscles but my hands are not so adaptable these days. Robin has already installed the vacuum pump in the barn on the other side of the wall that divides the milking parlour. It's been tested and works well. In fact it is rather larger than we need and we could run six clusters for six cows at the same time if we had a larger herd and a larger milking parlour.

"Would it take much to finish the installation?" I ask wistfully. I have a mental picture of drifting into the parlour with a serene cow, barely needing to replace my glamorous evening dress before clipping on the equipment and waiting till it's all over.

In the evening I hand-milk another ten litres from Buttercup and again first thing next morning. Robin is succeeding well feeding Betel with warm milk straight from Buttercup; he has more patience for this than I do.

All next day Robin works on the piping and plumbing for the milking machine, finishing with installing new food-grade hoses. Next he flushes the system several times and sterilizes it.

"It's all hooked up," he says proudly, "and everything's working fine; do you feel like trying it this evening?"

My honest answer should be, "Not really, I'm dreading it." Instead I say, "Oh yes, let's give it a go, we've got to brave it sometime."

I have a number of invaluable skills when it comes to farming. Training a novice cow to the milking machine is not one of them. I try not to project my inner turmoil onto Buttercup. I smile at her, for heaven's sake, as I secure the stanchion and she inclines her neck to eat grain. First I wash, dry and sterilize her teats. Robin already has the vacuum pump running and it's making soft sucking noises in the background. We've decided to attach the cluster of suction cups, or 'claw', as a joint effort—Robin will take the port side, and I'll do the starboard. Amazingly, with beginners' luck we manage to get the nipples sucked into the cups and the milk starts to flow—for a few seconds. Then Buttercup, realizing something is amiss in her udder region, perhaps realizing that she doesn't have four calves simultaneously feeding, lashes out a foot and we lose suction. The contraption clatters to the floor of the stall and she promptly clamps off her milk supply. Ribbons of residue milk dribble from the suction cups. I continue milking by hand for a few minutes until she relaxes a little and lets down her milk again while the vacuum pump still makes its slurping noises in the background. When things are going well I call Robin to help me try again. Alas, it is rather less than successful and Buttercup manages to flop four times in the process. We are splattered and the stall is slippery with partially digested green matter.

This isn't going well. If she'd behave then the milking would take only five minutes instead of twenty. How do we get that through a bovine skull? It takes us a further hour and tanks of hot water to wash down the stall, and wash and sterilize the milking equipment. When it's all finished Robin says, "it was a good decision to put in that water heater, so we have instant hot water!"

"Yes, we must count our blessings but I'm *so* not looking forward to tomorrow."

At 7:00 a.m. the electric motor of the vacuum pump whirrs into action. I wash and dry Buttercup's teats and milk a few squirts from each into the fore cup. Working together, we hold our breath and hook up the suction cups. Fabulous. Three of the quarters are working well, and Robin makes an adjustment to the fourth then she's firing on all four cylinders. We get about 11 litres. Buttercup is very good. Now we've got the hang of it.

Robin takes a calf bucket of milk to Betel instead of the usual bottle. It will make redundant the task of sterilizing his bottles. First he offers his finger to Betel who latches on and sucks hard as all calves will. Incidentally, we discover this is the foolproof way to walk young calves if they're too big to be picked up—just insert a finger in the calf's mouth and lead it. To train him to drink from the bucket, Robin lowers his finger and Betel's muzzle into the inclined milk bucket then he wiggles his finger a bit so that as Betel sucks the finger he's getting some milk too. In time, Robin can remove his finger and Betel continues sucking. In short order he has mastered bucket feeding and can suck up four litres of milk in a matter of seconds.

Evening barn comes around and, full of confidence, we set up the milking equipment. As Robin bends to attach the suction cup, Buttercup's right hoof strikes sideways with a lightening piston action and catches him on the eye. Next she gets him on the shin. Then she kicks my wrist and arm. She can piston backwards, sideways and forwards, like a kung fu artist. Amazing. Once suction is lost on one of the cups the whole cluster falls off. I revert once more to hand-milking. We shouldn't let her win but at least we do get nine litres of milk, even if everything else is plastered with liquid poop again. I feel like slapping her hard on the rump but fortunately common sense overrules ire. When we've cleaned up we try a dry run without the cow and think we have the solution with the clusters. The trick is to have the neck of each suction cup hose bent double to maintain suction, only straightening it as it is offered to the teat.

I did not sleep well. During the night I was worrying about this morning's milking. With good reason, it turns out. Once again, Buttercup kicks the cluster off. I try hobbling her, tying her back feet loosely together with a soft thick rope, and anchor the tie to the side of the barn. She's so mad, and, let's face it, scared, she fights and kicks and yanks off a barn board which clatters down onto her back. Robin tries hand milking for me, but she's not used to him, so she's still unhappy.

"I'm absolutely not letting you out today until we've done this," I tell her calmly, "So you might as well relax, put your mind to it and behave. I know you're scared, I am too, but if you can stop acting like a cantankerous old cow we'll do just fine."

Twice more it's suction, kick off cup, milk spray everywhere, poop: suction, kick off cup, milk spray everywhere, poop. Finally I sit on the three legged stool, keep my head jammed in her flank and we apply the cluster once again. This time, there's no kicking and the job's done in another five minutes.

Over the next three days of battles Buttercup finally adjusts and accepts the milking machine, only occasionally lifting and replacing a foot, but not kicking out. If truth be known, it's probably us who have done most of the adjusting and we're obviously approaching it in a more acceptable way. So following a rather tough week for all three of us, Robin and I are black and blue with bruises on our arms and legs. Robin has a hoof print round his eye and I have an impressive lump on my forehead, but we're getting about 10 litres of milk twice a day. We did it!

After their week apart, we put a halter on Betel, a finger in his mouth and lead him back to the cows' field. Catching sight of him Buttercup makes some baby moos then bellows and gallops towards him. Mother and son are overjoyed to be reunited and so is Blossom. They all run a victory lap round the field. Betel is now sporting his special nose band head collar to prevent him from suckling from

Buttercup. It contains some punk-looking, but blunt, spikes so that when he searches underneath her she feels something alien and lifts a foot to prevent him suckling. After all, she knows very well how to do that.

The next day the barometer drops rapidly and the sky is ominously black when we go to do the morning milking and feeding. During the day the barometer continues falling steadily and by late afternoon great gusts charge across the landscape picking up leaves and twigs and hurling them into the sky. Then the rain starts and is driven horizontally by the increasing winds. It continues all evening, howling and flinging steel pellets at the windows and on the skylights. Above this we hear a great crack and a giant of the forest falls over, followed by a blackout. It's fallen on the power and phone lines.

This evening is a log fire and candlelight affair, and we are well equipped with headlamps for reading. At least this time we don't have to finish incubating chicken eggs in the kitchen range, so it's relatively relaxing. We picnic on cheeses, crackers, fruit, chocolate, and glasses of red wine. There's no point in going outside or worrying about damage, if a tree hits us, it does. But I'm always unnerved by loud noises after being in the cyclone on *Orca*. Another glass of red wine puts paid to those worries. Fortunately Acorn is not concerned about the brouhaha outside, and snuggles up on his blankets at Robin's feet. He absolutely loves Robin who can sit still without moving for several hours reading a book, unlike me who bobs up and down continually as 'things to do' flash in and out of my mind.

In the morning it's not quite so rough as we complete our chores in the rain. Through gaps in the clouds we occasionally catch a glimpse of Mount Hal and notice that the snow line has crept to one third of the way down; winter's almost here. It's wet and dismal all day and the ideal time to be making butter from the cream I've saved over the past four days, enough to make three and a half pounds.

Despite our initial trials with Buttercup things are soon running smoothly which makes our customers at the Farmers' Market happy, as they've been patiently waiting for raw milk and unpasteurized Jersey butter. Robin is researching cheese making, and as it's a lengthy and time-consuming process, and as we're very fond of cheese, we'll probably keep them all to eat ourselves. There have to be some perks to farming.

Always eager to improve our milking technique, we finally clue into the fact that when a cow gets up from a night's rest a chain reaction is set in motion and soon afterwards it will lift its tail and flop. However, even if we take Buttercup straight from her stall in the morning for a short walk round the field before milking, she can often hang onto her bowel contents and reserve them to do an almighty flop while she's being milked—she's always ready to make a statement. Our only reliable remedy is to invest in an oversized shovel and while one of us milks with the machine the other stands behind her with the shovel ready to catch the offending manure when she lifts her tail. Now we rarely suffer mishaps.

17. Epoch's End

Give me the end of the year an' its fun
When most of the plannin' an' toilin' is done;
Bring all the wanderers home to the nest,
Let me sit down with the ones I love best...
~ Edgar A. Guest

November arrives with persistent grey skies and a depressing stillness following the latest wind storm. Trees drip relentlessly and mists are slow to clear. There's a smell of decaying leaf matter in the woods and wet, slippery leaves cover the fields.

A frightful sight meets us when we get to the barn to feed and milk the cows this morning. Liquid green manure is running in rivulets down the walls and forming thick puddles on the ground.

"What on *earth's* the matter, what's happened?" I say.

"No idea," says the ever-practical Robin, "but we're shit out of luck using the milk we get today."

The cows' legs are slick with muck and I can't help feeling very sorry for them and imagine that they may have terrible gut ache. We *must* milk, so we do it in haste, discard the milk, and then embark on a big clean-up of the barn stalls with hoses and brooms and Robin uses the tractor to dig out all the bedding and replaces it with clean shavings.

It's too early for the vet surgery to be open and I don't want to call the emergency number so as soon as we're back at the farmhouse I call our friend, farmer John, and explain the scene. He knows immediately what the problem is.

"They've got winter dysentery. It's highly contagious. It's just made its way through my herd." He hesitates a moment, "I wonder if I brought it to your farm when I came the other day to artificially inseminate (AI) the cow."

"Is there anything we should do? I haven't called the vets yet as the surgery's not open."

"No, it's not serious, and they'll get over it in a few days."

I go straight to the heavy tome, our Merck veterinary manual, and turn the flimsy pages to find bovine winter dysentery and start reading to Robin.

"It's a viral disease with an acute onset of profuse watery diarrhea in adult cattle, typically in the winter months from November through March."

"Yep, that sounds like it."

I continue to read, and tell Robin that it's not *so* bad, the cattle can remain bright and alert and generally continue to eat but milk production will be severely reduced and may not ever return to the normal levels expected.

We check them again, and on close inspection the cattle look just fine. It seems as if they haven't *suffered* the disease so much as *rejoiced* in it as projectile fecal matter continues to be squirted while they stand contently munching fine hay.

"I really hope we don't permanently lose milk production," I say to Robin, "we need that milk."

The vet confirms the diagnosis when he hears the symptoms.

"Is there anything we should do?" I ask.

"Not really, but there's something you shouldn't do. Don't walk behind the cows with your pockets open." —Oh, you've just got to love that sense of humour— "Other than that, wait it out, your cows are in fine condition and will throw it off quickly."

Although calves aren't normally affected, he advises the administration of extra fluids and electrolytes for any youngsters as a precaution and we are to administer this directly into the stomach using a funnel attached to a long tube fed down the throat.

Armed with the electrolyte mix and a funnel pushed into a 60 cm long tube we return to the barn and enter the stall with the calf. I back it into a corner and pry its mouth open so there's a straight line down the throat and Robin can slide the lubricated tube into the stomach, being very careful not to pass it down the trachea into the lungs instead. Robin is just about to pour the liquid into the jug-type funnel when I yell, "The tube's slipped off. IT'S GONE!"

Robin drops the funnel and wrestles the calf to the ground and wrenches open its mouth. I thrust my hand into the sticky salivary mouth and just manage to dig my nails into the last centimetre of slithery tube at the back of the tongue and yank it out. Poor little calf, how panicked it must be. When we've recovered our composure, Robin says, "Do you think he's poorly, do you think he needs this?"

"No, he looks just fine to me, and on reflection I don't think he needs electrolytes through a tube after all—just lots of milk." We couldn't put the little creature through that fiasco again we might not be so lucky a second time.

Happily all the cows return to robust health after a couple of weeks and milk yields are once again stable. We just hope that the AI farmer John performed on Buttercup, when he inadvertently introduced the dysentery, will be successful and a calf is forthcoming next year.

It was wishful thinking. A few days later Buttercup is again in heat, but perhaps it's not surprising since she was afflicted with the virus. Farmer John suggests we take her and Blossom, her 16-month old calf, to visit his bull. Buttercup can only stay for a few hours in between milkings, but Blossom will go for an extended visit among the other young heifers. John says it's a free service, "otherwise my bull will be coming over the fields to visit your cows and bring all my heifers with him." We have no great hopes from Buttercup's short visit to the bull, so she may need to visit again in three weeks, near Christmas time.

It is a rare event, but Robin has gone into town on a Christmas shopping expedition and I'm busy with a big pot of milk and rennet warming slowly on the stove for cheese making, when the phone rings.

"Hello," says a resonant voice, "do you keep a big pig?"

That all-too-familiar rush of adrenalin crashes into my bloodstream. Since the Colonel's two escapes earlier in the year Robin has always dealt with the boar and we've managed to keep him confined to his field. The caller is our neighbour to the south.

"Er, yes."

"Well, there's one roaming all over my pasture right now so you'd better come and get it."

Hoping that this time maybe it's just dear old Whitey, I load up with bucket and treats and run to the south fence to look into the next field. Contrary to my greatest desire, I can see my nemesis, the Colonel. To say that I'm frightened would be to engage in careless understatement. I'm torn between an overwhelming desire to run home to the bathroom, or try to collect the Colonel on my own before he causes any damage. I must be brave and attempt the latter, so start calling and rattling the bucket. He turns in my direction and decides he'll head for home. I'm not sure why because we share a mutual dislike and distrust. Perhaps he's coming because he wants to finish the job he started a while ago, knocking me over and trampling me into the ground. Pigs are very smart and have good memories. This time, though, he behaves reasonably well and once I have him locked again in his field, I return to my kitchen chores. One week later, when Robin is trying to pour breakfast into the boar's food trough, the impatient Colonel slashes the back of his leg. That does it. His fate is now sealed: the bad-tempered Colonel will have to be despatched in the New Year.

We're looking forward to this year's Christmas celebrations as we're having a family gathering. It's the first time we've been together with both our children for Christmas for many years and it's a great bonus to also have two spouses and two new grandsons.

The afternoon Bill and Laurie arrive from Nova Scotia with baby Mitchell, our seven Muscovy ducks don't return to the duck house by the pond for their late afternoon snack: just a solitary Lucy Goosey is sitting near the feeding area.

The ducks often tramp to all corners of the farm but always return before nightfall for their grain. I'm very concerned as we have lots of raccoons around and they have a fondness for chickens and ducks. I make a few quick phone calls to neighbours and they all promise to keep a lookout.

Billy helps me scout round the farm, but we can't find them anywhere.

"Something's not right," I say, "They've never done this before. I can see we could lose one or two to vermin, but it's not likely we'd lose seven at once."

"I'll drive you round the neighbourhood if you like," says Bill, "and see if we can spot them."

We take the Land Rover, Billy at the wheel. "I love this vehicle," he says, "it's just like the one we had when I was little, only that one had a soft top."

"Hmmm, we had a great time with that, on Land Rover trials, and cross-country expeditions with the Welsh Land Rover Club."

"Didn't we all spend a night in it once on the Brecon Beacon mountains?" Bill asks.

"Yes, those were the days. That's why we couldn't resist buying this one when we saw it. It was definitely an impulse purchase. We saw it parked outside a house, stopped, looked at it, took it for a drive and shook hands on the deal. It's the perfect vehicle for the farm."

Up and down the road and tracks we trail, checking with binoculars, gradually increasing our area of search. We're just about to give up and drive home, when I spot movement—something white. We're adjacent to an almost derelict property, full of broken farm equipment and old vehicles that have rusted into the landscape. I get out and use the binoculars.

"Over there—I can see a duck. I bet it's ours."

Billy backs the Land Rover to the driveway, and we walk onto the property, closing a rickety gate behind us. A couple of chained Rottweilers lunge and bark, bringing out the owner from a trailer next to the broken down house. He looks at us with a vacant, mildly inquisitive air.

"Can I look at those ducks over there? They look like mine." I don't wait for an answer and stride off with Billy towards the pen. Yep, they're certainly my ducks.

"Why have you got my ducks penned up?"

"They were just wandering about and I threw some food in the pen and they went in."

"You didn't think to phone around and see if anyone was missing some tame ducks? You can see they're not wild ones."

"Why would I? Ducks make good dinner."

There's no arguing with that. "Yes, well they'll make good dinner for us, not you."

I'm not *too* sure that we should be eating SPCA rescues, but rather us than the neighbour.

We pick up a couple at a time, load them in the back of the Land Rover, shout, "thank-you very much," and drive off.

"What gall," Billy says, "they have no shame."

"That's true, but to them anything moving on their land is fair game in all senses of the word. It's surprising one wasn't already plucked for the pot."

"Perhaps they did have a fire going ready," Billy adds. "Am I mistaken, or was there a pungent sweet smoky smell in the air?"

When we return home, Robin says, "I think the neighbours must have lured them. Possibly when they were out hunting they spotted our little band on the borderline of our property, and gradually set a trail of treats for them. That's why they've been missing all day lately, only this last time they got penned up so they couldn't come home."

"Good old rural BC, eh?" says Bill. "That place reminds me of the old joke, if you've got 14 vehicles on your property that don't move and only one that does, you could be a redneck."

The ducks will now be contained in the orchard with a small pond. All, that is, except the pure white Muscovy who repeatedly outmaneuvers our attempts to capture her. We call her Lucky Duck as she will escape the pot and stay to become Lucy Goosey's firm companion.

For days we've been watching the snow line creep inexorably down Mount Hal. The last of the Christmas shopping has been completed and tomorrow it's Christmas Eve, time for final preparations and Lisa, Pete and Alexander will arrive to join us. The live Christmas tree on the deck is hung with lights, a log fire is roaring in the grate and brightly coloured parcels tumble in a heap beneath the indoor tree. Mitch and Alex, our 3- and 4-month old grandchildren, are blissfully unaware of the season and upcoming historic change in the calendar, happily bouncing, facing each other in their jolly jumpers hanging from a beam in the living room.

Robin and I return from the cows' barn after the evening milking to join the family.

"I can smell snow," I say, "there's definitely something in the air."

On cue for a picture-perfect Christmas, a heavy moist snowflake falls from the leaden sky and soon the air is thick with dive-bombing flakes piling up rapidly to make a white world. The mini Christmas lights outlining the animal barns twinkle in the snowy darkness.

The New Year arrives and the transition to the new millennium, which had been in the backs of our minds for some weeks, has come to the fore. The media has endlessly promulgated the *Y2K Bug* hype, doing its best to frighten us all silly. It's been a lucrative time for computer experts who've been paid millions of dollars to check computer systems.

Computer problems or not, for us the year 2000 will be even busier on the farm than 1999 with new calves, a new boar, more piglets from the three breeding sows, lots of new ducklings, and chickens, a new puppy, orphan lambs, and the inevitable tragedies too. We've weathered our farm start-up and love it despite the really hard work. This is the stuff of farming life. We're looking forward to a bright new century and epoch with lots of new plans and projects.

18. Puppies and Orphans

Until one has loved an animal, a part of one's soul remains unawakened ~ Anatole France

"I'm going to the SPCA, Rob, to take some free-range eggs for them, would you like to come so we can have a look around?"

It's January 2000 and the beginning of the new century. The world hasn't come to a crashing halt because of the threatened 'millennium bug'—there wasn't even a blip. Our families have gone home following the Christmas festivities and I'm entering the winter doldrums. Skies are heavy with cloud and rain turns the remaining snow to slush. I need something to look forward to and I believe that something is another puppy.

Our new SPCA premises are a great improvement on the old, bright and airy with heated floors for the pens but I don't really enjoy visiting. It's always heartbreaking seeing the appealing dogs just begging to be taken home. Today there are the ubiquitous lab-cross puppies—always appealing but we have one, Acorn, who's now eighteen months old.

One grey dog, huge, shaggy and of indeterminate heritage resembling a lurcher, is not available for adoption yet. He has a terrible coat condition, eye infections and the most awfully misshapen paws with floppy toes.

"Oh, whatever's the matter with him, poor chap?" I ask the SPCA officer.

"He was badly abused by his owners, who repeatedly stood on his feet and broke his toes."

"That's disgusting," I say, "I would like to do real evil to people like that."

"Unfortunately we see more of this type of thing than we should, but we'll get him better and find him a good loving home."

We've been wondering about getting something like a Jack Russell terrier, thinking it would be good for the farm if we had a problem with vermin. At the shelter all shapes, sizes and ages of canines present themselves, many barking, saying, "Pick me, pick me," but there are no little Jack Russells. There is one funny little puppy in a huge pen all alone. It's light tan with a white chest and feet and a very short coat. Its ears stand up from its head and comically fold down forwards either side of its forehead which seems furrowed with a worried frown. It doesn't jump or make a noise, but sits upright by the front of the wire cage, watching. As I bend to its level a pair of meltingly beautiful brown eyes bore deep into my soul. It seems to have the weight of the world on its small shoulders, way beyond its tender age, and is not expecting life to bring miracles any time soon.

"This one's a pit bull mix," the officer tells us, "found wandering along River Road near the reserve. We think it's about 8-9 weeks old."

We continue our inspection of the dogs and as we leave Robin says, "Thanks for showing us around, we'll go and have a think about it."

On the way home we discuss the pros and cons of the various dogs.

"We should really adopt one of the puppies," I say, "as Acorn does love mothering babies. There was nothing there like a Jack Russell, though."

"What about the little pit bull," Robin suggests, "that's a Staffordshire Terrier isn't it?"

"Very similar, and I gather it's their turn for a bad rap. It used to be German Shepherds, then dobermans, then Rottweilers, now it seems to be the pit bull." I wonder if there's any truth in the rumours? That little pup certainly doesn't look mean.

By the time we've reached home, I'm really warming to the idea of the pit bull. In fact, I've decided it will be ours, but I think I'll let Robin be the one to make the decision so I jump to the computer to do some research.

"It won't be as big as you'd hoped when you were thinking of a mastiff some time ago," I joke, "but it says that Staffordshires make faithful companions and are very protective of their families, and in well-to-do England they were used as companions and guards for the children in the nursery. Doesn't sound very dangerous, does it?"

"OK, let's go and see the pup again," Robin suggests.

"Right now? Great! I'll call the SPCA to tell them we're on our way."

"Is it a girl or a boy?" I ask the manager over the phone. She's the same person who visited our farm and who brought us the Canada gosling and Muscovy ducklings. "I'm not sure, I think she's a little girl," she says. "I'm glad you're thinking of taking her, because we can only place pit bull breeds in specially approved homes."

Well as we've now got nine creatures from the SPCA, besides Acorn, I guess we qualify.

"Great, we'll be along soon to pick her up."

Humming a little tune I busy myself preparing the indoor crate for her, and put in woolly blankets, and toys. Acorn watches me, ears pricked, head cocked on one side, wondering what is happening to his old crate.

"We'd better stop at the feed store to pick up new bowls and puppy food on the way to the SPCA," suggests Robin.

Before going into the office, we wander through the kennels to take another look. What an engaging little pup. Not barking or leaping in her cage, but just standing up, looking out. I put my finger through the wire for her to smell and she licks it.

"Yes, this is definitely the one we'll have," I tell the manager, "we've already chosen a name for her—Cricket."

She unlocks the door and I reach in for the puppy who advances and licks my hand again. As I pick her up I say, "Ha! Doesn't look much like a little girl to me, he's definitely a boy. Oh dear, what are we going to call him now?"

I hug him as we walk through into the office to complete the paperwork and he now gently licks my ear.

"Don't forget," the manager says, "you must have him neutered when he's six months old. He's had his baby shots and you have a free visit to the vet for a check-up and booster shots."

I cuddle him all the way home. He's relaxed but alert. No sign of fear or distress. The name 'Cricket' sticks. At home in the kitchen we introduce him to Acorn, who gives him a comprehensive sniffing. Cricket subjects himself to the scrutiny and has a little exploratory sniff of his own. He mops up a little food and water before we take him outside, then he's happy to retire to his fluffy blankets in his crate to sleep.

Cricket has a pretty rough time for the first week. He vomits after eating, has diarrhoea, coughs and makes gagging noises so it's straight to the vets. It transpires that he's contracted the kennel cough virus. We receive worming tablets to rid him of his belly full of worms, and antibiotics to prevent secondary infection from kennel cough. Throughout it all, he's stoic and maintains his chirpy spirit. His digestive disorders disappear and after a week or two he's coughing less. He's such a trouper. We discover that he came from a house with a grow-op where his mum was used as a guard dog. His siblings were also found wandering and the owner was taken into custody and is now residing in custody at Her Majesty's pleasure.

When he joined Oak Tree Farm both Cricket's ears folded forwards. As he's grown a little, however, they've change and now both fold towards his left side. At this time we have to take him to the vet for his scheduled checkup. The vet remarks on his placid nature and cute appearance, casually adding, "Look at those ears, where d'you keep him, in a wind tunnel?"

Cricket adapts well to his crate. After Robin takes him for a stroll round the garden last thing at night he willingly settles in his den, and never makes a sound until we rise at 6:00 a.m. He's a model puppy and follows the lead of his big brother Acorn in all things. They escort us on our feeding rounds, and I take them both into the chicken houses when I collect eggs, so they become used to flapping birds and don't consider them prey. Yes, Cricket's arrival has been the perfect antidote to the winter blahs.

As the days gradually lengthen, the earth remains in the grip of frosts; pipes are frequently frozen and we regularly carry hot water to the animals. Unfailingly Cricket and Acorn accompany us. While Acorn sometimes scoots off on an errand of his own, Cricket stays close as if he knows he has an important job to learn and he's not going to let his new family out of his sight. We teach him to respect Buttercup and the other cows and to keep his distance from hooves and heads.

This year, however, as we approach spring and have no sheep, I'm really missing the anticipation of newborn lambs even though I know they can become difficult to contain within fences, especially the last ones after we'd sold their mums. I spend an idle moment reminiscing. They were such a plucky, energetic little flock cavorting in the pig pastures, carrying out raids on the vegetable garden, jumping and springing on the clean shavings in the shavings barn and playing hide and seek in the milking parlour. With Acorn's help we would round up the adventurers, enticing them with food and usher them back into their field in time to shut them into their house for the night.

What seemed endearing at first, especially to visitors who were overjoyed at their antics as they popped up all over the farm, later became a source of mild annoyance and then a worry when they had to be fetched after wriggling under the fence into the swamp area. Then, following a phone call from a neighbour to report that they were galloping up her driveway without concern for her flower borders, we started to look forward to them going to market.

Winter has at last lost its grip and a few days into March the weather is mild. Yellow, gold and purple, the primary colours of Spring, bring hope and cheer after winter's monochrome landscapes. Days can still be punctuated by some frosty snaps but I dream of sunshine and lots of work with newborns. Madness, I know, but the piglets, calves and lambs skipping and jumping in the fields brings me such joy.

Ebony and Ivory, though, don't exactly skip and jump into our lives. One evening the telephone rings. It's a call from a young neighbouring sheep farmer overrun with lambing problems in the fields, and who has just had to bring another new mother and lambs from the field into her barn. She's exhausted as her husband is working away from home.

"I've got two newborn lambs that I just can't handle," she says, "would you be able to take them? I'm already bottle-feeding several."

"We'd love to have them," I say, barely able to contain my excitement. "When shall we come?"

"Can you pick them up first thing in the morning, please? I've just given them some colostrum, but now I've got to go out again and check another ewe in the field."

I can hardly wait to set off in the morning. Everything's prepared. The pen in the warm basement has a soft bed of hay; a tiny manger and a water bottle attached to the wall. Sterilized bottles are lined up in the kitchen with special lamb teats, and we have plenty of cow colostrum stored as frozen cubes. I'm cautiously optimistic that we'll be able to rear the little chaps.

Ebony is large, black and beautiful, born yesterday. He was disowned by his mother and has a bloody navel. Ivory is white and tiny, born the day before, but sadly her yearling mother has no milk. She appears rather downtrodden, forlorn and her face looks bruised. Not much fun in her life so far. Her navel has already dried, but we treat them both with 7% iodine solution. After we gently bathe Ivory's face, they snuggle together into a box of hay in the kitchen under a heat lamp. They shouldn't need heat for too many days. If lambs survive their first few hours, have dried off and are receiving nourishment, in normal circumstances they are rugged little things. Keeping artificial heat on them for too long can be detrimental.

I make up an interim mix of food for their bottles; a blend of full cream Jersey milk, extra cream, colostrum cubes, eggs, castor oil and sugar, store it in the fridge and embark upon a two-hour feeding schedule, just 2 oz. each at a time. They're both very keen to drink but we mustn't feed them too much at each meal to begin with, or they'll scour. This is very difficult because they suck the milk down so greedily they give the impression they're still starving. Very soon, though, it reaches their tummies and they flop down to sleep.

Gradually they adjust to their new food and become very active jumping out of their box and running around the kitchen, much to Acorn's delight. So it's time to transfer them to their pen in the basement, where the wood burning furnace lives that keeps the whole house warm. When they've been with us for three days Ebony weighs in at 10 lb. and Ivory 6 lb. They are doing well and we change to an increased amount of food at 3-hourly intervals; a little easier schedule. A break in the rain and some welcome sunshine allows them to come outside for some fresh air and exercise in the field with Acorn and the hand-reared piglets.

Just when I was missing the joy of lambs, I was lucky to have two drop right into my arms. A farm just doesn't seem right without puppies and lambs.

19. New Millennium Farming

To my mind, the life of a lamb is no less precious than that of a human being ~ Mahatma Gandhi

Ebony and Ivory have been with us for four days when we have a late evening emergency call from another sheep farmer. The largest lamb of a set of triplets is not feeding and is fading away. He is, in fact, a half-brother to our Charlie the Ram who was killed last year while at stud.

Rain is sheeting down as we set off into the night. At the farm we've arranged to meet at the barn, leave the Land Rover and pick our way through the puddles to get into the warm, pungent atmosphere where mothers and bleating lambs are everywhere. Patrick, as he becomes known because of his Irish heritage, is in a pen with his family but is tucked into a corner while his lusty siblings punch at the ewe's udder to feed. Patrick has been supplemented with a bottle.

Soon we're bumping over the rutted lane to the road, homeward bound to a warm kitchen and I cradle Patrick in a blanket in my arms to cushion the jolts as the wipers work overtime to clear the windshield. At home we offer him some feed, which he takes hungrily, and then settles down for the night in the kitchen box. Ebony and Ivory are now comfortably housed downstairs in their basement pen.

Before we'd owned sheep I'd imagined that the woolly coats of tiny lambs were, well, soft like lambswool but that's not so. They have tight little wiry curls, not soft in the slightest. Like all neonates, though, they are totally captivating.

I'm so tired I sleep right through the lambs' 2:00 a.m. feed, blissfully unaware, so am very happy to discover that they're all well and eager for their 5:00 a.m. breakfast. Unlike two- to three-day old piglets and calves, lambs don't readily learn to drink from a bowl or bucket unless the bucket has teats sticking out of it. Lambs left with their mothers will naturally suckle for four to six months. Early weaning is the aim for orphans, at around three months. Until then it means lots of bottles to wash, sterilize and administer.

We now have the three lambs on lamb milk replacer which is calculated to give them the correct balance of nutrients. We've also injected them with Vitamins A, D, E, and selenium, as required for our location. Many geographical areas have selenium deficient soils, and this trace mineral is essential for normal development of brain cells. Lack of it causes white muscle disease in young lambs, resulting in inability to move, heart problems, and frequently death. So now our lambs are covered for everything.

In four days Ebony and Ivory have each put on a pound in weight and as Patrick is quite large for a triplet lamb, we don't need to follow the two-hourly schedule we use for tiny lambs, so increase the amount of their milk per feed and give them their last bottles at 10:00 p.m. and then not again until 6:00 a.m. just before morning barn. This gives me a good night's rest. I write all their feeding details and lamb behaviours on their three individual information sheets pinned up on the wall, so if I make mistakes they are recorded and I can avoid them in future.

There's no going back to winter weather now. The breaking leaves of the alders are spreading a pinkish haze over the dark tree skeletons and soon they'll be a bright young green. When the wind is in the right direction there's a scent of slurry being spread on the fields of a neighbouring farm to boost the year's growth of pasture. At dusk, frog songs from our ponds and swamps serenade us, continuing all night. It is a wonderful time of regrowth and rebirth. Ebony, Ivory and Patrick can now go into a pen in the multi-purpose barn where we already have three hand-reared piglets called The Three Musketeers: Athos, Porthos and D'Artagnon. The door of the barn is wedged open so they can all go in and out at will. Cricket continues to work round the farm with me while Acorn just loves being with the babies and will spend his whole day with them if he's allowed.

Young animals seem to love the company of other young even if they are of different species and the lambs get along just fine with the piglets. Ebony, being the largest, enjoys head-butting the little ginger boar, who's quite able to give as good as he gets.

Whenever they see me the lambs rush to the fence bleating loudly as if they're starving and it's virtually impossible for me to simultaneously bottle feed three lambs. As soon as #1 has latched on, #2 or #3 will punch #1 off and grab the teat. The stronger they get, the more boisterous and vocal they are. Eventually I discover that the easiest way is to separate them from the piglets and dogs, put them into their pen and wedge the three bottles between the slats of the gate and give them all the same amount. This way they can each take one. It goes well until they've nearly finished and they punch the bottle with a massive head butt to encourage the release of more milk and the bottles are knocked out of my hands. In well under a minute the fun is all over until next time. Soon we introduce young Cricket to the clan in the field and he fits right in, quickly discovers how rewarding it is to lick the milk residue from the lambs' chins. A practice he continues for as long as there are chins to lick.

He has also become fascinated by our duck and goose and if there's nothing more pressing to do he'll trail round with them. However, recently Lucky Duck and Lucy Goosey don't seem to be spending much time together and we're told by our elderly neighbour, Elsie, that Lucy often visits her. She wanders down our driveway, saunters across the road to Elsie's house and follows her around as she works in the garden. Twice Elsie walks the goose back to us, but as she really enjoys having the goose around and finds it flattering, I tell her not to worry, we're happy for her to share Lucy, who'll return when she's ready. Lucky Duck is spending time alone around the farm and on the ponds now, and twice we've had to rescue her from wandering into the chickens' yard. The chickens dislike ducks and have pecked at her. If we're not careful and intervene immediately, they'll mob her and kill her now that she's on her own.

"Hey," I say, when Robin comes in for a cup of tea one day, "I think I know why Lucy is hanging out with Elsie, and Lucky Duck is going solo. Come with me, I want to show you something."

Robin follows me to the shavings barn, and tucked in the back of the barn, fashioned from a pile of dried bracken is a perfect nest containing nine duck eggs.

"Aah, that's great," says Robin, "but what a pity we have no male and the eggs are infertile."

"Why don't we keep our eye on her for the next few days, and see if she's going to sit on them. If she does, then perhaps we can source some fertile eggs or perhaps day old ducklings to pop under her at the appropriate hatching time."

This certainly explains why she's been rather aloof. I consult the reference books on gestation time for Muscovy eggs and discover that it's 35 days, a week longer than regular ducks and two weeks longer than chickens. We also discover that, unlike chickens who lay eggs during daylight hours, ducks lay at night. Each morning, when Lucky Duck shows her face round the farm, I creep to the barn and check the nest. She's laying an egg every night. Isn't the urge to produce young amazing?

Now we also have two new daily visitors, circling overhead and then dropping down in to the farm. Two more Canada geese. They honk frequently and Lucy honks in return, yet she's very shy and hides behind the truck or Land Rover when they land. The geese are persistent for several days flying round and round the farm, calling. Then one day, Lucy takes off with them and flies around for a time. Soon, only one goose arrives and judging by its size it's a male. He becomes bolder and visits her right by the deck.

Sometimes they fly off together for an hour or two, but she always returns. We're hoping that she'll build a nest somewhere on the farm and have her own offspring.

Lucky Duck, meanwhile, has laid more and more eggs until there are 25 in total and then she settles down to incubate them in the nest that she's recently lined with down from her chest. Partly to insulate and cushion the eggs, and partly to allow the heat of her sparsely covered chest to come into direct contact with the eggs. We can now calculate the hatching day and set about finding some offspring for her to fulfill her, and my, motherhood desires. Lucy Goosey still divides her time between her suitor and Elsie, who is concerned that her neighbour's Jack Russell terriers are now paying all too much attention to the goose.

Cricket is nearly six months old and it's time for him to be neutered and to have two floppy dewclaws removed since they stick out at precarious angles and could get ripped off when he's powering through the bush. He's a model patient at the vets for his overnight stay, but refuses to go out and urinate during his visit. He's ecstatic to see me again in the morning and on the journey home insists on sitting really close to me on the front bench seat of the truck, bolt upright. When he squeaks I stop to walk him on the verge where he has a very long pee. At the farm a joyous reunion with Acorn ensues but then he refuses to let me out of his sight. He didn't transfer all his love and affection to us only to be parted from us yet again.

We are to watch Cricket carefully for two weeks because the vet's instructions say he must not get his bandages wet before the stitches come out. Really? We live in a rain forest with bordering salmon streams and large areas of intriguing swamp. Our intentions are good but on the second day Acorn takes off over the swamp after a rabbit with young Cricket in hot pursuit. There's nothing we can do short of penning him up for two weeks, so Robin tells me we'll just ignore the instruction. When we return to the vets to remove the stitches I feel compelled to confess that he might just have got a tad damp.

Snip, snip, snip go the scissors and the bandages fall to the table along with bits of moss, twig and other detritus. My cheeks burn and the vet laughs. "It's a good job you owned up, there was no hiding the proof." He examines the scars, which are beautifully healed with no sign of infection. "I might have to say that these are in much better condition that many I've seen that have never been wet."

"Ah-ha," I say, "it must be our pure, Hal Creek water!"

It's not long before Cricket makes it clear that it's his intention to be in his rightful position outside at night in his own insulated kennel under the deck, alongside Acorn. He watched us build it and wants to take up ownership. Although it has rained steadily all day and is really soggy and damp outside, he no longer wishes to be treated like a puppy, and would rather listen to the 'dog radio' at night broadcasting the latest happenings across the valley as various vocal exchanges take place between neighbouring farm dogs. In the kennel, he can keep an ear out for predators, too. He runs by his own internal clock and won't wait for us to take him to bed at 10:00 p.m., but promptly at 9:00 p.m. he jumps up and asks for his biscuit and carries it down the basement stairs and outside into his kennel and we latch the doors. It's time for his canine news programme.

Robin has been working in the forest cleaning up some scrub and comes rushing in with something cupped in his hands. "Look at these, I'd given up on them and was about to throw out the logs." They are beautiful specimens of shiitake mushrooms and although some from the logs resting at ground level have the odd slug bite, the ones from the hanging logs are perfect.

Now we're watching for the fruiting day by day. When conditions are just right for them they can grow from tiny bumps to full sized in a week. We promise each other to take much more care of them in future and discover that to encourage the logs to fruit prolifically a couple of times a year they need to be soaked for two days to force fruiting. I have a ready market for the mushrooms at the Farmers' Market where people can't get enough of these delectable fungi, although we make sure we keep lots for ourselves as they can be dehydrated and reconstitute so well. It's rewarding to be cruising along yet another learning curve with a very positive outcome, although the more we learn, the more we realize we don't know.

We're also into full butter production again, even selling it to one of our neighbouring dairy farmers and I'm on the lookout for an electric butter-maker to use instead of the food processor. I insert an ad into the Agriculture section of Buy, Sell and Trade, but with no luck. It's when I phone Lori, the source of our original Buff Orpington chickens, about fertile eggs to put under a broody Buffy that I discover that she has an electric butter maker which she no longer uses. I ask if I may purchase it and pick it up when we call for the fertile eggs. We still breed Buff Orpington heritage chickens and there's a great demand for them as they're good old-fashioned all-purpose birds and delightful to look at, unlike the commercial egg layers who are rather small and drab. Bringing in fertile eggs from other breeders increases the size of our gene pool too.

Lori tells me I can buy the butter maker but there is just one drawback. It comes with attachments, but not the butter-making kind. She'll sell it to us if we will also buy her Jersey cow, together with an old-fashioned milking machine, a small mobile vacuum pump and other bits and pieces. The cow is indeed lovely, with curving horns, and is the one we so much admired when we collected our first chickens. Lori's going through a rather messy separation and confides to us that her estranged husband won't leave the farm premises while they still have the cow. After all of a moment's discussion with Robin, I say, "Let's do it, I can happily use the extra milk and it'll be great to have another Jersey." So to help out Lori we agree to visit the farm to discuss things. Her husband wants to sell the whole lot for $1700, which is a hefty price. I offer him $1300. He says no; Lori says yes; adding that he'll come around to the idea pretty quickly. Lori will keep the calf.

We return to Lori's the next day with our little horse trailer to collect the milking equipment and our new milking Jersey. 'Cow' as the husband called her, will have her own proper name now that she's ours, and called Bluebell. Lori is greatly relieved that her estranged husband, Bodo, has now left the farm. She doesn't intend that he ever returns. Bluebell has been with us for two days when we're called again to the farm, this time to collect her calf. As he's rather wild, he's proved too difficult to rear without his mother. Lori tells us she has named the calf Bodo after her husband, because in due course Bodo will be going to slaughter. Meanwhile, Bluebell and her calf will be happy to be reunited at Oak Tree Farm.

I've always been a little concerned about horned creatures, but Bluebell proves to be very gentle and fits in well with the others. Right now she's giving us 16 litres of milk daily, and luckily is already accustomed to a milking machine. I'm so glad not to have to go through another initiation ceremony. It crosses my mind that I'm glad Buttercup doesn't have horns, as we'd have been gored by now, as she's just a tad cantankerous and fond of the head flick.

Buttercup is still proving difficult to get into calf. The vet has tried every trick he can think of to impregnate her, including hormone shots but still nothing. She's visited Farmer John and the new young Hereford bull to spend an amorous night with him—the bull, that is, not the farmer—but still nothing. We've mentioned beef and other dire consequences within earshot but she remains stubbornly open. Finally we decide to gradually taper milking to dry her off so she can make an extended visit to the bull. She quite enjoys a trip out. Indeed whenever we use the trailer for anything she trots up and seems to say, "are we going to see that young bull again?" and we have to restrain her from clambering inside. When she has pretty well dried off two days after Bluebell's calf arrives we indeed give her a ride in the trailer for a 4-day visit to the bull then bring her home and notice that she's still lactating, so we start milking again and are able to continue for a further two months. That's a real bonus. Thankfully, this time she's definitely in calf, her girth expands rapidly and she's looking distinctly tank-like when viewed from the front or rear. Perhaps we are expecting Jersey/Hereford twins.

Lucky Duck remains dedicated to egg incubation in her bracken nest at the back of the shavings barn. She still has three to four weeks to sit, but we must make a concerted effort to line up some offspring for her at her due date. Meanwhile we're very careful not to disturb the nest when collecting shavings for the animal houses, and fortunately won't need a new delivery of shavings for several months yet.

20. Hard Knocks

Never, never, never give up ~ Winston Churchill

Summer is in full swing: trees are heavily leafed, sheltering a myriad of creatures from insects to tree frogs. Swallowtail butterflies flit in the flower borders and fragrant honeysuckle clings to the barns. Blowsy red peonies with overfull skirts start dropping their magenta petticoats to focus energy on growing large plump seed pods. The strawberry plants are heavy with shiny ripe fruit and must be picked daily. I love the fruitfulness of the farm.

Acorn and Cricket are happily cavorting on the grass for a while but then a horrible sight catches my eye. They are rolling over and over together engaged in a terrible struggle. It looks as if Cricket has

Acorn by the neck. We race outside and scream at them, but they don't hear. I'm ashamed I briefly wonder if the pit bull rumours might be true. Locked together they roll down into a drainage ditch and then we can see the problem. Cricket's teeth are caught under Acorn's collar and they have rolled so many times, that the collar is tightly wound round Cricket's lower jaw and round Acorn's neck like a tourniquet. Their eyes protrude as they fight for life. We talk calmly and try to undo the collar but it's too tight. Robin whips out a knife but we still have no room to get the blade between neck and the collar. Acorn falls limp, his blueing tongue hanging out; Cricket is white eyed and frothing. While Robin anchors Acorn I fold Cricket's legs under him and flip him three times to unwind him like a candy wrapper. Only then can I unhook Acorn's collar from Cricket's lower canines and release Acorn.

"He's breathing!" Robin says as Acorn's chest rises. Robin carries him indoors and I lead Cricket and we check them carefully for damage. Fortunately there's no lasting harm done but it was a horrible scare for us all. I dread to think what would have happened if I hadn't noticed. From now on collars are worn very loosely, like chains of office.

Over the next few weeks, though, we lose so many collars when the dogs put their heads in the bush, down holes or under logs to investigate wildlife and return home with no collar that we dispense with collars altogether.

On a cloudy day in midsummer, a month before Acorn's second birthday, Robin is cleaning the cow stalls while I'm milking Buttercup in the parlour. I can hear a whining and scrabbling sound in the barn just behind the parlour partition. I picture one of the dogs has found a vole but the noise doesn't stop so I jump up from my milking stool and look over the partition. Acorn is lying on the floor, foaming at the mouth, crying and paddling his legs.

"ROB!" I scream, "Acorn's having a seizure." Robin runs from the cow stall to the other side of the milking parlour by which time Acorn is on his feet but disoriented, wild-eyed and pacing about. As soon as I've finished milking I rush to hug him but then stand back as the thought *rabies* flashes through my mind. Robin brings the Land Rover to the parlour and we take Acorn back to the farm. When I call the vet he says to just watch him and report back later. Acorn has three more seizures before bedtime and tries to wander off into the swamp. He has no idea where he is and when I call again, the vet says he'll admit him first thing in the morning.

We put Acorn and Cricket into their dens for the night, but very early in the morning Acorn is in a terrible state – wandering around inside his pen, eyes glazed, bumping into things. He's lost control of his bowels and bladder and no longer recognizes me when I scoop him up in a blanket. Robin drives us to the vet who administers Valium and Phenobarbitone as anti-convulsants and puts him on IV fluids. "We'll just have to wait and watch," he tells us.

For two days he's in a coma but holding his own. I call three times a day for reports. At 6:00 p.m. on the second day the vet tells me that he's much calmer. The blood work shows some liver damage related to the seizures but he thinks Acorn is coming out of his coma. "Thank goodness, Rob, perhaps we can pick him up tomorrow."

Less than an hour passes before the vet calls again. "I guess the little chap just didn't make it." I hang my head as tears brim over and run down my cheeks. A brain tumour, the vet concludes, unless he's been poisoned, but we have nothing poisonous on our farm. Could he possibly have wandered away and picked up some anti-freeze? We're fenced, though, and I'm sure we would have missed him.

There's nothing worse than going to pay the vet's bill and being handed an empty collar and leash. Again I can't stop the salt tears coursing down my cheeks as I shake my head to a postmortem. We expect to see Acorn at every turn as we work round the farm and Cricket searches for him for a week or so but then falls into being the man of the house. Young though he is, he takes his responsibilities very seriously.

Lucky Duck has been diligently sitting on her infertile eggs for a few weeks; rather longer than for the normal 35-day Muscovy incubation, but so intense is her desire to hatch the eggs she hasn't counted the days as we have. Happily we've discovered that Lori's white Muscovy is just hatching her own eggs so we arrange to visit and collect three, day-old ducklings. We hope Lucky Duck will hold on for another day or so.

The newly hatched Muscovy ducklings we've collected are simply gorgeous—acid yellow in colour. We keep them in a box with a dish of water and some food for the day. They jump in and out of the water and scatter feed all around with their tiny webbed feet. At dusk Robin carefully picks up Lucky Duck from her nest and I collect some of the warm infertile eggs she's been sitting on. We carry them to the pen in the grape arbour where Robin places her into a nest we've prepared and I pop the warm eggs beneath her. He then hands me the day-old ducklings one at a time and I place them beside her. They immediately scuttle underneath and disappear from view. Before we retire for the night we go out in the semi moonlight with flash lamps to check her and she's sitting tight on the eggs and babies, but has pushed one egg out of the nest. Possibly I cracked it when I moved them. Very slowly and gently I feel under her body and remove the rest of the infertile eggs, leaving her with her three babies.

"It's worked, Mags," Robin says next morning, "I can see them peeping out from under her." Lucky Duck is supremely proud of her offspring and the next day is waiting at the pen gate to be let out so she can march the daffodil-coloured balls of fluff around the farm. What a heartwarming sight, bobbing like corks on the pond and furrowing their beaks through mud puddles for tasty morsels. They are born with the instinct to search for food and the Muscovy variety aren't vegetarian so it's a bonus that they'll eat slugs and so be good for the garden. The ducklings grow rapidly and their yellow down is replaced with pure white feathers. We have one male and two females. Our numbers are increasing.

We have a new calf, too. It seems impossible that two years have already passed since Buttercup's daughter, Blossom, was born at the Vancouver Island Exhibition yet she has just presented us with her own adorable little heifer calf, called Beauty. The calf shows her partial Dexter heritage and is a miniature only weighing in at 45 lb. Her coat is fuzzy and dark brown but she'll lose the fluffy coat to become a sleek black with telltale white sprinkles, like a large snowflake and tear drops, on her face—inherited from her father's Hereford white-face genes. As she's a heifer we'll have to keep her, of course, and add her to our breeding stock.

Things have improved recently and life has been calmer until something happens that makes me erupt like a volcano. Our neighbour who has a house on 50 acres between us and the mountain has access over our driveway, and on this clear sunny late summer Monday he's having gravel removed from the huge creek on his property. I've asked that the gravel and pick-up trucks drive slowly past the animals' fields, but do they? No. Cricket is walking with me on the grassy verge beside the drive when one of the contractors roars past. I hear a great bang and Cricket is lying in the driveway. The bastard has run over *my* dog on *my* driveway and he hasn't even stopped. Snorting with fury I rush to Cricket as he starts picking himself up. He's only 10 months old and has an imprint of the truck's oil pan on his chest, where he was rolled underneath. How lucky we are the wheels didn't run over him.

I take him to the farmhouse, and check him carefully, bathing his multiple cuts and abrasions with hydrogen peroxide and smearing them with Polysporin, bandaging the wound on his chest. I'm still trembling with ill suppressed fury. How could that person not even stop? I call the neighbour to tell him what has happened and he passes along the message. Apparently the contractor is told to come straight away to apologize to us but still doesn't bother until the end of the day. When he does eventually slink up he says he knew he'd hit something and offers the lame excuse that he thought he'd hit a rock.

"You absolutely disgust me," I say, my heart thumping in my chest because of the confrontation. "I'm having a hard time not punching you, you're a low down, unprincipled bastard and I'm sending you any vet bills."

Fortunately Cricket is from tough stock and recovers well over the next weeks, never complaining or showing he's in pain, despite his collection of scars—now badges, attesting to his devotion to duty. Nothing slows him down and the routines of the farm are imprinted on his mind, so one morning when he's indoors with me he seems agitated and won't settle. I go outside with him to see what's worrying him and he shows me that I've forgotten to let chickens out. How we adore this little guy.

A mellow and colourful fall has been uneventful and it's a shock when icy winds blast through the valley bringing hard frosts, frozen water troughs and pipes, and ultimately a massive fall of snow.

Lucky Duck flies onto the driveway but as the snow is too deep to walk in, she only succeeds in making duck angel wings. We rescue her and take her to an area we've cleared near the pond. In the evening all three females decide it would be prudent to roost on the deck railings. The young male, however, is too big and heavy to fly up but manages to beat his wings and, with the aid of the claws on the toes of his webbed feet, climbs his way to the top of a low fence close by Cricket's kennel. Lucy Goosey, who never did accept a partnership with her suitor also flies up to the deck to sit on the rubber mat outside the sliding glass door.

Christmas is a quiet time for us this year, spent with animals, a log fire, good books and cups of hot chocolate. The millennium year of 2000 slips quietly away and we're now well into the new century and so far we've seen nothing but dreary monochrome days with gusting winds, rain and an occasional snow shower, the temperatures hovering around 0°C. The rawness and constant damp makes it seem much colder. Even the animals look out dejectedly from barn doorways then stay in their houses from choice.

In the middle of January things on the farm seriously deteriorate. Lily is due to farrow and during the night we can hear over the intercom in our bedroom that she's restless, going into and out of her house, but no sounds or little squeaks to indicate farrowing has started. We get up early in the morning darkness to investigate.

"We have piglets, Lily's already farrowed," Robin says. I'm about to join him in the farrowing house when I catch something in the beam of my flashlight.

"Oh no," I wail, "there's a piglet out here in the cold." I gently pick it up. It's still alive, but deathly cold and I tuck it inside my jacket. Robin comes out of the pig house and we both start scanning the uneven, icy ground with our lights. It's a disaster, Lily has farrowed six piglets outside, one of them is very tiny indeed and almost lifeless. I scoop it up and place it inside my shirt, next to my skin hoping to impart some warmth to it. The other five we carry inside our coats and into the basement where we already had heat lamps on in case of an emergency. Once we have them tucked up together under the lamps, I prepare some warm colostrum milk and feed them one by one with a syringe. The tiniest piglet doesn't survive until the first feed, and mouth to snout resuscitation won't restore life. We've never had a sow do this before, farrowing some indoors and some outside, and fight valiantly for their lives, feeding them a small amount every hour, but by the end of the day we've lost all six babies. How cruel to have been born into a frozen wasteland and not find their mother's warmth and nourishment. The little creatures never stood a chance.

My lower lip quivers as I try to voice my despair. "If only we'd stayed with Lily all last night."

Despondent and exhausted we climb into bed and have been asleep for no time at all when Cricket's frenetic barking wakes us at 12:45 a.m. Something is really wrong. I open a window to listen and can hear Buttercup bellowing in the barn. Is something attacking her? Dragging on boots and coats we race to the barn and find her cast on her side on the floor, flailing her legs. Her abdomen is already bloating. She can't expel the natural gases formed during rumination and is inflating, compressing her lungs. We struggle to take hold of her kicking legs or her head to right her, but she's thrashing so wildly. Robin stays with her while I run to the farmhouse to call the vet. The answering service quickly gets him out of bed and just as I'm explaining the problem to him, Robin comes indoors, head bowed, shoulders sagging.

"It's too late, Buttercup's gone."

I burst into floods of tears, "Oh no, Robin, how could this happen?"

Robin's too upset to answer. Our cherished first Jersey cow, with her big character, was six weeks away from delivering twin calves. She'd lain down in the stall, rolled onto her side and being so rotund was unable to get any purchase with her feet to right herself.

"You did nothing wrong," the vet tells us, "it's just one of those tragic unfortunate accidents."

How I wish I'd know how to puncture her rumen to release the gases that compressed her lungs. I don't think I'll survive this. There'll be a big hole in our lives now that we've lost our matriarch— no beautiful Buttercup and no adorable twins.

Stunned, we mechanically attend to our farm chores. The seven piglets Lily gave birth to in the farrowing house have survived for her to nurture, and we must now arrange for Buttercup's disposal. At the end of a harrowing day at 9:30 p.m. when all I want to do is curl up in a ball and wallow in sadness, Portia starts farrowing. We stay with her into the early hours of the morning as she delivers her piglets, six alive, two stillborn and four tiny embryonic fetuses. More tragedy. I didn't think my heart could break any further. Sometimes it all seems too much to shoulder.

"How can farmers bear the losses and heartaches?" I say to Robin who is doing his utmost to put on a brave face. Our morale is at an all-time low following the worst two days of farming causing us to seriously question whether we've made the right decision and are competent enough to take on these responsibilities.

A new day ushers in a welcome change in the weather banishing the grey landscape. Skies are clearing and shafts of weak sunlight shine onto a mild frost. Our spirits are boosted a little and we have no more tragedies. In the evening we receive another Mayday.

"Can you help us? We're in the middle of lambing and we've got a tiny triplet born a couple of days ago and he's not doing well because he can't suckle. He's declining fast. Could you try hand-rearing him? I'm already hand raising other lambs and I'm afraid this one's probably not going to survive."

"Of course, we'll come and pick him up." This has happened at an opportune time after so many losses of our own. It gives us something to focus on and fight for—a helpless lamb who's losing his fragile grip on life. We jump into the Land Rover and head for the farm that Patrick came from last year. Fortunately this time without the lashing rain. Instead, our headlights flash up and down like wartime searchlights with every bump, picking out a frosty rutted track and winter blackened skeletal trees. Again we meet at their barn and collect the wee scrap, bundle him in a blanket and quickly bear him home to warmth and nourishment. We choose another Irish name and call the lamb Fergul. The absence of Buttercup and her twin calves has been central to my thoughts and I haven't even had time to start lamenting the potential absence of newborn lambs. Now I'm happy to be bottle feeding once more.

Young lambs possess a piercingly pitiful bleat no one could ignore and this familiar sound breaks through the mists of sleep when Fergul calls plaintively at 2:00 a.m. and again at 6:00 a.m. from his box under the infrared heat lamp. His tiny tummy is empty. It's wonderful that he's survived the night and has a fighting spirit. We're over the first hurdle.

However, he does have a problem with sucking: he accepts the teat but his tongue slips out of the side of his mouth and doesn't curl round the teat to create the vacuum necessary to draw the milk into his throat. He *is* able to swallow, though, and his tongue doesn't flop out of his mouth all the time. Robin suggests enlarging the hole in the teat and we feed him very slowly, poking his tongue back inside his mouth and cradling his lips round the teat, allowing the milk to trickle in as he swallows. It's a lengthy process but we succeed with only modest spillage from his lips which Cricket will happily clean up.

As we have Bluebell's Jersey milk, we're starting Fergul on that instead of lamb replacer, boosting it with beaten egg, cod liver oil and glucose. While not being quite as rich as sheep's milk it is the next best thing to lamb milk replacer. We don't anticipate it will be easy, and he does scour a little but his system gradually becomes accustomed. He's sleeping in the basement pen and within three days is lasting all through the night from 10:00 p.m. till 6:00 a.m. and during the daytime he gets plenty of exercise galloping round the house with Cricket who has turned out to be our best nursemaid ever, even surpassing young Acorn. He'll wash the orphans, play with them and sleep with them.

Since Acorn died Cricket is now the man of the house, and is earnest about his perceived role, balancing his duties as nursemaid with those of defending the property and livestock. As Fergul flourishes with care and he gains strength his sucking problem resolves and he's transferred to the pen in the multi-purpose barn where, during the day, he can come and go into the field with freedom. As we don't have a companion for him Fergul often accompanies us on our chores about the farm and wears a collar with a small bell so we can keep track of his whereabouts, not that Cricket would allow us to lose him.

21. Room for One More

It's always too early to quit ~ Norman Vincent Peale

We're still feeling despondent about our recent animal losses and the reduction in milk production and I mention my doubts about farming when chatting to a friend. The village drums start beating in the valley and amazingly, via the farming network we locate another Jersey cow who will soon have abundant milk as she's about to calve. At least that's what the owners originally thought, but now they're doubtful. On the phone the tell us if she does give birth they'll be happy to loan her to us for four months as they really don't have the time to milk her at present. We agree to board her and bottle feed the calf in return for keeping the Jersey milk.

"I'm afraid to raise my hopes again in case she's not really in calf," I say to Robin.

"Only one way to sort this out," he says, "let's go and have a look at her."

In between animal chores and feeding Fergul we drive to see the cow, Nell, who is about eight years old.

"We thought she was pregnant," the owners say, "but today is her due date and nothing has happened and she has no milk so now we're not at all sure."

They open the door to her stall, where we see the most beguiling silver and sable-coloured Jersey slowly chewing hay and not showing the slightest bit of concern.

We inspect her from all angles. Her sides are large and she has sizeable hollows in front of her hip pin bones which can indicate that a calf is dropping into position prior to birth.

"She certainly looks in calf to me," I say, "even though she hasn't bagged up yet. When was she served, exactly? Cows can wait right until the last moment before they start producing milk for the birth."

It transpires that the owners have been working on the assumption that a cow has a nine month gestation period, when in fact it's nine and a half months.

"So don't worry," I say, "she's got another couple of weeks to go yet." We feel optimistic that a calf will be forthcoming and we'll be able to have Nell to board with us for a while.

Although it may not be spring just yet, it shows promise of arriving with imminent births. Lucky Duck too has made another nest and started laying eggs. This will be the first of her own offspring, as she's paired with the adopted male Muscovy, Donald.

Two weeks after visiting Nell I'm reluctant to call her owners in case I receive bad news, but I muster my courage and place the call.

"We're so happy," the owner says, "she calved at 1:00 a.m. and has a lovely bull calf."

"That's terrific, and are you still willing to loan her to us?" I ask tentatively.

"Of course!"

Next day we drive the horse trailer through a light fall of fresh snow to collect the most serene cow we've ever met. Nell calmly walks into the trailer with her day-old calf and we drive them home and settle them into a stall.

Then, just as we're leaving them she suddenly drops to her knees and can't get up. Frantic, I run to the house and call the vet.

"Sounds like classic milk fever," he says, "and we mustn't delay, I'll be right out." Within half an hour the vet is dispensing a litre of calcium into her jugular vein via a drip. It's nothing short of miraculous when, within a few minutes of the litre being absorbed, she climbs to her feet and goes to the manger as if nothing has happened, and yet it would be fatal for cow and calf if not remedied promptly. The vet explains that it happens when calcium is drawn from the blood for milk production and the cow can't mobilize calcium from her bones fast enough to maintain blood calcium levels. It often happens in heavy milkers and older well-fed cows.

"You might always have this problem with her," he adds, "it's common in Jerseys and she's certainly a heavy milker." He leaves us with a few more litre-bottles of calcium with instructions to inject it subcutaneously in different spots along her flanks for the next couple of days, and then massage each place well to disperse the fluid. Oh, how I hate to do this to her but she doesn't complain, just looks back over her shoulder at us with doleful eyes. Nell, from now on called Daffodil, is a delightful calm addition to our farm. We fall hopelessly in love with her and she's a dream to milk by machine. We will hate to see her leave.

Now we can fulfill all the requirements of our customers for raw milk and butter. It's always in great demand despite, or perhaps because of, the fact that I'm not officially allowed to sell raw milk or unpasteurized dairy products, but it's generally felt among our farming community that the authorities should allow customers to make their own choices and decisions where they purchase their foods.

There are altogether too many bureaucratic rules in farming that have no logical foundation and should never have been brought into existence. Much better to allow people to use common sense. Yet, on the other hand, there are several unwritten rules that are very important in farming. One such is that it's not good husbandry to use a boar to service his own progeny and soon the Colonel's daughters will become ready for breeding so we need to increase our gene pool. Our hand reared red Tamworth boar, D'Artagnon is now a year old and we'd like to organize a young-boar swap with someone, so put in a call to a few farming contacts and are given the name of a young man in Cedar.

Rob Palfry does indeed have a young boar for sale. We give him details of D'Artagnon, agree to make a swap, and will transport our boar to his farm and return with his. On the appointed day we load D'Artagnon into the horse trailer and set off, stopping en route to shop at a superstore in Nanaimo.

"I don't like leaving him in the trailer, Robin. Perhaps I should stay with him. If he gets bored he might want to fight his way out, or he may be upset when someone peers over the doors at him."

"Stop worrying, he'll be fine, we won't be long." Indeed all is well when we return to the truck and trailer and we continue to Cedar.

Robin backs the trailer up to Rob P's very large wooden barn and we're invited inside. It's an astonishing sight. He has several pens on either side, all spotlessly clean and all containing animals. There are different sheep breeds, various goats, several varieties of chickens and all the creatures are behaving calmly. At the rear of the barn are the pigs.

"This is the little boar," Rob P tells us, and we look over the gate to see the smallest boar we've ever seen, about the size of one of our six week old weaners. Robin and I exchange glances with raised eyebrows.

"He's a bit small, isn't he?" I say, "we're hoping to breed the sows in a month's time."

"Well, he's only three months old, but he'll grow."

Since we've brought D'Artagnon all this way, we really don't want to have to take him home again.

"Tell you what," says Rob P, "if you take this little boar I'll let you have the services now of my old boar, Big Al, for your girls and I'll deliver him to your farm."

"Yes, that could work," Robin says, "OK," and they shake hands on the deal.

The little boar we call Burt, settles into a pen in the barn with deep straw and a heat lamp as the weather is frigid and he has no siblings to snuggle up to, but as he loves his generous food and milk meals he'll soon grow to his proper size.

Meanwhile word has spread in the community and it seems that Fergul's arrival was just the start of a larger lamb orphanage for us this year. When he's three weeks old we receive a call from another farmer. "We've got a first time mother who's had twins and rejected them. We didn't find them fast enough and she's killed one already but we've rescued the other. Would you like to have her?"

"Absolutely," Robin says, "when shall we pick her up?"

"No need, we'll deliver her shortly."

That's a pity. I do so love to see other farms. Anyway, I prepare the baby box and lamp in the kitchen and sterilize more bottles. I'll be starting night feeds again, tonight.

'Flora' is two days old and arrives in a cardboard box. She's a sorry looking little scrap, pummelled, droopy and dirty. I take her from the box and wrap a towel around her.

"We'll do the best we can for you," I tell her, "you haven't had much fun so far, have you? How about we start with a little warm milk?" Robin cradles her while I prepare the bottle. She appears to be another little Hampshire, like Fergul. After a small feed, we spot-bathe her with warm soapy water, trimming off the worst of the stuck-on dung and detritus and dry her before popping her under the heat lamp.

"She's looking much better already," Robin says as her eyes close for the first safe sleep of her life. The sheep-rearing book tells us that it's not uncommon for a yearling ewe to reject her first offspring, but those that do certainly don't always attempt to kill their babies. Next year the young ewe should be mature enough to bond with her infants. Flora's eager for her feeds and after one day she's able to launch herself out of her box so takes up residence in the basement and we bring in Fergul from the barn to keep her company. Cricket frequently visits to carry out his protective vigil and is always present at meal times in case any washing is required.

Cricket is a calm dog around our animals and also in general, but he does alert us when visitors approach the farm. Today he tells us there's a vehicle arriving. It's a local dairy farmer and his son who've come to collect their free-range eggs. They own the largest dairy farm in the valley and are good people, as are all the farmers in the neighbourhood. They are unfamiliar with pit bull type breeds and are enchanted by Cricket who gives them abundant gentle attention. I'm keen, too, to show them our latest orphans, Flora and Fergul, especially with Cricket there.

After they've seen them all together in the basement the farmer puts his head on one side and slowly rubs his chin as he looks at us for a moment, considering what kind of people we are. He's fascinated by our love for the animals. Large-scale farmers, of course, can't afford to become *too* emotionally attached to their charges.

Flora remains quiet all night after her last feed and when I wake at 5:30 a.m. I fleetingly wonder if she's faded away and I should have been more attentive. But she's fine and *very* keen for breakfast, rushing out of her pen bleating, and plugging straight onto the bottle without having to be held. Fergul too guzzles his bottle in a few seconds. Seeing Flora's remarkable recovery and spirits proves to us how important companionship is to these young flock animals and bringing Fergul in with her has probably made all the difference to both of them. That's why, if we can avoid it, we also never hand rear only one piglet at a time, as they too are social creatures.

For the past four days the weather's been cold, foggy and wet but at last the sun breaks through and we can let Flora have her first sight of the great outdoors accompanied, of course, by Fergul. And they can now be transferred to a pen in the barn with the addition of a heat lamp.

Our lamb family is doing well when yet another distress call comes in. A ram lamb has been rejected by his mother; he's already three days old and in critical condition. It's sad that the owners wait until the lamb is likely to expire before they call us but it's human nature to keep hoping for the best. We know these farmers can't afford to lose a lamb and offer to care for him as they don't have time with their other animals and commitments. If he survives we're happy to return him to them.

'Liam'—we're staying with an Irish theme this year—is like a wet noodle. He flops in our arms and doesn't appear to have any muscle tone or stamina. He's beyond being on his last legs and just lies in a heap. He's stopped sucking and, like many animals near death, appears to be resigned to his fate. We start giving tiny amounts of food to him at two-hourly intervals round the clock. We won't give up on him. He may have white muscle disease and so it's essential that he has a selenium shot immediately, and also vitamins A, D and E.

After two days, he bleats for the first time before his feed at 4:00 a.m. This is a breakthrough and we begin to believe that he might pull through, but he needs to thrive, not just survive. Although he's accepting his feeds, he's still limp, and can't stand like other little lambs. But he *is* surviving and we persevere and in a further three days he's a bit perkier, popping his head up to look around, drinking better and for the first time he sleeps through the night.

"I think we've done it" I tell Robin, "He's definitely improving, he just stood on his feet for his bottle." But our rejoicing is premature. Liam becomes lethargic, loses his enthusiasm for feeding and has developed a cough. It sounds as if he has pneumonia. With tiny hand-reared lambs it's possible that they will inhale a little milk which can cause the problem. Or perhaps as Liam had virtually no muscle tone maybe his swallowing muscles haven't been working well so any residual milk in his mouth could be inhaled. After checking with the vet we give him the recommended tiny dose of antibiotics to help prevent secondary infections, and soldier on. He does call out in the night for food, and we manage to get a few ounces into him in little bits.

"Please hang on," I croon to him as I cuddle him while he takes his bottle, "you've come so far. You're nearly two weeks old. It hasn't been fun for you, but it will get better."

I call his owners to alert them about the pneumonia in case he doesn't make it. The farmers feel very sorry that we're having problems and they thought it would only be a case of bottle feeding for a day or so. They tell us we can keep him if he survives and ask what they owe if he doesn't.

"Absolutely nothing," I say, "at the very worst this is excellent experience, but I'm really hoping he'll pull through. We'll do our very best."

He continues feeding, but is still only taking small amounts, so we feed very frequently. It's another two days before he starts showing signs of being hungry. Now after two and a half weeks, we weigh him.

"He's put on a whole pound." Robin says, "he's not fading away, this is a great achievement." After two more days of continuing improvement we are able to add him to the barn with Fergul and Flora as he'll probably do a whole lot better with siblings. This is indeed the case and his cough clears up. He can now walk and even perform standing jumps as befits a young lamb. When the weather is suitable, little Liam even starts to frolic outside in the field with the other lambs.

What a roller-coaster ride farming is turning out to be. The new cow, Daffodil, and her calf have settled in well and best of all, the owners decide that they would like to sell her to us but want the bull calf back when he's weaned to rear for beef.

Now that she's officially our cow, the most pressing task for Daffodil's care is to get the hoof trimmer to call. It's often impossible to schedule him to visit a small farm even when we book over a year in advance. His time is usually taken up with profitable large farms in the mid-Vancouver Island area. We try to arrange for him to call in to our little herd on his way to or from neighbouring bigger farms, but, of course, it's not an economically viable stop for him. However, we are in luck and he arrives on his way to Farmer John's dairy herd. Cows need healthy feet and it's important to trim their hooves annually. Poor Daffodil has arrived with what are described as 'Persian slippers,' hooves badly overgrown and curling up at the front, which causes her to distribute her weight incorrectly involving her heels in walking rather than just the hooves. It's very sad to see, but common in pet cloven-hoofed creatures. As Daffodil is placid she accepts the hoof-trimming contraption without complaint and walks in with only one finger hooked onto her halter.

Over the weeks she has become a serene and steadying influence on the rest of the herd and the kind of beast who will let other calves suckle from her if they choose. Without complaint she carries out her daily routines and gives us buckets of milk.

How glad we are that we persevered and didn't give up farming.

22. The Cougar Chaser

It's not the size of the dog in the fight, it's the size of the fight in the dog ~ Mark Twain

March has gently drifted in as the lambs graze contentedly on the growing pasture. The sun peeps between the clouds, smiling on early white fragrant peonies spreading their bouquet as the breezes ruffle the petticoats of their pink-tinted skirts. The skies are alive with birds bent on their annual rush to create new life.

After breakfast, lying with nose on paws, Cricket looks longingly out of the patio doors, in his quiet way telling us it's time to get out and enjoy the day. Abruptly, he pushes himself upright, ears pricked. Then our less sensitive ears pick up the slow grinding of an elderly vehicle driving along the curved driveway and an ancient Ford Econovan appears. It draws to a stop half way along the drive and Rob Palfry hops down as his wife, Rita, who barely weighs 100 lb. slips down from the passenger seat. We join them in the drive and they open the back of the van. Reclining there is the largest boar I've ever seen. We're both staring wide eyed as we register that there's absolutely no barrier of even the flimsiest sort between the boar and the two old seats for driver and passenger. He can pick up his head and just rest his snout, complete with massive tusks, on a shoulder or between the seats on the gear shift, if he so desires.

"Aren't you afraid of having a boar loose in there with you?" I ask, when I recover my ability to speak. "What if he gets mad?" Thinking, but not voicing, that the van looks so old that it could break down at any time and if it did, there can't be too may tow companies who'd pick up a van and a boar, and what would they do with a boar at the side of the road?

"No, he's fine, he's like a baby." Rob P gives a husky laugh. "It was quite funny, though, when we stopped for gas. Al sat up like a dog and stuck his head out the window to look around. You should've seen the face of the guy at the next pump. His hand was locked on the trigger and his expression was something in between disbelief and panic. A bit like yours, really!"

We immediately rearrange our facial expressions and laugh.

Rob P pulls a makeshift ramp from the van, wriggles it into position and gently backs Al out onto the drive and leads him into our waiting horse trailer so we can drive him round to the sows' field. It's agreed we'll keep him for a month, or until it's a suitable time for Rob P to have him back.

Al wastes no time and immediately serves Prickle who, conveniently, is in heat. It won't be long before Portia will be served too. No messing around, no fighting, just getting the job done.

He vacations contentedly with the two sows, and what an angel he is. While the Colonel was the pig from hell, Big Al is the converse and positively wears a halo.

Five weeks later, Rob P and Rita arrive in the aged van to collect Big Al. We walk him from the field into the horse trailer where he waits patiently for his transfer to his travelling van to go home. Rob P rigs up his rickety makeshift ramp again, which not one of our pigs would have ever trusted or walked on, and Al slowly lumbers into his mobile home. If he could, I think he'd be smiling. He does enjoy a ride.

"I'd offer you tea and cookies but I expect you'd like to be off quickly with Al," I say, eying the rusty lacework adorning parts of the vehicle. Al really does look a whole lot stronger than the van.

"Oh no, we'd love tea and cookies," Rita says, "Al will be fine."

"If that was one of our pigs," I say, "it would use the time shredding the interior into little pieces and rewiring the electrical system. When we had the horse trailer in their field they stripped the wires out like they were long roots to be eradicated from the ground."

We spend a pleasant hour drinking tea, eating fresh baking and chatting while I keep a watchful eye on the van. Then, with a cheery wave, they drive off down the drive.

Sometimes I have to wonder about the benefits of free-ranging animals. It's always been a tenet of ours, but Al, who spends most of his life in a barn, is beautifully behaved, whereas our creatures left alone in the van would have regarded it as a play thing. They did fleetingly mention that D'Artagnon, the boar we swapped, was doing just a *bit* of nibbling on the wood of his pen.

A whole month has passed since Liam came to us and we are very happy with our three-lamb family when we receive the next cry for help. Two lambs, each three days old and rejected by their respective mothers, are proving too much to hand rear for their owner. "Welcome to the clan," I say, and prepare two more record sheets for 'Little' and 'Large' and initiate individual feeding plans for them too.

We now have five lambs, all different ages and weights, all on different feeding schedules with different amounts of feed. It seems every hour I'm sterilizing bottles, making feed, warming bottles and feeding someone. The top of the old kitchen range is devoted to bottles, teats, sterilizing equipment and other paraphernalia.

It's good that our latest arrivals, Little and Large, haven't been injured. The biggest challenge for them is changing them onto our Jersey milk based diet.

They've been with us for two days when very early in the morning a new diminutive lamb arrives. She's as light as a baby's toy. I wrap her in a small blanket and tuck her into bed with Robin for warmth, while I prepare her heat lamp and box. We try to feed her a minuscule amount of colostrum using an extra small teat, but it trickles from her lips, and she just lies under the heat of the lamp. Her eyes gradually become glazed and within two hours the life has ebbed away from 'Little Lady.'

"Oh, Robin," I cry, unable to stem the flow of hot tears, "why couldn't she have had a chance?" I am overwhelmed by the sadness of it all, she weighed less than 5 lb. and we were helpless to save her. Our first orphan loss.

Lambing season is over for the valley. It's the beginning of April and daffodils and narcissi bloom in drifts, the trees flush out and pink apple blossoms start opening in the sunshine for the bees.

Day by day Little and Large gain in strength and enjoy some sunshine in the garden. They look tiny compared with Fergul, Flora and Liam who occasionally inspect them when they take a break from charging around in play, or chasing Lucy Goosey and the chickens, and we think our five-strong lamb family is complete.

I am, therefore, greatly surprised when a local businessman approaches me one Saturday morning at the Farmers' Market stall where I sell our organic produce: eggs, meats, mushrooms, and under-the-counter pre-ordered butter and raw milk. This particular man only ever comes to my table if he wants information or advice. In the past it's always been about his pig or piglet problems. It irks me sometimes that he never comes to just pass the time of day, although I see him every week when he buys bread form a baker friend of mine. Today he leans over my table to speak in confidence. He tells me his brother, who is also a businessman, is a part-time sheep farmer and has a month-old crippled lamb who self-feeds from a bucket with a teat, but he has no mother, no companions and isn't thriving. Naturally we open our hearts to the forlorn lamb.

We call him Freddy. At birth he was healthy but his navel wasn't immediately treated with iodine and he contracted the devastating infection 'navel ill' where, in less than sanitary conditions, the bacterium enters the navel and attacks the joints of the new born who is susceptible because of its weak immune system, especially if it hasn't had colostrum from its mother. The joints become swollen, then distorted, arthritic and exceedingly painful. Freddy is the sweetest fellow and has a particularly severe form of this debilitating disease. His front legs bend outwards at the knees, and his forefeet meet together in the front, the underside of his hooves facing each other. His 'elbows' and lower legs rest on the ground, and he looks something akin to a lobster with large claws as he inches along on his swollen, twisted knees and forearms. He also has pneumonia, with a severely rattling chest, which we treat with antibiotics. Just one more in a series of crosses this little chap had to bear.

All of his problems, which might have been avoided with good initial care, prove too much for the man to bother to continue rearing him. Yet despite his pitiful situation in solitary confinement in a pen, and having had virtually no interaction, human or otherwise for his one month of life, he's very happy to have contact with us and chuffs and grunts when we approach to feed him or give him a scratch under the chin. He is totally engaging. When we bottle feed him we hold him and talk to him, stopping frequently to allow him to breathe through his mouth. We watch that the other youngsters aren't boisterous with him, but mostly they seem not to bother him, and he can get around quite quickly. For the first time he's putting on weight and wee Freddy is learning what it's like to enjoy life. He shuffles round the pasture happily eating fresh grasses and is adept at lying down to nibble, yet shows a good turn of speed when he spies a human with a bottle. Another example of thriving in the fresh air and sunshine with the benefit of companions.

Bottle feeding is finally over for us at the end of May. At the peak we were feeding 40 bottles a day. It's quite a relief but what will I do now with all this free time? The lambs grow rapidly and become ever more mischievous, poking their heads through fences into the garden to eat whatever is in range, escaping into the cows' field to cavort and gambol and create general mayhem, and leaping the low fence to get into the flower garden. Of course, once they taste forbidden fruit they never forget it. By late summer they will be ready for market.

Our livestock numbers continue to swell and we're thrilled when Lucky Duck hatches nine ducklings in her nest tucked between two straw bales. Donald accompanies her as she takes them for a walk down to the pond where they straightway launch themselves onto the looking glass surface, rippling the reflection of the trees and flowers lining the banks into a kaleidoscope of colours. Nine mini yellow watercraft already perfectly able to float and navigate using their tiny orange paddles. Within two days Lucky and Donald have them marching round the farm, the ducklings sometimes finding a deliciously muddy piece of ditch where they can run their beaks through the slurry to find edible morsels before the family tramps home in the late afternoon for grain.

I'm not sure what it is that draws the ducklings to the chickens' field, but one afternoon they wander through the wire and in with the chickens while Lucky Duck remains on the outside the fence. Muscovy ducks don't quack, and she gives a high pitched peeping sound to signal her distress. I glance up from my gardening. "DUCKLINGS" I yell, and Robin and I rush in as a chicken makes an initial lunge and the others are mustering for the kill. We dart this way and that, hefting chickens out of the way and picking up ducklings, launching them over the fence where they plummet to safety with their mother. All, that is, but one. Cricket is with us and decides his job is to help us catch the duckling, so rushes into the fray. Being much quicker than us, his jaws snap closed on the body of the last little duckling, whereupon its entrails, like coloured curly telephone wires, shoot from its rear. "Nooooh," I scream at Cricket, who drops the duckling and backs off, wondering why I'm shouting at him when he's only helping. The duckling died instantly, of course. In future we must never chase or catch birds when Cricket is around to help, and he has yet to fully learn that he must ignore any prey drive with chickens or ducks.

Cricket does have a strong prey drive for small creatures like mice, voles and squirrels, yet a nurturing nature with the lambs, and he also exhibits the classic Staffordshire 'protect my master' trait and will confront any adversary he sees as a threat, irrespective of its size.

Each day around 4:00 p.m. we scatter a few handfuls of grain in the pasture for the lambs and do a head count as they eagerly nibble up the treats. Today, Liam is late on parade. "One of the Hampshires is missing, it's Liam," I tell Robin. We conduct a search of the property, checking the fence line looking for telltale bits of wool where he may have squeezed through into the swamp, then I climb over the fence and squelch around shaking a bucket and calling his name, but no luck. I phone to alert the neighbours, in case they spot a lamb where he shouldn't be.

When I go outside again Cricket is agitated, skipping and darting around my feet and keeps running behind the house and barking up at a fir tree. I assume he's found a squirrel—the cheeky things always excite him when they chatter from the branches of the trees and throw bits of cone down at him.

Eventually I humour Cricket. "OK, boy, what is the matter?" I follow him to the rear of the house. There, on the ground behind a fallen tree at the edge of the forest, just 7 metres from the back of the house is Liam, lying on his side looking peacefully asleep. He's dead, of course, and only recently so, still warm and supple with no apparent damage. I praise Cricket and call Robin. We pick up the lamb who weighs about 60 lb. and manoeuvre him into a barrow for a closer inspection.

"There's a small hole in the back of his neck," Robin says, "but I can't see anything else." He fires up the tractor to dig a pit so we can bury Liam. Farm life is full of sadness as well as joy.

We report the death to the conservation officer, as we have no idea as to the cause. "Sounds like a cougar kill to me. I hope you've left the carcass where it is because the cougar will come back for it. I'll bring my cougar hounds and wait for it to return." Alas, Liam is already buried and for that I'm not sorry. With all the livestock around I don't want to think of the cougar returning.

Next evening just as dusk is gathering we're sitting at the dining room table sipping a Shiraz and looking out over the cows' field when we witness a bizarre sight. On the brow of the hill the cows are galloping across the field towards the band of second-growth trees. As we peer into the failing light we notice that there's something in front of them and they are actually chasing it. Robin grabs binoculars and says, "It's a cougar, and I think the cows have treed it." Bluebell, who came to us along with the butter maker is near to calving and at times like this the herd, although only small, is very protective and aware of the vulnerability of one of their kind. Robin grabs his gun and ammunition and we race outside, through the fields to the base of one of our taller trees—a 30-metre Douglas fir. Cricket races along with us; whatever it is we are doing, this is his work and he should be involved.

"Be careful," I tell Robin, as I shine a powerful flash lamp high into the branches. All we can see are golden disks of light from two reflector-like eyes to prove the cougar is actually there. Cricket is tense, one foot trembling, waiting for something to happen and ready for anything. He doesn't bark despite his agitation. He can detect the scent of the cougar although we can't. The cows have retreated to their field now that there is no longer any imminent danger to the herd.

Our gun is intended for predator control, and we always hope we'll never have to use it but in our early farm days Robin enrolled us both in a gun-handling course so we could gain Possession and Acquisition Licences, and I could learn to use firearms. He learned to handle guns when he was enrolled in the army cadets at school. However, Robin can't just kill a magnificent wild animal, this is the cougar's territory too. Instead, he fires a warning shots to startle it. Cricket's shaking with suppressed excitement as the cougar slips down the tree, metre by metre, using its claws as anchors. As it gets closer to the ground I call Cricket to come back to me well out of the cougar's reach. He ignores me. "This is *exactly* what my job is," he seems to say.

The cougar hits the ground and bounds off away from us towards some cross fencing a hundred feet away. Despite being not much more than a puppy, Cricket's sturdy little frame flies along right at the cougar's heels. It's almost dark and the cougar fails to see the fencing, slamming straight into the paige wire and falling on his back. In the flashlight we see Cricket powering into the cougar. I'm terrified, but instead of attacking Cricket the cougar springs up, leaps over the fence and is gone. Our young hero returns to us triumphant, spattered with cougar spit, but totally unharmed, and very proud. The foe is vanquished.

"What really bothers me," I say to Robin on reflection, "is that while I was ignoring Cricket barking up at the tree behind the house the cougar was probably still up there. I never think to look up, do you?"

"No," he says, "who walks around looking 30 metres in the air?"

"In future I should just trust Cricket—he's never guilty of barking up the wrong tree."

23. *The Tax Gestapo*

According to the government, a taxpayer is someone who has what it takes ~ Anonymous

It's not surprising that we haven't paid any farm income taxes yet, because here's the thing: we haven't made any money, only losses, lots of losses from starting up the farm. Despite that, as instructed, we annually complete several different tax returns. I doubt any farmer, small or large, will disagree that the worst part of farming is paperwork, and the worst of the paperwork is tax returns and their attendant problems. Tax time is something that is foreseeable, must be scheduled, and *endured* at Oak Tree Farm. It is a time when things can get a little stormy in the household. I try to make myself invisible, spending as much time as possible outside or away from the farm while Robin virtually shuts himself away for three weeks. When the returns are completed and filed, Robin smiles again and regular order may return to the farm.

In the early days we started our farm records in hand-written ledgers, keeping every receipt stored in labelled polythene bags. Robin had a unique system whereby his columns ran horizontally rather than vertically. His unusual systems seem to be a relic from his childhood. His father, an accountant of some accomplishment, insisted, when Robin was old enough to write and do simple arithmetic, that he present a weekly balance sheet account of how his allowance was spent.

We still have an account book, laboriously penned in Robin's 8-year-old hand. One page of which is heavily scored through with the annotation in capitals: DOES NOT BALANCE. Perhaps this trauma in some way accounted for his adoption of horizontal tallying, whether by accident or by design. Henceforth, the system worked just fine for Robin until, after a couple of years, he graduated to maintaining farm records on the computer.

Following the annual filing of tax returns, in due course we receive notification that the taxes we must pay amount to $0.00, and we have tax credits in hand to be put against future years. We dismiss taxes from our minds for another year, vowing to be a bit tidier and deal with things month by month which, despite resolutions, never actually happens. Farm life continues at its erratic pace as we pass through the seasons with never a tax worry on our minds.

At the beginning of November a rare fine day appears like a pearl emerging from a grey oyster. The sun warms our backs and those of all the animals who happily soak up the golden rays. For the past few days we've been preparing for a good bonfire, returning to our childhood roots to celebrate 5th November, Guy Fawkes Day.

The potatoes are pricked, oiled and salted, wrapped in foil and put in the embers then sweet onions join the potatoes and lastly the steak. We sit by the bonfire long into the evening, mulling over the day with a glass of wine and watching the stars appear brightly as a frost begins to form. The cows visit us for a while then retreat to their barn. Cricket is constantly on the move, checking into the dark recesses and shadows away from the flames.

Next morning after her breakfast, Portia, our current resident porcine matriarch, discovers the bonfire site and lies down on the edge of the warm embers and we fear that she'll turn into pork crackling. Everyone enjoys the benefits of a bonfire.

From that point forward the month deteriorates. An unexpected phone call comes from Revenue Canada telling us our farming operation has been *chosen* to be audited. They tell us with great precision what they require. An auditor will come to audit the books covering the years 1999 and 2000. "Have all relevant documents, books and receipts ready and in date order for inspection."

We are given two weeks to assemble the documents and accounts. At first we are mystified, then outraged. Is it because we haven't paid any income taxes? How typical to pick on a very small farmer trying to scrape a living from the soil. We are further annoyed that we have to spend valuable time struggling to get all the documentation together in the appointed time when we need to be sowing fall seed, lag the water pipes and complete other pre-winter chores.

For the two weeks, in every spare moment Robin works on the Canada Customs and Revenue Agency demands in order to have everything ready for the 'Revenue Canada Verification and Enforcement Officer'—yes, that's her title. Don't you just love the sound of 'Enforcer' or 'Enforcement' in job titles? It immediately translates in my mind to 'Power Crazy Petty Bully.' The reality not only lives up to but seriously exceeds my expectations. Robin is in mental turmoil anticipating this visit of the federal fiscal gestapo. If he didn't have ulcers before, he probably does now.

The dreaded day arrives and Robin has escaped outside working with heavy machinery on the other side of the farm. Best to keep away from it; he has surely already played his part. I stand to attention by our polished mahogany dining table with everything requested lined up in date order, pages squared with mathematical precision.

The enforcer, a matronly woman with contours resembling a potato, introduces herself and I think she seems pleasant enough and offer her tea or coffee and fresh muffins or cookies, but the reply is "No" to everything, accompanied by vigorous head shaking, like a dog with ear mites. It seems she's everything-intolerant and will be going to her hotel at lunch time (twenty minutes' driving each way plus the time spent consuming her chosen comestibles) returning in the afternoon.

"Where's your computer?" she asks as she imperiously scans the area.

"Upstairs in the office, but the accounts aren't on the computer," I say adding with warmth and an inner glee, "everything's handwritten." Oh dear. She takes on the aura of a thunder cloud and inhaling deeply through flared nostrils, says, "And *where* is Mr. Ansell?"

"Outside working," I say, grinning sheepishly.

"Call him in, he must be here to assist me."

"What about his work? We're behind already spending so much time on these papers for you." The auditor is unmoved. It appears we are legally bound to do her bidding. I feel like clicking my heels together, standing to attention and saluting before marching off to summon Robin.

He unhappily presents himself to the enforcer. I hang around in the background to buffer proceedings between them, and to be generally helpful or to obfuscate matters if needed.

The agent assigned to us is endowed with the charms of a snake, slithering and hissing her way through the appointed years 1999 and 2000 making random strikes accompanied by condemnations, venomous comments and probing, invasive questions. Such tutting and cursing issuing from the lady as she looks at the books and she a public servant at that. She despises our hand-written ledgers, but can't fault the content or math. Robin's horizontal columns have upset her sense of order and she complains bitterly about the difficulty of totting up columns. She's really quite rude to us. This doesn't bode well for her opinion of our farming venture.

Then she starts making a foray back into 1998, *not* a year in question.

"How did you come by the money to buy the farm when there's no evidence of a bank loan or mortgage?" "When did your father die?" She has no business delving into matters outside her domain and we gently point out that 1998 is not under review but she says she's trying to come up with answers that her team leader will accept. Once she has departed for her lunch we discuss her possible motives.

"What do you think she's looking for?"

"I reckon," says Robin, "she's been told to find the source of what they think must be dirty money used to buy the farm."

Sadly for her they've chosen one of the honest guys and won't unearth any sooty little secrets for which she can receive a pat on the back and a bonus from her team leader. Robin conducts his business 'by the book' even if it *is* handwritten.

Late in the afternoon when it's cold and foggy, Ms. Enforcer returns, looking not one jot happier. I try to be pleasant to her to steer her away from her suspicions and implied accusations, but it doesn't work. If anything, she seems even more bitter. I might as well be hostile to match her mean spirit even though that probably won't improve matters.

Unable to find any trace of illicit money she changes tactics and starts fishing. She's distressed because there are certain purchases for which we've claimed exemption but for which we have no printed receipts. Things like a cow, the milking machine (a work tool) and especially the hay purchases from local farmers we've claimed as legitimate working expenses. She's *extremely* bothered about the hay.

"Why would you buy hay for several hundred dollars and not ask for a receipt?" she says. Why, indeed? Because that's how the local farming community works. We help each other: we barter and trade if necessary.

"Write down the names and addresses of any farmers you've bought hay from in such a manner so I can verify your claims." It's obvious what she's after now, she's looking for local farmers who might be selling hay without declaring it and so avoiding being squeezed for more petty taxes. The poor farmer works hard enough for a pittance as it is, and imagine the paperwork involved in the selling of a few bales of hay at a time.

It's a strange thing, really, but my mind has suddenly gone blank, and I can't remember the name of one single farmer. "How did you find the farmers selling hay?" she prompts.

"By looking in the Buy Sell and Trade paper at hay time."

After a noisy in-drawing of breath and a facial adjustment to her nostrils, she says, "Well work on remembering and I'll get back to you."

I have no intention of aiding her fishing exercise so she can harass other farmers, but she hasn't finished yet. We receive a salvo of questions about more things outside the designated years, and for which we haven't lined up pieces of paper, printed or hand written. What was the farm purchase price? *Why* don't we have a mortgage?

Robin patiently explains that we have no mortgage or bank loan, because by having debt we subordinate ourselves to the debt holder, so we used our own capital to finance ourselves. As she listens to Robin she pulls her neck back, tucks in her chin, lowers her lids and closes her eyes for a few seconds, breathing audibly. A little yoga tactic perchance. Then she restarts her planned attack.

"How could you afford to purchase this little farm? Where did the money come from?" She's roaming *well* beyond her scope of powers. However, with scarcely concealed anger and contempt now, we do our best to turn our records inside out to find and provide evidence of the sale of shares and liquidation of the RRSP for homeowners. Next she wants a copy of the currency transfer from Robin's mother's estate in England and a copy of the Foreign Transfer Credit, and so it goes on. And on. And on. Finally we've assembled a modest pile of papers on the table and she resorts to her calculator to tot everything up. What a surprise. The total from the papers that we've provided at short notice doesn't *exactly* match the figure she perceives we needed by a few hundred dollars. Now she's looking for evidence in our bank accounts as to how we support our current operations. She's really harassing us and I want to tell her to stop but we are powerless.

Still dissatisfied, she eventually retreats to her hotel to work on our 'case' and we are released at last to attend to milking and feeding the animals. What a sinful waste of a day.

During the evening we discuss the day's events and Robin again wonders what she's after. She knows, of course, that we have lived and worked for five years in the Cayman Islands. Has this thrown up a flag on our files with the revenue agency? It's public knowledge, as is the fact that we bought from the Cayman Islands government an ex-drug smuggling boat, from which the authorities confiscated 900 kg of cocaine , (valued at that time at 172 million dollars) and in which we then sailed the South Pacific. It's never been a secret—I published the story in the Readers' Digest and I'm currently writing the book. What she's probably looking for, then. is evidence of laundered money. Good luck with that. Putting children through ten years of boarding school and university so they could graduate debt-free, coupled with buying a boat that, courtesy of Cyclone Justin, is now at the bottom of the Coral Sea took care of all those funds earned.

The enforcer phones the next day wanting yet more information from Robin. We were working outside as one mostly does on a farm, and receive her answering machine message later in the day. Robin locates the information requested, calls her back and asks if we can fax the papers to her. She's upset that we weren't in all day sitting by the phone in case she needed us. "No," she says, "don't fax them, I'm coming to the farm again and will pick them up tomorrow." She also wants the price of certain shares sold on a certain day in 1997. "She could find that out herself, the lazy woman," I say, "but I bet she wants to check out more things here too."

I'm busy washing eggs downstairs when she arrives so I let her in via the basement door. I won't take her upstairs to the living room, I'm too busy. She decides that as she's here it will be a good opportunity to inspect the basement to see my egg-washing set up and equipment (mentioned in dispatches sans receipts, of course). She also needs to see the milking equipment which we also paid for with cash, but she won't believe exists until she sees it. That, of course, resides in the milking parlour. It doesn't matter that she won't be able to differentiate the milking equipment from a sewing machine being an obvious city girl, despite the numerous dairy farms in her native Holland.

She seems ignorant of all bovine matters and we get to wondering why she was selected for our audit (we later surmise that she must have been a naughty lady and this is her punishment) but whatever the reason, she's not doing well gathering information for her team leader. After seeing the milking equipment that we explain in detail, she decides that she hasn't yet seen any of the cows either that we claim to have.

"Right," says Robin, "let's go find the cows," and calls Cricket to accompany us.

Sadly she's underdressed for a damp day on the farm and clutches her cardigan to her chest as Robin takes her round through the wet, soggy fields spotted with a few cow flops. While we are wearing rubber boots she's wearing beige leather pumps, having declined the offer of borrowing boots, and within minutes her footwear, more suitable for performing a ballet, is first saturated through and then thoroughly mucky by the time we find the cows. Robin introduces her to them by their names, including the extra calves we've bought (oops! no receipts). As the cows assume this surprise visit is intended to share treats, as it usually is when we bring visitors round the farm, they mill around and jostle us. It's truly heart-warming to see their enthusiasm for the newcomer. She comments that our matriarch has been busy having all those calves! Aaah, the blissful ignorance of this sweet city person is surpassed only by her winning smile and generous nature. I don't think she has any idea that a cow only has one calf a year. Perhaps she thinks they have three or four at a time, like sheep. I don't want to be empathetic, but I actually feel sorry for her.

On our return trek to the farmhouse I ask, as she's outside anyway, if she'd like to come and see all the pigs. "They're only down this track, and they love to see visitors. Better take some treats, though." My question sets up a muscle tic in her cheek but receives a frosty silence. We hope by now she realizes that the farm isn't a front for some nefarious dealings and this is indeed our only business and yes, making an impressive little loss.

She's ready to leave the farm and we are liberated for the time being. She'll submit her reports about us but will wait two more weeks before doing so to give me time to rack my brain and see if I can remember the hay-selling farmers' names so she can follow up with them. By now we've had all we can take from her. "Don't bother," I say, "I can tell you now I won't *ever* remember and don't intend to try. Do what you have to do; penalize us if you must, we'll pay whatever penalty you impose."

Whatever she decides, the cows will enjoy their barn full of illicit hay. At least she didn't confiscate that.

She never does return to the farm. Life is so busy as we head towards the year's end we don't waste time giving her another thought. We know we've done nothing wrong apart from the heinous crime of keeping hand ledgers and missing a few petty little receipts.

A week before Christmas the official Canada Revenue Agency letter arrives. The items that we'd claimed as business expenses without receipts will be disallowed and they are deciding whether to rule that we aren't running a bona fide business but just doing it to reduce tax implications. What a splendid Christmas present. We await our sentence.

It's another three months before any further communication. Our favourite tax enforcer telephones saying that she, Verification and Enforcement Officer of the first order, and her *Uberführer* Team*

Leader have reviewed our files once again and decided *not* to pursue penalties. The decision has been rescinded.

No explanations given, no official letter, only the phone call.

"That's so very kind of you to tell us," I ooze, like liquid cow manure in a bad dose of winter dysentery, "thank you *so* much." I forbore to let her know who we thought behaved like a *real cow* on this farm. Their treatment of us is enough to make you spit. She just couldn't understand that we wouldn't succumb to her threats and implicate others in order to avoid penalties. In the evening we crack open a bottle of wine to celebrate the end of all this stupidity.

We're still awaiting written verification rescinding their former threat. It's been more than a decade so far. Another classic example of a waste of tax-payers' money.

* While editing this chapter I looked up 'Uberführer' in Google. I didn't have to look further than the first entry from an urban dictionary. This is what I found. (No offence intended to my German friends.)

Uberführer

A psychotic self-obsessed female team leader from an international profit making company. She would need to be small minded, brain dead, stuffy, anal, terrorizing and controlling without substance to back up any of her words. Would be very good at organizing pointless exercises for personnel and even better at changing processes constantly to confuse everyone...

... I rest my case.

24. Dog Tails

BADGERED

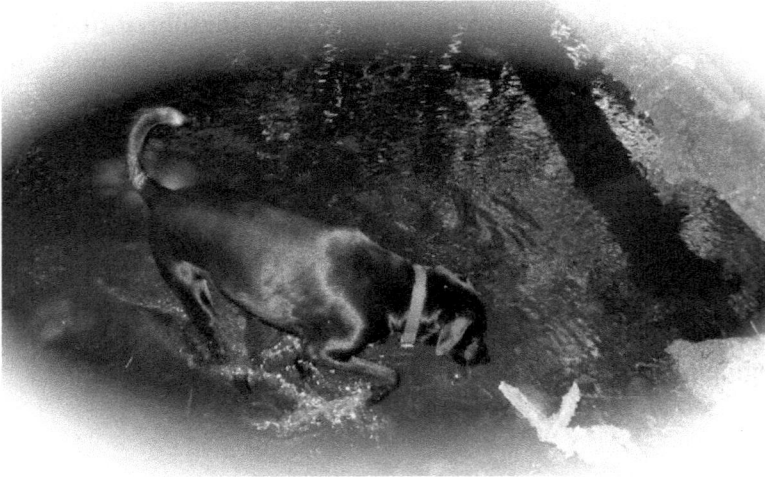

It's just the most amazing thing to love a dog, isn't it? It makes our relationships with people seem as boring as a bowl of oatmeal ~ John Grogan

I feel we should have two dogs on this farm, so it's time to replace Acorn and find a friend for Cricket. I settle on a day at the end of April to broach the subject to Robin. A spell of warm spring weather has brought the tulip bulbs and early shrubs into bloom, the birds are singing and all nature is smiling.

"As we're not in a rush today, Robin, can we check out the SPCA for another puppy?"

"Sure," he replies.

Good, I've chosen the right day!

The manager greets us warmly and asks after the farm and the animals. "We're looking for a second puppy and we'd really like another pit bull type," I tell her, "because Cricket's so good on the farm."

"We do have a litter of puppies," she says, "the mother was found wandering on the street and was brought here and delivered her pups the next day. We call her Jazz and think she's part pit bull."

Jazz, who looks more like a small lab, has seven black puppies napping in a heap.

"If you're interested, they'll be ready for adoption when they're eight weeks old."

"Oh yes, we're definitely serious and would love more pit bull genes."

On our third visit to the litter we find they've moved to a foster home in the country so make arrangements with the foster mum, a friendly Scottish woman, to visit the next day.

A driveway curves off the rural road, winding towards a charming house and outbuildings set in a field of green surrounded by hemlock, fir and cedar trees. The pups are romping outside in a pen when we arrive while their mum has a break, relaxing close by. They're all appealing, but one puppy waddles over to us, sniffs round Robin's feet and licks the toe of his boot. He bends to pet it and it sniffs his hands.

"Seems to like you, Robin," the foster mum says.

Robin picks up the pup, "Let's have a look at you," he says and peers into its face then cradles the wriggling bundle in his arms. "This one's a little girl—that would be good with Cricket."

Her foster mum suggests painting one toenail with nail polish, so we can identify her again. They're all very similar in appearance but she's one of the smaller bitches, with a white chest and thumb print on her chin.

We wonder if we'll recognize her on our next visit, but sure enough when they're let out to play one pup heads straight for Robin's feet. He's flattered, bends to check and sees she has the remains of red nail polish on one toenail. This black and white pup will have to be ours, and will be called Badger. By the time she's had her shots and is ready for her new home June has arrived and the lilac is in full bloom, its heady scent hanging on the air.

Badger immediately adopts Cricket who, after the initial shock of having a little sister constantly following him, seems happy to have a buddy. He'll pick up a toy and take it to her, so that she latches on and he can drag her around the room. He teaches her to play tug o' war and how to disembowel teddy bears; he shows her where it's shallow enough to paddle in the pond and paw at salmon fry, and how to wriggle under the tarpaulin covering the manure heap, for a spot of rodent hunting. Not that she needs encouragement to hunt rodents. At every opportunity she busily digs holes to expose small furry creatures living in the bank of the drainage ditch. We keenly wait for her pit bull traits to surface. She does have a very sweet temperament and there's no doubt she's a labrador cross, but crossed with what?

Sublimely happy to defer to Cricket in all matters, Badger knows her place is being his sidekick and soon graduates from sleeping in a crate in the kitchen to her own pen with an insulated kennel right next to Cricket's under the deck, trotting out to bed behind him each night, although if she were an only dog I'm sure she'd be happy to stay indoors at night.

Some things she's learned quite without help. She'll snatch licks of chicken poop in passing and sometimes can't resist rolling in it. We try to be alert for her adopting a lowered-shoulder attitude swiftly followed by the sliding of an ear, neck and back in the delightful treat. It's fortunate that she likes water because outdoor baths are frequent.

Nevertheless, she doesn't learn to swim because Cricket dislikes the water and we don't want her to disturb the fish in the pond and creek. She did fall in as a very small pup and Robin had to haul her out by the collar. Although she'll happily tramp around outside in the rain, when she comes in she has quite an obsession about being thoroughly dried. I rub them with towels in the basement but if it's not completed to Badger's satisfaction she'll sit in front of Cricket's face and he'll obligingly lick her to complete the drying process. Something that persists throughout her life. Sometimes she can be such a wuss, if allowed.

Sadly her predilection for chicken nutrients doesn't diminish as she leaves puppyhood behind and we finally reckon that Badger chose Robin because his boots probably had a certain chicken *bouquet* to them. In time we have to fence to keep the chickens and Badger apart. If we find Badger's fascination with chicken manure unpalatable there is, and this might be hard to believe, something rather worse.

At the end of the summer the salmon return upstream to their spawning grounds in the gravelly streams nearer to the mountain. We're quite close to their destination and some who've made it this far pass through our pond en route to Little Hal Creek. From the thousands making the pilgrimage few succeed and by the time they are on our farm they are beaten up and very tired. Several don't make the final few hundred metres to complete the journey their forbears have made for generations. These salmon disintegrate and rot by the sides of the pond and creeks. The eagles, who are not picky whether their salmon meal is fresh or well rotted swoop down to feast on them, carrying away chunks and sometimes dropping the rotting flesh where the dogs can find it. This make the most delectable, highly nutritious, fetid snack for canines. If you've never experienced a dog vomiting up a large piece of putrid fish, skin and skeleton on your area rug, then count yourself fortunate. It's not something you need to experience. On the scale of disgusting, nauseating smells it's on a par with the putrid turtle Robin once found on the beach and brought home and put by the gate because, 'the ants will clean up the shell.' The ants would not. In fact they kept a very respectful distance from the shell, just as all our neighbours did, crossing the road rather than walk in our vicinity.

When the dogs are not eating the rotting fish, they are dressing themselves in it, daubing their cheeks, necks and shoulders, luxuriating in the disgusting slimy stinking mess. It's a time of constant awareness for us, and numerous baths for the dogs. We try to remove any fish before they find them—an impossible task because of their vastly superior sense of smell and dedication to the cause.

The annual returning salmon become a lifelong obsession with Badger and Cricket, although he's rather more circumspect about adorning himself, unlike Badger who abandons her self wholeheartedly to the pursuit. Fortunately the season is relatively short.

There's no doubt about it, we were hoodwinked. We'll never spot a single pit bull trait in Badger. She's a lab through and through with her figure inclining to stoutness because of her predilection for food. Any food from dog kibble and cattle cake, to scavenging a freshly killed limp mouse the cat has just deposited at her feet. The funny thing is, if she's picked up something she knows she shouldn't have she can't help giving herself away. With the offending item still in her mouth, she inclines her head and looks sideways at me from under a raised eyebrow, with perhaps the tip of a rodent tail between her lips. "OK, give it to me," I command, and she'll obediently open her mouth and eject the creature. Cricket will guiltily hang his head as if he's the one to blame. "It's OK Cricket," I say, "it's not *your* fault, she just can't help herself."

Dog Tails continued...

THE DOG WHO WOULDN'T BARK

Man is rated the highest animal, at least among all animals who returned the questionnaire ~ Robert Brault

Cricket rarely does anything wrong. He's gentle with all humans, other dogs and livestock, especially the very young. If he has a failing it's that he rarely barks; only when it's vitally important to alert us to a human or wild animal intruder. He particularly dislikes raccoons, though, and on one occasion barked frantically, refusing to stop until Robin finally got out of bed at 3:00 a.m. to despatch one in a tree near the chicken house. Not being lovers of noisy dogs, we enjoy his quiet demeanour, but it doesn't always work to his advantage.

One day the dogs accompany us as usual in the late afternoon to do the feeding and, following our routine, they come with us along the farm track, through the gate and into the field to the barn where the cows stand at their feeding stations, waiting patiently to receive their rations.

It's been a heavily overcast, raw day, and I won't be sorry to return to the warmth. As I work I catch glimpses of Cricket and Badger running this way and that, following the scent of rabbits or deer. Robin's in the barn tossing hay for the cows' manger, while I wheel the barrow around picking up manure and tipping it on the pile before returning the barrow to the empty stall where it's kept.

The cows finish their grain and I untie them to let them go to their hay manger while Robin washes their food buckets.

I whistle for the dogs and set off for home. Badger comes bounding up to join us.

"Where's Cricket?" I say.

"Oh, he must have taken off chasing something through the woods." Robin continues walking homeward. "He'll be back shortly."

I hang back calling and whistling. Badger can't understand why I keep whistling when she's right here beside me.

After a few moments I admit defeat and go home to warm milk for lamb bottles. Cricket won't be long: he likes to be in his kennel when the daylight has gone. We have a job keeping him in the house past 7:00 p.m. these days. He loves to lie in his insulated house in the pen under the deck, snuggled in his heap of blankets, so he doesn't have to miss the start of his dog soap operas which can be heard way off in the distance many evenings, as the neighbourhood dogs up and down the valley talk to each other, passing their latest news.

As I prepare supper, I keep one eye on the sliding door leading to the deck, where he'll surely appear at any moment to tell us he's vanquished a foe. After supper it's totally dark and I go onto the deck to call and whistle yet again, but he doesn't appear so I sit at my computer toying with my work, so I can keep my eyes glued to the glass door. Of course he'd come if he could, I reason. Something is very wrong and I can't settle to anything. "I'm just going to check outside again," I tell Robin, who's sitting in his chair reading a book. "If I need you, I'll call."

I dress warmly in coat, gloves and boots, pull a headlamp over my woolly hat, grab another flashlight, and walk all over our territory, calling and whistling. I check the barns, flashing my light over the half-doors into the stalls, to the furthermost reaches. The cows in the lean-to turn in my direction, blinking in the sudden light before returning to their hay. Then I work my way through the bush to the salmon-bearing creek which provides our water, cross over the plank bridge and into the swampy woodland beyond. I'm wondering if he's hurt himself, chasing something through the bush. I have visions of him lying with a broken leg but not making a sound. But surely if he had a broken leg he could still make it home? Perhaps he's been shot—no, I haven't heard any gunshots so I try to dismiss that possibility even though we do have a few dubious neighbours who like to shoot and set traps. Oh no, now I've thought of traps I can see him in my mind's eye, lying with metal jaws clamped on a leg. Sadly, the reality of finding anything in the dark is virtually zero. Cricket just doesn't bark or whine. I could be standing right next to him and I'd only hear the thump of his tail on the ground or feel the lick of his tongue.

After shutting up the duck and chicken houses I have one last option to explore and climb into the Land Rover to patrol the roads nearby. Maybe he's gone through the woods and is lost, or has been knocked over and is lying injured on the road. But there's no sign of him.

Utterly dejected, I return home where Robin is still reading his book.

"I can't find him." I have to bite my lower lip to stop it trembling.

Robin switches on the TV, and I phone all the neighbours. No one has seen him, most don't even know what he looks like but say they'll watch out for him. I can't think of anything else I can do. Every few minutes I glance towards the deck, because when he does return, he certainly won't bark or paw at the window. He'll wait patiently, looking somewhat melancholy, until we notice him.

Badger's also uneasy. She's never been without Cricket and her time clock tells her they should have gone to bed some time ago. She leans against my legs, peering anxiously into my face. I take her out for her late evening stroll, calling again for Cricket. I doubt she'll settle in her kennel so I bring her indoors and ask her to lie down on her rug in the hallway. During the night she repeatedly pushes into the bedroom to poke me, telling me something's amiss. Not that I'm getting any sleep anyway. I know Cricket's not away by choice, he's virtually attached to me at the hip.

Images of him injured in the woods, or lying in a ditch stay with me all night. I never realized quite how much this dog means to me. I get up frequently to check the patio door, and put a sheepskin rug outside on the deck for him if he returns.

Morning arrives and my depression has set in. Still no sign of Cricket. We must deal with the other animals before starting a major hunt in daylight. I've not forgotten that the neighbour's dog, Sam, disappeared and later only his collar was found and I'm already trying to imagine life without Cricket. In this void I tackle the morning chores like an automaton. After feeding lambs, ducks, chickens and pigs we get to the cow barn, where the cows are waiting patiently by their feeding stations. Badger tags along, sedately for once. I run my hands along the backs of the cows, trying to gain comfort from their smell and warmth. Robin's inside the barn tossing out hay for the cows' mangers and I must clean the stalls.

I head to the empty stall to collect my wheelbarrow and shovel, unlatch the door and Cricket bursts out, leaping high and bouncing with joyous squeaks. He's been shut in all night, patiently waiting. Not a sound did he make when I searched and called last night. Not a sound when he must have been right beneath my nose behind the half-door as my flashlight's beam searched the far corners of the stall. Our reunion is nothing short of crazy. I laugh and cry all at once hugging him as he does some frenetic licking, then Badger and Cricket race round and round in frenzied circles.

"I thought I heard a slight rustling noise just then when I went into the barn," Robin says, "but I didn't want to raise your hopes. I told you Cricket wouldn't run off and there'd be a simple explanation." It's funny how often he's right.

Later I'm still feeling guilty, and brooding. "What went through his mind when I shut him in the stall?" I ask Robin, "Maybe he thought I was punishing him, leaving him there all night."

"Maybe he thought nothing of the kind," replies Robin. "Maybe he just bedded down in the straw listening to the cows munching on the other side of the wall, knowing that we'd return the next morning. We always do. Every... single... day. And don't forget, he could still hear his dog radio. Now, will you *please* stop over-analyzing everything?"

"I just believe it's good to think things through." I continue, "I wonder how a dog's mind works? Does Cricket think we humans are stupid? If he does, he's right."

Robin rolls his eyes. "Just accept that he's a devoted rescue dog. He'll never run away and he doesn't share all human feelings, especially yours."

"All right, but I really should teach him to bark on command."

Sounds simple enough, but proves much more difficult that I thought. He just doesn't want to bark, and who has time to play silly games when a dog has work to do.

25. Pig Tails

PIG MOVEMENTS

Never wrestle with pigs. You both get dirty and the pig likes it ~
George Bernard Shaw

One pig-rearing book tells us that to move a pig we need only a stick and a board. Guide the snout with the stick and hold the board at the pig's rear. Sounds easy. Not true. Another book tells us that to move a pig all we have to do is hold a bucket over its head and back it in the desired direction. Also not true. Makes the pig MAD.

With our sow the only way she'll go in any direction other than the one she has chosen is by dropping bribes from a rattling bucket. Big fat juicy tasty treats. Sweet apples and out-of-date cream buns and doughnuts from the bakery are her favourites, laid down along the trail not more than a metre ahead of her snout. Then her waif-like 500 pound body will trip daintily forward on pointy hooves, metre by metre, vacuuming up the delicacies as she goes. She can hear the bucket rattle; she can smell the food; she can see the food; she can eat the food. All is well. Unfortunately, this time I have misjudged her appetite and we have rather a long way to go, so I'm reduced to rattling the bucket with no treats forthcoming. This serves only to irritate Whitey who thinks we're teasing her. As far as she's concerned this game is over.

Now a pig is wedge shaped, and it's well known to pig lovers that the smallest hole through which the snout can pass, will in short order be enlarged and with consistent steady forward pressure and the occasional concerted thrust, the rest of the body will follow. Like driving a chock into a log.

Whitey has had enough of empty bucket rattling and, feeling somewhat replete, is ready for a nap in her comfy bed. With an astonishing turn of speed she leaps into the air making a 180° turn seemingly in one movement to bolt for home. She spies a little gap between Robin's legs as he's standing between her and her house. Unfortunately her squinty eyes have assessed that the shortest route to her target lies directly between his legs.

She charges, intending to pass through the gap but becomes stuck fast. Robin not being a yoga practitioner or double jointed or swivel hipped is unable to gracefully lift one leg waist high to give her passage, especially since he isn't wearing exercise spandex, but is restricted by jeans. Off they shoot together like horse and rider from the trap, she forwards, Robin backwards, the heels of his boots skimming the grass, a look of astonished horror on his face. I watch transfixed as Robin slams forward, his arms clutching at Whitey's ample girth. They are making quite good progress together until seeing her chance to rid herself of the unwanted rider, Whitey swerves and detours under the low hanging branches of the cedar trees en route to her old home.

Robin suffers a severe blow to his rump as a thick branch halts his backward motion. Whitey bolts forward, free and light as a dandelion seed, and Robin smacks face down onto the moist leaf litter. Pigs are not only powerful, they are smart. Whatever course of action they decide upon, that is usually the one that happens.

In the future we find it no trouble at all doing what we hitherto thought would be onerous, that is, spending two days luring Whitey into the horse trailer and hooking it up to the tractor in order to move her around from pasture to pasture. Anything's better than another backwards ride on a hot cross pig, and there are no books that we've discovered to help us out of that dilemma. Maybe we should write one.

Pig Tails continued...

STRANGE BEDFELLOWS

People must help one another; it is nature's law ~ Jean de la Fontaine

Four of our piglets are being raised in a new area of the back forty to give them full advantage of the vegetation while doing some ploughing work and fertilizing for us. They're nine weeks old and are usually eagerly awaiting my noontime visit with their meal. They live in a custom designed, no-expense spared, precision-crafted log house fashioned from existing trees, logs and old barn boards in their one-acre of woodland and swamp.

As I approach their log cabin, there's not a piglet in sight. Very strange, have they escaped? They're good time-keepers when it comes to food, pushing and jostling each other to be first in line. I stick my head through the doorway and the piglets are squished together at the back corner of the house, eyes wide, darting terrified glances from me to their strange bedfellows. Spread-eagled (now I understand where the term comes from) on the straw beside them is a large brown juvenile bald eagle with a wingspan of about two metres. It's motionless, its beak pointing down towards the straw.

I immediately retreat a few steps, then cautiously edge towards the entrance to take a second look. The eagle is breathing and the piglets appear unharmed although frozen with fear. I circle round to the back of the hut to peer in through a gap in the logs. It's an astonishing sight. Beneath the eagle's head is a large raven lying on its back. It has its left leg stretched up and backwards towards the eagle, its foot encircling the eagle's beak with two of the claws digging into the eagle's nostrils.

Stalemate. The raven can't let go, as the eagle will kill it. The eagle can't move as it's snared and anchored by the heavy raven. Catch 22: locked in deadly motionless combat. Only a matter of time before one or the other will succumb. It could take hours, or even days. I can't leave them like this with no way out of the impasse.

At Oak Tree Farm, odd situations like this only ever happen when Robin is out of town. Action must be taken, but what can I do? I swiftly dismiss my first impulse to get in there and separate them. Stupid idea. Raven talons and beaks are hard and cruel; eagles' are deadly. I have a gun and a licence, and have taken a gun handling course but I feel woefully lacking in what's required to fire a gun at a creature.

"Hold on!" I say to the piglets as if they understand me and hoping the familiar tone of my voice is a little reassuring for them. "I'll be right back." I run to the house to telephone a good neighbour a few miles down the road. Fortunately I catch him just before he leaves for work.

"Have you got a gun, Rod?" I ask.

"Sure," he says.

"I've a bizarre situation of life and death." I explain the dilemma, adding, "can you help me?"

My neighbour arrives, and he saunters across the field reassuringly calm as is his way. My heart's racing, but I know Rod can deal with anything. I just have time to take one quick photo as he walks to the rear of the hut. He peers through the boards, assesses the situation and says, "I'll shoot the raven." A man of few words.

Poking his gun through a slot is the last straw for the piglets and is the necessary catalyst to galvanize them into action. They pop and bounce out of the hut like beads of mercury from a broken thermometer and then re-cluster for comfort in a mercurial blob just outside. I'm glad they're out of harm's way, and I chase them further from the area.

One shot only and the raven is despatched and releases its death grip. The eagle remains motionless, slow to gather itself together as if it's already resigned to its fate. It seems disoriented and weak but discovers that its head is free, and gradually drawing in its extended wings by stages, it drags itself around to the entrance of the cabin. In a short while it has composed itself and makes its way outside the hut. It beats its wings experimentally, and I smile as it rises into the air and away over the trees to hunt another day.

The ravens are smart and terrible thieves. They take much of the piglets' food from their bowl if I am not in attendance for the whole of the meal. To try to outwit the birds I had tucked an extra bowl of food inside the house. We can only guess that a brazen raven hopped into the hut for the food. I can imagine the eagle witnessing these comings and goings and deciding that raven could be on the menu for lunch. It was an opportunity too good to miss.

The eagle has not been back. I can't say I'm sorry; if he becomes accustomed to easy food here his next step might be to help himself to a free-range chicken. Although I couldn't have killed it myself, I now have a dead raven to hang up as a warning to others—I'm told it may just work for a while to keep them away until the piglets are bold enough to chase them off.

There's much truth in old saying; nature is *indeed* red in tooth and claw.

Pig Tails continued...

PORTIA'S LAST STAND

It's sad when someone you know becomes someone you knew ~ Harry
Rollins

A brisk cold spell has enveloped us in mid-November. Actually, not just enveloped but overwhelmed us. We are experiencing an uncharacteristic temperature several degrees Celsius below freezing, with foggy mornings that sometimes end in sunshine.

It's inevitable that the time should come for our beloved and pampered 600 lb. pig to go to the butcher, prompted somewhat at this pre-Christmas time by the demands at the Farmers' Market for organic ground pork for the French Canadian Christmas Eve classic tortières—pies with mixed ground beef and ground pork, combined with special spices and baked in a pie case.

A few days before the appointed time, we lead Portia into a new field with a stream for extra spoiling and fun, and also bring in the little horse trailer we use to transport the animals. The doors are propped open and we can accustom her to feeding inside so she's not frightened of it. The first day she marches in, rearranges the straw bedding inside, then promptly lifts off both metal doors from their three hinges, and stomps them into the ground. Apparently they're not to her liking. Robin patiently replaces them and locks them closed. We should have drilled and pinned the hinge pins so they could not be lifted off again—something we are to bitterly regret later. Next day Portia rips out the emergency brake cable, followed by trying to liberate the battery installed on the fender to power the emergency braking system. Finally she chews off the wiring for the rear lights and bites them off.

"She's only being playful." Robin says. Well he would, after all, she's a favourite pig. I think he's being uncharacteristically calm about the whole affair. Sadly, though, she must be banished to her original field until the due date, while Robin rewires and repairs the trailer.

On the arranged morning it's very cold and foggy. Robin tempts the hungry, and correspondingly ill-humoured, Portia up the short ramp into the trailer with sticky buns, closes and bolts the rear doors, flaps up the ramp and secures it with a cross bar. We set off and have travelled about three of the ten kilometres towards our destination, when we hear an almighty bang.

"My God! Something's fallen off the trailer." I shout. A vision of a loose pig on the road immediately charges through my mind and my gut lurches in a most unsatisfactory manner.

Robin stamps on the brake. As he draws onto the shoulder I leap out before the truck stops, and race to the back. The ramp is down, one door is missing and Portia is testing the ramp with a forefoot. I fly at her and smack her on the nose to startle her into backing up. Fortunately, the fact that she's five times my weight eludes her. I heave up the heavy ramp, swing it into upright position and lean against it as Robin reaches us. Portia is not in good humour, after all she's not had breakfast—a gooey cake or two doesn't fill the void.

A hundred metres behind us in the middle of the road lies the door—metal, lined with wood. Robin takes over with the petulant pig, trying to keep her captive. Portia wants out—NOW. I run down the road and try to pick up the door, which seems to weigh a ton, and start back towards the trailer half carrying and half dragging it. My lungs are bursting with the exertion; my head pounds and mental images of a rampaging pig in the neighbouring flower and vegetable gardens won't go away. The damage one pig can cause is tremendous—I know some of these people, they are my customers at the Farmers' Market. What will they say? Eventually I reach the trailer, gasping, and heaving.

Robin takes the door and I crawl into the cab to grab some cakes I had reserved for an emergency. This is certainly an emergency. I lob a cup cake into the trailer. It sails right over hear head to the furthermost corner. She'll not trouble with that because I have more in my hand, nearer her nose. I drop them on the floor and they divert her for a few seconds so Robin can lift the door over the ramp and try to re-hang it on its three hinges, but it won't seat properly. The impact of hitting the road has undoubtedly distorted something. We clamp the retaining bar across the ramp as securely as possible and I take over humouring Portia while Robin fetches a long rope to lash the doors, but there's nothing much to attach the rope to. The trailer looks like a badly wrapped Christmas parcel. It is not going to hold a furious pig.

I clamber on the outside of the trailer with one foot on the offside fender and the rubber booted toes of my second foot perched precariously on the thin edge of the ramp. I hook one arm through the open window as an anchor and I'm clutching a stick in my other hand. Portia doesn't find this at all amusing, in fact she's livid. My heart is hammering in my chest. Nothing, but nothing holds back a mad pig. If I were brave I would get into the trailer with her, but I recall a misquote of an old saying, *there are old swineherds, and bold swineherds, but no old, bold swineherds.*

Portia, having also practiced in the field before we left, is now thoroughly familiar with how to remove the rear door and sets about a repeat performance, worrying at the bottom edge with the dexterous floating ring of cartilage at the end of her snout evolved for just such purposes. I alternately scratch her behind the ear, or flick her on the nose with a twig, whichever seems necessary at the moment to focus her attention.

"Quick, drive on, Rob, I'll hang on here to keep her diverted."

Robin is distinctly unhappy with me playing limpet on the outside of the trailer but there's no alternative. He slowly pulls ahead and with hazards lights flashing we make slow progress over the next seven kilometres through the patchy fog. Robin constantly checks his side mirror, and I give him a stiff and frosty thumbs up. A few cars pass us slowly, rubbernecking, but fortunately there are no police on the road, although an escort with sirens and flashers might not be such a bad thing. To add to the discomfort, it's -7°C, and although I'm in a coat, hat and gloves, I am perishing cold.

It seems an eternity until we turn off onto the side road where there are small farms and rural properties. At least here farmers might be more understanding if she escapes.

Portia has finished every scrap of the comestibles that I've thrown in, and she soon tires of my antics; she isn't even interested in the loose end of the rope I've thrown in to her and is becoming testy again. She takes stock of her surroundings and, lifting her snout, senses some fresh air coming in round the perimeter of the groom's door—a slim door on the side of the trailer—and sets about attacking that. I envision her springing the narrow door open, and launching herself out, but getting stuck and hanging half in and half out of the trailer, screaming, as only pigs can scream. We're not even carrying a rifle or a sharp knife, in the event that a quick despatch is necessary. I shout at her, sing to her—anything to keep her attention and prevent her from escaping. Fortunately Robin can focus on driving.

It seems aeons later when we reach the slaughterer's yard, and thank goodness father and son are standing ready. Portia is madder than a hornet, and if I interfere with her one more time, I swear she'll rear up and remove my arm. I almost have to be pried off the outside of the trailer since I'm frozen solid.

"Quick! She's broken the door off." I say. The gravity of the situation is immediately understood, The rope is unwound and without more ado, the fellow stands on an upturned bucket to get a line of sight, fires one shot and the saga is finished.

Portia was an adorable piglet, a spirited juvenile, a contented mother and a cantankerous old lady. Right to the end, there was never a dull moment with Portia.

I can only wish my epitaph might read the same.

New Beginnings

Memories are the key not to the past, but to the future ~ Corrie Ten Boom

There are many more tales from Oak Tree Farm where we stayed for fourteen years. In the latter period we made a change and grew lavender, distilled it for oil and hydrosol which we used for making beautiful lavender products. The demand increased as the interest in the wonderful healing powers of lavender grew, and before too long we were selling worldwide.

Sadly cancer intervened, making it impossible to continue working on the farm with animals or lavender. However, those fourteen years were some of the happiest times of my life, and I often peruse the daily log books we kept of farm life, and chuckle or shed a tear at the memories of those animals and times. How soon I can publish more stories depends upon how long the winters are here in Nova Scotia, because when the weather is good, I still prefer to be working outside on the land!

About the Author

Farming was the latest in a long line of adventures. For many years she travelled with her engineer husband, working in the UK, Canada, Libya, Cayman Islands, Philippines and Australia. During her travels she learned to fly, scuba dive, sail, and gained a science degree from the University of Toronto. After their sailboat was sunk in a cyclone and they were rescued by helicopter off Australia, the author and her husband returned to Vancouver Island, Canada where they started farming. For several years an editor and writer, she's been published on five continents.

Now retired from active work she lives with her husband by a river in Nova Scotia where he keeps his latest sailboat and she spends time landscaping; growing organic food and lavender; walking their pit bull puppy and writing during the long winter months.

Another Book by the Author

When the Wind Blows—
Extraordinary adventures with a deadly twist

Available in print with online retailers and also in ebook form. Learn about it on the website *http://www.Maggi-Ansell.com* where you can also see a CBC TV video about the *Orca* adventure.

To connect with the author
email: Author@Maggi-Ansell.com

When the Wind Blows

Extraordinary adventures with a deadly twist

Maggi Ansell

1

Temptation—Grand Cayman, British West Indies

"Drug Alley, they call it!"

Robin sweeps his arm in a gesture of introduction towards a row of dilapidated boats resting on chocks along the west side of the desert-like expanse of Harbour House Marina, in Grand Cayman. "This is where all the drug boats are stored when they've been confiscated by the government."

The midday November sun blazes down. In the shimmering heat we wander along the row of broken dreams: small sailboats, home-built boats, antique boats—all in degrees of disrepair with vestiges of yellow, plastic police tape attached. I shake my feet to loosen the gritty sand and chips of old anti-fouling paint working their way between my bare, sandaled toes and step over the old paint-rollers, brushes, sanding disks and beer cans littering the ground.

"Have all these boats been caught running drugs?"

"Yes. They've come from Panama en route to the USA. They come via the Cayman Islands to throw suspicion from their Panamanian roots." Robin rolls his eyes. "What the drug runners fail to realize is that the Cayman authorities are naturally distrustful of all vessels from Panama."

"What happens to them?"

"The crew is removed, tried and jailed; the cargo is disposed of and the boat is impounded."

I don't think Robin has driven me 8 km from town during our lunch-hour, just for an entertaining stroll in the sticky heat. I wait expectantly, head on one side and smile at him.

"A new yacht came in a while ago," he says, casually.

OK, now he *has* managed to tweak my interest. "What was it carrying?"

"Oh, 900 kilos of cocaine," he says nonchalantly, "worth US$172 million dollars."

"A hundred and seventy-two million dollars? My God! What happened to it all?"

"Ah ha! The police have it under lock and key, still wrapped in oilskin packages. They unloaded it at the government dock, motored the yacht round to North Sound and hauled it out at the Marina here."

For once I'm speechless: overloaded with information swirling in my brain. "So which one had all the cocaine on it?"

Robin darts a meaningful glance further along the row, but instead of telling me, he draws a small slip of paper from his pocket.

My life is about to change for ever because of a three-sentence announcement in The Compass, our local newspaper:

FOR *SALE* by private tender: 17-metre yacht. Viewing at Harbour House Marina by arrangement with the Manager. Sealed bids to the Cayman Islands' Government offices by noon, December 1ˢᵗ, 1990.

"So *this* is what it's all about. I thought you seemed extraordinarily well informed."

"I do my homework," says Robin looking off into the distance, "it won't do any harm to take a look at it. Let's get the keys from the manager."

"You mean we can go on board?" I glance behind as we walk back to the marina office, keen to know which vessel it is.

We poke our heads into the gloomy interior of the plywood and corrugated iron shack, thinly disguised as an office and boat supply shop. Slowly our eyes adjust. Crowded, dusty shelves support paints, resins, fibreglass, shackles, chains, nuts, bolts, zincs, tools, mouse traps and a few mouse droppings. A cat snoozes in a coil of rope on the floor. Roger, the manager, sits behind a desk littered with stained invoices and old coffee cups, the telephone to his ear.

He drops the phone in its cradle and examines us. We must look incongruous. Robin, with his neatly-trimmed, brown hair and short beard, is dressed in grey pants and a white, short-sleeved shirt with the Caribbean Utilities Company (CUC) logo on the sleeve. He has a brightly-coloured bow tie—his personal trade mark. I'm wearing a summer dress suitable for the office, and sandals.

"You've come for the keys of the latest drug boat," Roger says in a rich Devonshire accent. I smile at him. Robin has obviously planned this meeting as a nice surprise for me. "Be careful," Roger continues, chuckling, "don't fall orf. We don't carry insurance for you, y'know!"

Outside, we squint from the brightness of the sandy yard and walk past the boats again. On our right are a couple of non-drug, long-term nautical inhabitants still waiting for work to be completed, long after money for restoration has run out. This time we walk further than before; past piles of rusting, corrugated iron, paint pots, old batteries, torn disposable overalls, cardboard and strips of paint-spattered masking tape. There's no end to the richness and diversity of the environment.

One man is spray-painting his boat. A cloud of spray hitch-hikes on the air and envelops us.

"Nothing toxic here." I smirk, but Robin's not listening.

"This is it!" His eyes are aflame as he points towards something the size of a dinosaur.

"My God! You've got to be kidding." We stand beneath it, dwarfed by the hull. The tip of the mahogany bowsprit at the front of the yacht is 4 metres above the ground. Orange streaks from rusty deck fittings stain the once-white hull and blue keel.

"What's it made of?" I ask, still stunned.

"Ferro cement."

"A concrete yacht! Won't that be a little heavy?"

"I'll have you know," replies Robin, "some very fine yachts have been made from ferro cement, especially in New Zealand."

Stepping away, I bend my head back as far I can to look at the masts. "My God!" I say again. My vocabulary is somewhat limited in times of stress. "How tall are those masts?" I feel a moment's unsteadiness as a small white cloud drifts past, giving me the impression the mast is slowly falling over. I put my hand out to touch Robin for support.

"The main mast is 18 metres," Robin is in his element, "the mizzen mast is only 12 metres. It's a ketch, you see."

I trail Robin round the vessel as he inspects the exterior. The stern is buried in a stand of mangrove trees and we have to fight our way through a tangle of scratching branches. A beautifully carved wooden nameplate spans the transom, showing the name and port of registry: *Cowes, Isle of Wight, England.*

"Uh-oh! I hope this is not an omen, Robin. You used to work in Cowes, Isle of Wight."

Robin continues with his own musings. "We'd have to re-register under the Cayman registry, of course. Let's find a ladder and go aboard."

The keys jingle in his hand as he searches the boatyard for a typical 'Caymanian' ladder—two 3-metre 2x4s with irregularly spaced pieces of wood nailed across, for steps. Whistling through his teeth, he leans the heavy construction against the hull, quickly climbs up and steps onto the deck. I follow, challenged by the wide spacing between the rungs and the need to clutch at my skirt.

Chained to the handrail at the stern is a rusty, fold-up bicycle that has seen better days. An ancient Zodiac inflatable dinghy wheezes its last breath as I poke its crumpled form with my foot. Interesting algae have colonized the puddles in the black fabric. I peer into the murky depths and can see squiggling creatures.

"The mosquito larvae like it here." I say, but Robin is busy.

"The equipment looks a bit grim, doesn't it?" I continue as I straighten up.

Against my better judgment, I'm beginning to feel a tiny bit interested in this leviathan and rather sad at the state of the gear.

Our tour of the deck starts on the starboard side. "Deck's recently been repainted," Rob observes, "and isn't it interesting that she has black masts."

"What's special about that?"

"They don't show up at night under searchlight; they're not so reflective as bright shiny aluminum if you're trying to avoid detection."

We step up 40 cm onto the upper deck, which forms the roof to the main cabins and to the midline of the yacht. The sails are still in place on the booms, but the black Sunbrella sail covers have chafed through where they are bound by rope lashings, exposing the sails to degrading sunlight. A couple of small heaps of guano on the deck indicate that some birds have found convenient roosts.

"They should have taken the sails off," Rob muses. "Hmmm. All the sail covers are black too!"

I stare up at the main mast again, towering aloft. "Hey Rob, it's got steps all the way up, can I climb it? There must be a heck of a view from up there."

"We're not doing any climbing before checking the state of the rigging wires supporting the masts," replies my ever-practical husband. "Anyway, you're wearing a dress."

At the bow, the anchor chain locker lid is set into the deck. Robin opens it and peers inside. "Lots of rusty anchor chain but no sign of an anchor."

"Come on!" I urge. "Let's look inside. I want to see what the accommodation is like."

"All in good time."

Robin continues his inspection, returning along the port side of the yacht. I should know by now, there's no way I can rush him, just because I want to satisfy my curiosity.

At the stern is the 'dog house' covering the deck steering station. It has a one-metre-diameter spoked wheel, bound in fine rope and finished with a Gordian knot (see Glossary for terms). It is superb craftsmanship—evidence of many hours at sea and much patience. Behind the wheel is a series of instruments I don't even ask about, for fear of a detailed description which will delay us.

"Shall I turn the wheel?" I'm eager to do something.

"Try it gently." Robin replies. "The rudder didn't look fouled when we were below, but you never know." I turn it as far as it will go to port, then to starboard and back to the middle.

"Three and a half turns each way," I report, "and the rudder is in midline position when the Gordian knot is at the top."

Hooray! At last he has completed his tour and inserts the key into the lock of the companionway cover. A couple of clicks release the lock and Rob pushes back the hatch top. He slides up the duck boards—which act in lieu of a hinged door to the interior of the vessel—and places them aside.

I can't explain it, but as I'm about to go inside, I feel a shift in my long-held negative opinion of boats. Not a tectonic shift, but a shift all the same.

Heat billows up from the interior accompanied by a strange, unpleasant smell—something mixed with diesel fumes.

"What's that?" I say, wrinkling my nose.

Robin is impervious to unworthy comments. Our eyes scan rapidly and eagerly as we cautiously step down the three-step ladder into the cockpit containing the inside steering station. Here there is a small traditional wooden wheel. The interior of the cabin is striking, crafted in polished mahogany; the bench seats on two sides look like church pews, although their royal-blue velvet seat cushions are tossed on top in an untidy pile.

"I love all this rich woodwork, it's really beautiful!" I say, as I run my hand along the silky contours.

Nautical charts and books of sailing instructions are strewn haphazardly on the chart table, with pens, pencils and scraps of paper everywhere. Cupboard doors hang open. A bundle of multicoloured electrical wires protrude from a control panel behind the chart table, like a bunch of tendons, veins and arteries left hanging, where equipment has been removed and the wires severed. A bicycle seat, flashlight, pop cans, tubs of bearing grease and a few baseball caps complete the scene.

"I guess it's too much to expect the drug police to put everything back in order when they've searched." I say.

Two steps down from the inner steering station is the galley and dining area. On the starboard side in the galley is a double stainless-steel sink, with crockery still in drying racks. There is a gimballed propane stove with pots and pans stored beneath. Above and behind the stove, small shelves are crammed with provisions: peanut butter, flour, cashews, parmesan cheese, herbs, salt, syrup, pancake mix, there's no end. Trails of food run everywhere, mixed with rodent droppings.

"Yuk, look at this," I say. On one of the counters a dirty fridge is bolted to the bulkhead.

Robin makes a brief inspection, not of the inside of the fridge, but of the back. "This is a special nautical fridge," he tells me, "it runs on either 12-volt batteries or bottled gas."

"Oh, perhaps we can clean it up, then." Opposite the fridge there's a new microwave oven set in mahogany surrounds. "This would be useful too," I say, this time to myself.

In the dining area across from the galley is a mahogany pedestal table fixed to the sole of the yacht. Set into the pedestal is a miniature mahogany door with antique brass fittings. This *Captain's locker* is stacked with partially full bottles of liquor—gin, vodka, rum, brandy and tequila.

"Hey, shall we have a drink?" I ask. "Maybe I could fix something to eat too if you're hungry. There's lots of food and we haven't had lunch yet."

Robin smiles indulgently and continues exploring. Moving forward, we find a single cabin on the starboard side. Sliding open the louvered wooden door reveals a comfortable-looking bunk, again finished in polished wood. A non-opening port light lets in the sunshine. Bedding and clothes are strewn on the bed and tumble onto the floor, books fill the shelves of the cork-lined walls and a goose-necked reading lamp sticks out over the bunk.

"Just imagine lying here reading when you're off watch—that would suit me." I say.

"OK. If you like that, wait till you see this." Robin says as he peers through a narrow open door opposite the single cabin. I squeeze past him and look in. A splendid turquoise half-bath claims pride of place, complete with a shower head. There's also a little stainless steel sink and a toilet. "Nothing but the best for you," he continues, "you can even have baths!"

"This is great! I'd thought life on board had to be Spartan, but I think I could handle this."

A few steps further and we are in the forward stateroom in the bow of the yacht. A double bunk fills the starboard side, with drawers and doors to storage space underneath and on the port side a tabletop and more storage. At the far end of the cabin is a child-sized door set 35 cm off the sole. I cautiously open the door and see coats and clothes hanging inside.

I lean into the locker, push the clothes aside and feel beyond. There's a 60- by 45-centimetre hole in the wall, into a further storage area, maybe it is the sail locker. If I climb in past the clothes, I wonder if I might find myself in the Narnia of my childhood.

I return to the present. Everywhere brass fittings and handles compliment the rich woodwork. "There was no expense spared when this was built. It's lovely."

We retrace our steps over the shiny, cork-tiled floors back up the two steps to the inner steering station. Robin lifts two large brass rings set into the floor and removes two floor sections, creating a 2- by 1.5-metre hole, revealing a massive new Volvo engine. He whistles, hops down into the 'engine room' and looks around. "Good God!" he says. "There's enough power here—165 horse power and it's turbocharged. I bet the drug-runners put this in so they could outrun the authorities."

While he is admiring the engine and checking the layout, I go towards the stern, past the steps that would return us to the deck, to the last area to explore. Two steps down, on the port side, is the louvered door of a wood-panelled two-piece bathroom. The toilet is set high up on a pedestal.

"Hey Robin, guess what? We've got a *real* throne in here! Why is it so high off the floor, with a step up to it?"

Robin peeps in. "Well if it weren't, it would be below sea level and the ocean would siphon into the yacht through the heads."

O.K., I'm not a nautical engineer, but it makes sense. I'm learning.

Together we gaze into a spectacular master stateroom spanning the stern of the yacht. Beneath the tangled mess of clothes, bedding and books, there is a large double bunk, with inset mahogany cupboards beneath, spilling out more books and sailing directions for many parts of the globe. There is also an upholstered seating area for five to six people and a large clothes closet. Two portholes on each side of the stateroom have little curtains to draw across when in port. It is all so charming, like a miniature house.

Am I beginning to get a warm fuzzy feeling already? Did I say *we've* got a real throne? This is ridiculous; no way could we afford to buy something like this under normal circumstances. Yet I start to picture it as our home. Settle down, I tell myself, this is a pipe dream and anyway, it won't belong to us.

Back on deck, I force myself to concentrate on a few areas of peeling paint and flaking varnish, and imagine all the renovation work that needs to be carried out.

"I suppose we'd better get back to work," I say as Robin re-secures the lock on the hatch. "We're really late."

He descends the ladder ahead of me, as a gentleman should. We take a last look from below, and then return the keys to Roger.

"Had a good look then, did you?" Roger is trying to gauge Robin's feelings but he's wasting his time. Robin's expression is not easily read.

"Yep," Rob answers, "thanks for letting us see her." Now it's Robin's turn to probe. "What sort of price do you think she'll go for at tender?"

"Ah well," Roger appears lost in thought for a moment, scratching his chin. He then throws out a preposterously high figure. I say nothing.

"And where are the anchors and radar?" Robin asks.

"That's a long story," says Roger, "I'll tell you when you're here another time."

We get back into the oven-hot car, turn on the air conditioning and head for town.

"What do you think?" Robin asks.

"Well, if you want to put in a really low bid and you can afford it, go ahead," I say, and put all thoughts of boats out of my mind.

Robin obviously does a lot more research and thinking than I do. Unlike me, he's not impulsive. A few days later, as we leave for work, he casually says, "Tomorrow's the deadline for the sealed bid for the yacht. I'm going to write a cheque for 10% of my bid price and take it down to the Government Offices today."

Is this what he really wants? Could I feel happy owning a boat? What a liability! Why am I even considering it? If I'm honest, I'm disturbed at the superior feeling it's giving me.

"OK," I say, "that's fine. Don't forget to be home in good time tonight. We're going out to dinner."

2

A Monstrous Christmas Gift

Thursday, December 20th rolls around and we're not prepared for Christmas. When it's hot and sunny all the time, it's difficult to get into the mood, even though our children have arrived for the Christmas holidays. I've taken the day off work, to do some baking.

"Can we borrow your truck and go diving?" Billy, our son aged 21, is up bright and early and has decided the order of the day. He is entering the Air Force as an officer, and while waiting for his call-up papers, has been working as a waiter in a restaurant in Waterloo, Ontario. Lisa, our daughter, and her boyfriend, Pete, both 22, have just arrived from university in Guelph, Ontario. With only a couple of weeks at their disposal, they need to put their days in Cayman to good use. Scuba diving in these beautiful waters is top priority for all of them.

Today is also decision day on the sealed bids for the yacht. We have money tied up in the bidding procedure, money which I could very well use for this Christmas season. I'd like to buy diving accessories for the kids. It's been niggling at the back of my mind, so at 10:00 a.m. I call the government office to see if we can pick up our deposit.

A lady with a sense of humour—a rare commodity among some government officers—answers the telephone and I explain my plight.

"Yes," she says, rustling through some papers, "I understand. There was a decision made this morning about the tenders. Just a minute and I'll check the file."

"Uh—no," she says, "you can't have your money returned."

"But it's Christmas!" I plead.

"Sorry, in fact you owe us money; your husband was the successful bidder. We need the balance of the funds by 31st December. You are also responsible for the Marina storage fees immediately. I hope you enjoy your yacht and your Christmas."

I know instantly that my life will never be the same. Where is a massive yacht going to fit into my world? The children are out, so I can't tell them the news. I'll just have to call Robin straight away.

"Hi Mags!" says Rob's voice at the other end of the line. "What's up?" I have his attention, as I rarely call him at work.

"Are you sitting down?" I ask, my heart thumping. "Get ready for a shock."

"What's the matter?"

"You're the owner of a huge yacht."

"Really?" Robin's voice rises an octave. "That's great!" He knows I wouldn't play a cruel joke on him.

I pitch the next question. "Does that mean that now we own the yacht and everything that is on it?"

"Yup—well, when we've paid the balance."

"Then we'd better get to the marina as soon as possible to tell Roger, before anything disappears from it, now it belongs to us," I say. It's never too soon for practicalities.

"You're right. I'll take a cheque to the government offices at lunch time and get home a soon as I can. We can go before it gets dark and then we can start inventorying it at the weekend." Now it's Robin who's racing ahead.

Against my better judgement, I'm excited. We suddenly belong to the 'yachting set,' a group of people I'd hitherto thought were rather overtly affluent. They, of course, won't know that we don't really belong in their bracket. Our new status could be hard to live up to.

Robin arrives home with a fistful of boat papers and we start sorting through them, piecing information together. When the kids come in an hour later they whoop, holler and dance around when we give them the news—they have a million questions. At 5:00 p.m. we're heading to the marina, crammed in our Nissan Patrol.

Roger, the manager, has already been notified that we're the new owners and has a bill prepared for the moorage fees. Sometimes he can be really on the ball. "You'll have some fun with her," he says knowingly, "just a bit of work to do."

We drive through the marina and pull in between two neighbouring boats.

"Which one is it?" the kids are impatient.

We walk up to our acquisition and pat her bulky cement hull. "This one!"

"Holy Shit!" says Billy, his eyes like archery targets.

"You're kidding!" says Lisa. "You don't even sail, Mum!"

"Wow, this is great!" Pete, who has the most sailing experience, is already assessing cruising possibilities.

Saturday can't come soon enough, so we can see what we have and start cleaning up. In fact, not everyone waits till Saturday. At supper on Friday, Billy admits that they've all been to the marina and climbed aboard to inspect everything possible without actually going inside.

I don't have to drag anyone out of bed in the morning. Breakfast is early, then boxes, garbage bags and all the cleaning materials we can lay our hands on are stuffed into Robin's car and my truck. I include notepads and pens for list making and the boys pack lunch and beer into coolers.

This is the first of hundreds of trips to the marina we'll be making over the next year.

It's another clear day and not yet too hot. On board, Lisa and I start with all the clothing, bed linen, towels and sundry rubbish. Stripping the beds and emptying all the closets and drawers, we create two massive piles. One is to throw away immediately and consists of unappealing items, like pillows, toiletries and underwear. The other pile is for 'launder then check,' including sheets, towels, blankets and good clothing, like T-shirts and shorts.

"You're not thinking of keeping any of that are you?" Billy is horrified when he sees our efforts. He wants nothing to do with it.

"Suit yourself." I tell him. Lisa and I can see the bargains that are to be had. So now we only need to share stuff between four of us, not five. The former crew really had good taste in designer casual wear.

Billy and Pete work on the noxious job of bagging and throwing out all the food. After running extension cables to the nearest power point, they use the yacht's shop-vac to suck up trails of flour, nuts, other packaged foods and, of course, the ubiquitous rodent droppings. Canned food gets tossed, as do all the half-full liquor bottles from the Captain's locker. It's a pretty disgusting job and although we've thrown open all the hatches, it's hotter than Hades inside. At least that's the excuse given for the copious amounts of beer being quaffed.

Robin is busy boxing up books, sailing directions, charts, tools, boat spares, rigging spares, engine spares, lifejackets—everything that will be useful to us in our new life. It all has to be transported home for assessment, logging and storage, to give us room to work in the yacht.

We've been hard at work all day and we still haven't emptied the interior. At dusk we head home to get cleaned up.

"Anyone for a gin and tonic?" Pete offers to mix us a drink to sip while we're getting showered and dressed to go out for a celebratory dinner at a Mexican restaurant. The table talk accompanying our Coronas and enchiladas is, 'the sailing adventures we will have.' Funny how we've managed to embrace a new life, just like that.

Sunday finds us eagerly returning to the Marina and Robin and the boys take the sails off the booms and pack them. As befits a heavy vessel weighing 36,000 kg (40 tonnes) the sails are correspondingly large, heavy and difficult to handle. Lisa and I soldier on below decks.

"What's that gluey smell?" Lisa asks when we're poking around in the forward cabin.

"It's what gave away the crew," I say, "and perhaps what saved the yacht from being totally wrecked by the drug squad. In Panama, an artificial dividing wall was built in the sail locker in the bow. The drugs were loaded through a hole cut in the deck into the concealed compartment. The hole in the deck was filled in and painted over and they made a panel to hide an access hole at the back of this closet. They glued on thick cork tiles to match the lining of the hull, to disguise the entrance. Amazing that we can still smell the contact cement, isn't it?"

Lisa frowns. "What happens if we find any more drugs?"

"I don't think we will. Drug dogs have been over the entire yacht, but if we do find anything, then we hand it in. If there is any more, I certainly hope we find it here in Cayman and not when we're entering another port."

"It's not funny, Mum."

"It was certainly quite a haul and somebody put a lot of money and effort into making this a drug-boat, what with the huge engine and repainting the waterline."

"What do you mean repainting the waterline?"

"Oh, didn't Rob show you? Come outside and have a look."

We climb out of the confines of the yacht and down the Caymanian ladder, glad of a break and some air.

"Come here you guys!" Lisa shouts to Pete and Billy, "Look at this."

It is clearly visible. The waterline at the bow was repainted about 20 cm higher than the natural waterline and slants back to rejoin the original about 4 metres towards the stern. Even thick applications of antifouling paint haven't fully disguised it.

"This way it wouldn't be immediately obvious that the yacht was nose-heavy," says Robin. "With 900 kilos of cocaine in the bow, it substantially alters how she sits in the water."

"They certainly tried to think of everything," says Pete.

"Yeah, but I guess they were too cocky, believing the Cayman authorities were naive," Billy chips in, "they obviously didn't do their homework. I imagine every boat coming directly here from Panama gets the third degree."

At the end of an exhausting day, most of the interior and the deck lockers are now empty. Our house and carport are filled with boxes and gear, all smelling of diesel fumes. It's hard to believe all this stuff fitted on the yacht.

In the evening, after a take-away supper of some particularly fine Jamaican jerk chicken, we sit around with beers, musing over the day's activities.

"So who actually were the crew?" The kids are keen for the full story.

"Well," I say, repeating some of the history Robin has researched and information we've gained from newspaper reports, "as far as we know, they were all Americans from Florida. Two fellows and one girl: the captain, Kevin Shawn McNulty; Alfredo Carmona and Frances Fox. They posed as friends out cruising. Hence the womanly touches, like the artificial flower displays, pretty curtains and wall paper on some walls, which were intended to lend an innocuous air to the ship's complement."

Robin takes a drink of beer and continues the tale. "The girl, Frances, tried to say she didn't know what was going on and only found out when the drugs were loaded in one of the San Blas Islands and she could do nothing about it because she was not in control. Judge Harre didn't wear that. He said that it defied belief that a crew member would be recruited in a haphazard fashion without some confirmation of the crew member's commitment to the enterprise."

"Where did they get the yacht from?" asks Pete.

"We're not sure of that yet," says Robin.

"How did they actually get caught?" Pete continues.

"There's more than one story going around about that," replies Robin. "One was that the authorities had a tip-off from somewhere, another is that the harbourmaster on duty was suspicious of the way the yacht was sitting in the water, and a third was that the customs officers boarding the vessel had a drug dog with them that marched smartly to the forward locker and just sat there. The officers could smell contact cement, from the recently glued cork tiles. The last theory was that the captain, in return for a break, owned up and told them what drugs they were carrying and where they were."

"There was probably a bit of truth in all the stories," I add.

"So what happened to them, where are they now?" Lisa asks.

"They went to court, were tried and convicted of drug-smuggling," continues Robin. "Judge Harre sentenced them all to 11 years with no parole, for possession with intent to supply 900 kilos of cocaine."

"They're here right now, just up the road in Northwood Prison," I add, "probably having a ball. Northwood is affectionately called a holiday home. It's fairly well populated and every weekend families go to visit their nearest and dearest and have a bit of a party."

"Well who stole all the equipment off the yacht when it was in the Marina?" asks Billy, frowning, "they had no right."

"The marina gave us a copy of the initial inventory so we know we've lost radios, radar, another dinghy, outboard motor and anchors," says Robin. "But it's really rather funny. Several months ago, the police launch went out through the North Sound passage. As you know, the passage has a severe dog-leg in the middle and the marker lights aren't anything too special. When the launch returned, it missed one of the outer marker buoys and powered in over the reef. Well, it didn't get far as it blasted right up on top of the coral and sat there, for all to see.

"They were embarrassed, naturally, so radioed to someone to come and pull them off the reef immediately before they became the laughing stock of the island. Now there is minimal tidal difference in Cayman, perhaps 30 to 40 cm, and it was low tide. Instead of waiting for the tide at its height, a cable was hooked to the launch and it was dragged off, lacerating the hull. As soon as it cleared the reef it sank in the channel, in 6 metres of water. Not good for the electronic equipment."

I take up the story. "Apparently the Brits gave them a new launch but there was no money in the budget for fancy electronic equipment. Then along came the drug boat with all her gear and the local wharf rats swarmed her and stripped off all the electronics, together with anything else they fancied. They rationalized that the yacht belonged to the government, so it was OK."

"How could they do that?" Billy thumps his beer down on the table. He has a strong sense of ethics and has a hard time believing that people in authority can manipulate the circumstances to make dishonesty appear honest.

"Quite easily," says Robin, shuffling some leaflets he's been looking at on his lap, "they have ultimate power. We know exactly what's been taken, of course, because of the yacht inventory. This is why we've spent two days removing everything from the yacht, except the standby generator and that's chained down. The really amusing thing is," he continues, holding out the handful of papers to Billy, "we have all the instructions and installation diagrams."

"So what happened to all the cocaine?" Lisa asks.

"Ah ha," says Robin, "officially, it was all taken to the municipal dump and burned in front of the MLAs, the Governor of the Island and select invited guests."

"They must have been as high as kites if they were standing downwind," says Pete, "and unofficially?"

"It's rumoured that some found its way back onto the streets. With such huge sums involved, it must have been very tempting. I don't suppose we'll ever really know."

"It may not seem much like Christmas," adds Pete, "but this has got to be the best Christmas present you guys have ever had!"

"Let's hope you're right." I say.

3
Marina Rats and Other Low Life

Christmas is over. Lisa and Pete have reluctantly returned to Guelph and we throw ourselves energetically into our task. We have persuaded Billy to stay and work for us on the yacht, rather than return to wait tables in Canada and sleep on the floor of a friend's apartment. We get the better part of the deal as we have such a lot to do and he is a willing worker.

One disadvantage to having the boat on land is that we're not the only ones who can board the vessel. We are host to a legion of cockroaches, one of the creatures I most dislike. I set down a batch of roach-bait cans under stairs, inside lockers, under the sinks and in the engine compartment and hope for the best. Unfortunately, they're not our only uninvited guests. While searching in a locker for some rags to use, I come across a fluffy nest with tiny babies snuggled inside.

"Robin, quick, come and look, I've found the sweetest little black mice in a nest!"

"Black mice?" Robin rushes to where I'm standing admiring the little ones curled together like chubby punctuation marks. "Don't touch them, they're not black mice, they're baby rats." He quickly pulls on some thick work gloves, grabs the nest and takes it down into the bush and despatches the young.

"That's bad news," he grumbles, "it means there's a mother somewhere and you know how quickly these things reproduce."

We think no more about it for a week or two, until one Saturday morning we arrive and throw back the hatch cover and are met by a disgusting smell.

"What the hell is that?" I ask, sniffing around.

"Something's decomposing." Rob frowns in disgust. "I wonder if it's a rat?"

"It reminds me of that putrefied turtle we had in Libya." says Bill. "You know, you brought the dead one home from the beach and put it inside the front gate and thought the ants would clean it up. People used to cross the street rather than walk by."

We split up and start checking lockers and storage areas.

"I've found it!" I say, looking into the locker which housed the baby rats in their nest. "God, it stinks."

"Here it is!" I can hear Robin's muffled voice coming from the stern heads.

"There's one in the bilge." Billy brings his great news.

In total we find four decomposing bodies, but it is a mystery as to why they died. We didn't set any traps or rat bait. Perhaps they ate the cockroach bait, or ate the cockroaches which had eaten the bait. Either way, we're glad they're dead. All we have to do is get rid of the lingering smell. A few days later, instead of improving, the smell is getting worse. We rip out all the floors of the cupboards and remove the heavy, insulated covers to expose the engine.

"I thought so," says Billy, who has volunteered to jam himself in the engine compartment to check. "I can see another body under the Volvo." He scoops it up with rubber-gloved hands, drops it into a bag then continues searching with his flash lamp. I can't take the stench any more and have to rush out on deck before I lose my stomach contents. Soon Bill emerges and he's retching.

"Oh God," he says, "I've found another one, but I'm not sure I can reach it. I have to press my face right up against the engine and I'll have to pull it out at eye level with a hook. Something like a scuba tank J-rod would be good."

Robin finds a suitable hook and poor Billy disappears once more in the bowels of the yacht. Some time later he re-emerges with a foul-smelling polythene bag.

"The worst thing was, Mum," he explains, "when I hooked into it I pulled the head off and I could only tease out little bits of putrid meat and fur and limbs, it was so friable. Then I had to check it to see if I'd got it all." He always did rather like biology at university. The 7th and final rat is located in a locker on the deck. Now we well understand the origin of the phrase I can smell a rat.

We clear out all roach bait and decide to bring 'TP' (Tropical Pussycat) to live on board, to act as the RRCO—Resident Rodent Control Officer. Despite our concerns that she might run away, she settles in well and immerses herself in her job.

Our first official visitors are Chris and Nik van den Bok, my bosses at Caribbean Publishing Company, complete with a video camera for the 'before' record. They are the start of a long list of visitors intrigued with the yacht, its history and our ambitious restoration schedule. It's amazing how they can watch us work and happily join us in a beer or glass of wine, without feeling the slightest urge to pick up a tool and scrape! It's a pleasure to see them all and to know they're interested.

The Marina is a blend of fascinating characters. The qualifications for working here are various, including a desire for a slow pace of life; the ability to drink Old Milwaukee for breakfast, lunch and dinner; preparedness to use ancient unguarded equipment in the machinery shed; adeptness with such things as oxyacetylene and, above all, an irrepressible sense of humour.

Rudi, a well-muscled, shy 'Honduranian,' lives aboard a little vessel by the harbour wall with his girlfriend. They have no running water or sanitation. He works for Roger and also for himself, on the side, in order to save money to send back to his wife and children in Honduras. His burnished brown skin is complimented by the gleaming, chunky gold chains circling his bull neck and the gold glinting in his smile. Rudi is one of the few who saves Old Milwaukee for supper, probably because his girlfriend provides him with plenty of real calories in the shape of food. She also always keeps him dressed in neatly-pressed khaki shirt and pants.

Rudi performs many tasks around the Marina. In fact he's a skilled craftsman in numerous areas. He drives the Travelift to haul boats into and out of the water and we've seen him in the bush, oxyacetylene torch in hand, converting an old fridge side into a hood for his car. One day while I'm at work, Billy is toiling inside the galley on a thankless task, trying to chip unsavoury one-inch ceramic tiles and grout from the walls and counter surfaces. Without warning he is pitched off his feet and the yacht is rocking, as if in the grips of a major earthquake.

He rushes on deck as the yacht continues to pitch violently and sees the Travelift on the starboard side. He races forward shouting, "Stop! Stop! Stop!"

Rudi has snagged the bowsprit side-stay with the Travelift and is frantically shifting from forward to reverse in a desperate attempt to free himself, oblivious to the fact that someone is on board. He almost falls out of his driving seat with fright when he sees Bill.

"What the hell do you think you're doing?" Billy shouts.

Rudi sits shamefaced, admitting defeat, then together they devise a plan to extricate the Travelift from the side stay.

"God, Mum!" Billy says when I arrive after work, "I thought he was going to pull us off the chocks. Come and look, I think he's cracked the bowsprit. This crack wasn't here before was it?"

The bowsprit, formed from a one-piece slab of mahogany, measures 30 cm wide, 10 cm thick and 4 metres long. It has a crack running from the side stay attachment to the pulpit attachment.

"No, it's a new crack—it's pink inside, not weathered, so it's newly exposed wood. We'd better report it to Roger."

I exert a little friendly pressure and Roger humours us and comes to see. Billy is looking like thunder.

"Nooh, not our responsibility," attempts Roger after rubbing a well-practiced thumb over it, "it's an old crack."

"I don't think so," I say calmly, "if you look closely the crack is pink and there's no flaking of varnish along the crack line. We'll expect to be reimbursed for the replacement."

Roger bristles.

"That bow sprit supports the self-furling jib, which acts as the forestay for the main mast," I continue, although he knows this perfectly well, but probably hopes I don't. "If the bow sprit breaks we'll be dismasted."

Roger mumbles something about coming to an agreement.

"Yes, we will." I state firmly.

The situation is defused. "Don't worry Bill, they'll pay for it, but we really don't need the extra work. We'll have to import a piece of mahogany."

Rudi remains sheepish and aloof when we see him, but we continue to be friendly. He's a nice guy—an intriguing part of our neighbourhood.

Work moves along slowly on the longest and worst job of all, scraping off the old blue anti-fouling bottom paint, centimetre by centimetre, metre by metre. It's a soul-destroying task, as all the little dimples and dents in the ferro hull must have individual attention. We wear overalls, gloves and face masks, but still the toxic dust covers us. For weeks our bath and shower water is cobalt blue. Billy toils on, with intermittent help from Robin and me.

A constant joy for Bill at the Marina are the puppies. A bitch has found it a safe place to give birth. As soon as they are big enough, every day they greet Billy ecstatically. They romp and play, are cuddled and cradled and sleep in the shade of the hull while he works. They pull the power cable around like a snake, run off with paintbrushes and sandpaper—every mischief they can devise.

Two months into our restoration, Billy receives his call-up papers. He and I make a trip to Miami, Florida to shop for everything he needs and all too soon he has gone. We'll miss the hundreds of hours of work, like those spent on the hull and the galley; the painstaking sanding of all the paint from the mahogany portholes and rub-strips and, of course, ridding us of the rats. All the nastiest jobs he tackled happily, often in the suffocating heat and without complaint.

Things are quiet around the house and yacht for a couple of weeks and we have to readjust to our extended workload. There's no more night-diving for me either now Billy's gone. Others in the Marina miss him too. The growing puppies rush to greet the truck, but wander off when Billy doesn't get out.

Not all the visitors we receive in the Marina are known to us. One Saturday, Rob is happily installing a new Northern Lights standby generator and I'm busy mixing some of the two-part Philadelphia Blue resin that we're using to coat the ferro-cement keel, for good protection. I can only mix up two tablespoons at a time, because the temperature is a lot higher than 21°C and the mix cures in about 15 minutes. Applying it with a scraper, I can cover a 30-centimetre square before it chemically hardens. Our keel is 85 square metres, so I have many days' work ahead of me.

The mix is just ready when a large man with a Dutch accent comes along and starts to chat. I excuse myself and continue with my task for a few minutes. Our visitor, a minister of religion, has a disturbing request.

"I'm a prison visitor," he tells us, "and I regularly visit the captain of this vessel at Northwood Prison."

We're shocked. What on earth is he doing here?

"Captain McNulty has asked me to bring you a message. He would like you to visit him in prison."

I feel as if I've been doused with a bucket of cold water. What possible reason could he have for wanting to see us?

The minister asks us to consider the request and let him know the answer. He then walks away, leaving us staring at each other in disbelief.

"Is this legitimate, or sinister?" I say. "Do you suppose he's going to tell us about more drugs?"

"I'll think about it," says Robin, "but I don't like the sound of it. How suspicious is it going to look if we go to visit the captain of the drug boat that we've just bought?"

The weeks rush by and Robin ticks the jobs off his long list: renew electrical wiring; overhaul the engine; recast the rear portion of the keel and remove a fake waste-handling system. I reupholster all the sitting areas, including cutting new seat cushions and mattresses from foam. I sew matching curtains, mend worn sail covers and make new ones. I also repair sails, using the Sailrite sewing machine we ship in from Miami.

Robin checks the rigging minutely, laboriously washes it all with acid and replaces a couple of turnbuckles. Now it is safe to climb the steps of the masts. What a wonderful view we have when we stand 23 metres above the ground at the top of the main mast! North Sound in one direction and across the island to the sea at South Sound.

If we have any energy left after supper in the evenings, I sort and catalogue the multitude of charts we have and Robin sorts through batches of papers. Gradually we piece together parts of the jigsaw of the yacht's history and also start planning our own first cruise across the South Pacific. It's all a game for me—we'll never actually do it.

"Well, it looks as if the yacht has been all round the world, but not with the three crew members who are in Northwood Prison." Robin tells me. "There are all sorts of papers from before their time. The yacht was built in the UK in 1978, and cruised round the world with a family on board. I think it was stolen in the Indian Ocean."

"What happens if the original owners ever find out and want the yacht back—are they the legal owners, or are we?"

"I wouldn't worry too much about that," he says, "we have legal title to it from the Cayman Government. Anyway, I would think if they had any insurance, they've long ago claimed the insurance money. I'm more concerned whether she'll be recognized in Panama. It is a singular design. Maybe the people who went to the trouble of making it suitable for drug-running will want it back and take it by force. The area's riddled with pirates."

It's fascinating unravelling the mystery, but I don't want to entertain the idea of being caught by an irate drug lord.

One evening Robin brings a large roll of paper into the living room and carefully opens it on the floor. It measures 4 by 2 metres.

"What's this?" I scrutinize the white markings on the dark blue paper.

Rob is grinning. "It's the blueprint of the boat's hull framing! We are the happy owners of a New Zealand-designed Hartley Tahitian, only this blueprint is of the 13.7-metre version and ours is a stretch model. It's nice to know what make she is."

A few days later, the minister turns up again and I can't say we welcome him wholeheartedly. He repeats the request, yet he won't tell us why the captain wants to see us. We had put it out of our minds, but now that he has reintroduced the topic, we are feeling distinctly uncomfortable about the whole thing. I wish he would just leave us alone. Robin politely asks him not to bother us again, but we can't help wondering what is going on. It will be good when we move away from the marina.

This Saturday is a milestone for us. We have finished the preparation of the hull and are ready to start applying the white epoxy top coat. The two parts must be mixed together well, poured into a tray and quickly applied with rollers, before the paint cures. It is incredibly sticky. Robin is more successful at applying it than I am, possibly because it takes such a lot of muscle power to overcome the friction, in order to get it on the hull. The temperature is far too high and curing is too rapid, but we have no choice but to continue. So I mix and Robin applies. By the end of the day we think we've done well on the first side. It looks superb.

On Sunday morning we are keen to look at the results of our handiwork and walk round to the port side of the yacht.

"Oh no!" I have to bite my lip to stop it trembling. The hull is sporting a rash of bubbles. "Oh Robin, what's happened?"

Robin's shoulders droop. He inspects one of the blisters. "I'm not sure; it seems as if it's cured on the outside but not on the inside. I don't know if it's temperature and humidity related, or whether it wasn't perfectly prepped underneath."

There are more than a hundred small blisters, over an area of about two square metres.

"We'll just have to scrape them off, fill the holes, rub them down and repaint," he says.

It's a laborious, disheartening job, but thankfully, the rest of the paint looks great. Subsequent coats go on without a hitch, so the bubbles remain a mystery. During the painting I only once drop the whole tray of paint. Robin glances down from his painting position on the scaffolding, says nothing then returns to his task. It is an atrocious mess to clean up.

During the many hours I spend working alone on the hull while Robin is at work, I often have the benefit of advice from Emile. He's a tall Romanian Canadian with curly grey hair and is the sign-writer in the boatyard. He also knows everything about all aspects of boat building and repair and freely shares his opinion. I admit that my knowledge is inferior to everyone in the marina—I'm not a sailor or a boat-builder—so I'm easy prey for do-gooders. I really do like hearing the opinions of others on the job at hand, but once Emile starts talking, there's no stopping him. At first I listen with rapt attention, but after fifteen minutes or so, I have to make my excuses and continue with my work.

Funnily enough, he never bothers Robin. Emile does give me a compliment one day though, when he says I'm the 'hardest workingest woman he's ever seen.'

Mostly, the marina workers let me get on with my business—I'm allowed to use any of the tools and equipment in the big sheds. It is a constant battle, though, to keep the use of the large oil drums and planks, or the scaffolding for the few days of hull painting. Often our first chore of the day is to round it all up before we can start.

Mr. Miller, a dour, elderly gentleman well over 70, is the antifouling painter on many of the vessels. I can see him from the corner of my eye, watching me work without making comment as I apply masking tape for the thin grey stripes I want on the white hull just above the waterline.

Centimetre by centimetre, I pull out the tape and stick it to the hull, making sure I follow the original line. Mr. Miller can't tolerate watching any longer. He strides over and without a word snatches the masking tape out of my hands, unravels it in an expansive gesture, strides about six metres along the hull and slaps it on.

"You can't do it bit by bit," he spits out and promptly stomps off leaving me to continue. He's never spoken to me before and has never said a word since. But, as I say, I like advice.

It is November 1991, and we have completed the major tasks necessary before we leave the marina and hit the water. As well as the boat work, we have to pack up and leave our rental house so the landlord can move back in. This time we're renting an apartment at Governor's Harbour because it has a dock where we can berth our 36,000 kg gem. It will be wonderful to have the yacht right outside our patio doors, so we can spend even more time working on her, without all the travelling.

The new bowsprit is finally being installed and bolted through the ferro cement, using two kilos of special caulk to seal it to the deck. We've renamed the yacht Orca after the whales around the west coast of Canada, as she is black and white, bulky and of a similar shape to a killer whale.

She is now registered on the Cayman registry and proudly flies the Cayman flag from the mahogany and brass flagpole at the stern. Emile does a superb job of sign-writing Orca on port and starboard bows in black, and Orca George Town CI on the transom in black and gold lettering. He adds the gold as a gift for me. It looks magnificent!

Robin has re-commissioned the engine and it is running smoothly. All that is left before launching is to apply the antifouling paint.

"Shall I call the Police and ask for the equipment back that they took from Orca?" I ask Robin. We have spent so much money so far, it would be good if we could get back the radios and radar.

"Yes, why not, it can't hurt."

"Good Morning," I say positively when I'm put through to the right police department. "My name is Maggi Ansell. I wonder if you remember the drug boat that went to auction last December?"

"Yes."

"You remember the accident with the police launch on the reef and a lot of the equipment was commandeered from the drug boat to furnish the new launch?"

"Yes."

"Well. we now own the yacht. Did you ever install any of the equipment of the new launch?"

"No." He's not being very forthcoming.

"So, as we have all the installation diagrams and operation manuals for the equipment, I wonder if we could have it back?"

I hear a chuckle at the end of the line, before he answers.

"No."

There's not much more to say, but I say it anyway. "Well, if you change your mind, this is my telephone number and we could come to the police warehouse and pick it up."

I never receive that call, but one police officer does come to the marina and gives us something very valuable. It is a picture of the unloading of the drugs with the hundreds of colourful waxed packages being pulled from their hiding place and stacked on the quay.

4

Launch Parties and New Docks

Launch Day! How we've longed for this. Monday 23 December 1991, just one year after we acquired the yacht. Our bowsprit negotiations with Roger come to a satisfactory conclusion when he deducts $800 from our final bill for marina fees, so we are happy. It is such a momentous time that we organize a party.

Invitations go out to friends and acquaintances who have visited us at the marina during the year and cheerfully watched our progress. Robin takes the day off to get things ready. I'm detailed to be in charge of bringing the 'bar' and food in the back of my Patrol.

At noon our friends arrive. A lot of Robin's colleagues at CUC have contacted me in advance to see if I will lend them bowties without Robin's knowledge. We have a hasty bowtie-tying session before they present themselves. One or two end up looking more like aeroplane propellers, but the intent of support is there. Robin is so involved with Orca and the tasks at hand that I'm not sure he recognizes they are wearing his 'signature ties' until much later.

The Travelift is positioned round the yacht and the giant strops secured under her belly. Four or five friends are on board with Robin, to man the fenders and throw mooring ropes. The rest of us watch, drink and take photos. With Roger in the driving seat—this trip is too important to trust to Rudi—the strops are tightened, the last chocks knocked away and a cheer goes up from the onlookers.

"Wagons roll!" Orca, at the upper end of the weight range for the Travelift, slowly progresses across the boatyard to the launching slip. Cautiously, Roger positions the lift straddling the slipway—there are only a few centimetres to spare on either side and he doesn't want an unscheduled entry into the water, especially with an audience. Peering out from the middle of the drinking crowd, I watch Orca lowered into the water, my fingers at my mouth, while the others continue with their partying.

Orca is floating free of the strops. Robin rushes from cabin to cabin below decks, to check that no water is entering though any of the stopcocks, but all is well and he returns topside, to oversee the mooring. The Travelift backs away and willing hands receive the mooring lines thrown from the deck and snug them up on the bollards on the dock.

I initiate the ritual of 'blessing' the vessel with champagne, spraying it over the hull, rather than smashing the bottle. I then leap aboard and fling my arms round Robin.

"We're floating, we're floating!" is all I can manage. Robin is grinning like an idiot, too overcome to say anything. It will be impossible for others to imagine how happy he is feeling, but I know. Designated bar tenders go into action opening bottles of Champagne—or whatever is the preferred tipple—for everyone to join in a toast. Our glasses are constantly refilled.

It's time for everyone to clamber on board and tour the interior. Food and drink are flowing freely, in every sense of the word and several people don't bother to return to work. Those who do have had a much-extended lunch hour. Heck, it's Christmas Eve tomorrow! People are lounging on the seats, making expansive gestures and slopping wine onto my new upholstery, but I'm too excited to care.

Some of the revellers drift away, leaving the stalwart. Robin, by this time being well fortified and deservedly relaxed, is ready to try the motoring capabilities of Orca. He offers them a trip, fires up the engine and motors a short way inland along the canal. It's a short way, because the canal becomes shallower and with a big 'clunk' Orca connects with an infamous rock. Nonplussed, our fearless captain executes a multiple-point turn in a restricted width of canal, testing the forward and reverse gears and finally moors in our appointed slot along the canal wall.

Orca is allowed to stay here for the next two weeks, to await the extraordinarily high tide we'll need to get over the extensive sandbar in North Sound, about one nautical mile from the entrance to the marina. It offers less than 1.8 metres of clearance at high tide. Although the difference between Cayman's tides is only a matter of 30 to 40 cm, a high tide will be invaluable as Orca has a 2.1-metre draft. The benefit to waiting is that it will provide us with a wonderful excuse for a full-blown party.

On 4th January, 1992, we arrive at the marina early. Our dock at Governor's Harbour is already decorated with black and white balloons, black and white streamers and tables set out under sun shades. The food is organized, drinks are on ice. We have boxes of black T-shirts and white T-shirts printed for the occasion with Orca Launch Crew. For us, it's a once-in-a-lifetime occasion.

Seven of our yacht club sailing friends act as 'launch crew' on board, and Robin's boss, Bruce, has offered to use his powerboat North Star to act as a support vessel. We arrange with him that if necessary, he'll take the end of our spinnaker halyard, motor off and use it to pull us over about 30° to reduce our draft. Our new neighbour at Governor's Harbour offers to bring his triple-decker, 14-metre sport fishing vessel, so if necessary he can rush up and down creating a huge wash to help lift us over the bar! Who are we to turn down offers of help?

At the marina Robin is even quieter than usual, checking out the systems and preparing everything for our epic voyage.

"Ok, I guess this is it," he murmurs.

Uncharacteristically, I'm too nervous to say anything at all. I flit from place to place ineffectually. Fortunately, our crew is so experienced they just get on with the job at hand. Lines are cast off and slowly we glide along the canal. Everything is going well as we approach the sandbar. At the first sign of drag, Robin uses full power and Orca dredges her way through the top layers of sand. Looking astern, we can see it churning in our wake. Robin continually checks the instruments for signs that the engine is overheating, but after a few minutes we break free and shortly the elevated engine temperature drops and we're clear.

"Hooray!" We whoop and cheer and holler and I break out the champagne—the rest will be plain sailing, or rather plain motoring. We only have 6 nautical miles to go across the sound to Governor's Harbour and our crew take turns helming.

This day ranks amongst the happiest of our lives. Months and months of hard work have paid off—we not only own a yacht, it is watertight too! Only 13 months ago, we had never heard of a ferro-cement drug boat. I should never doubt Robin's determination and ability to complete a project. I love him so much for his strength of character. I hope I'll be an asset to him.

Our voyage is uneventful. Guests are arriving for the party on the dock and for the second time in two weeks Robin and I are floating with happiness. Orca has come home. The afternoon passes in a blur of food and drink and happy chatter peppered with advice and sailing stories from those who have gone before.

Once the excitement has passed, we realize there's still much to be accomplished before we are ready to start voyaging. One of the first jobs is to re-attach the self-furling gear which had to be disconnected for Orca to fit into the Travelift. The mounting point is way out on the end of the bowsprit.

Before we start, Robin asks, "Have you got the pin?"

"Yep," I say, patting the breast pocket of my shirt, "it's right here."

First we drag the heavy self-furling drum as close as possible to the required position and tie it off to the pulpit. Robin then grunts and heaves and grunts some more to get it perfectly lined up. I lean over the pulpit to get close to his ear, to give some advice.

"Plop!" My mouth falls open as I experimentally feel my breast pocket, hoping the pin is still there. It is a fruitless task, as I know it has dropped into the water and sunk without a trace in the silt below.

"Oh God! You haven't dropped the pin have you?" snarls Robin.

I try to think of an excuse for my carelessness, but none comes quickly to mind.

"I'm sorry," I say, with tears threatening, "it just slipped out."

"Bloody stupid place to put it, wasn't it?"

"Yes. Well next time, do the job yourself, if you're so clever."

I leave the battle area, distressed, but the pin is etched in my mind. I have a sneaking suspicion that I've seen a second pin with the boat spares we inherited; it's just a matter of locating it. I find the pin and we install it together—it's an impossible task to complete alone. This time it goes without a hitch and all is forgiven. I immediately order another spare from the manufacturers.

We happily slip into the routine of office work and boat work. One task I've set myself is to keep up with varnishing the dozens of metres of brightwork. To this end I buy gallons of varnish and in some places achieve nineteen coats. It looks magnificent. But nothing is safe from the relentless Caribbean sun which destroys hours of hard labour with ease. At first, I inspect the mahogany minutely every week and sand down and touch up as necessary, but it becomes evident that this will take the rest of my working life. There has to be a better way.

"What can I do to protect the woodwork?" I idly ask Robin one day.

"Why don't you cover it?" Simply said, but expensive and time consuming. So I order a whole bolt of grey Sunbrella from Miami and make patterns for covering everything made from wood. It turns out to be a 'work in progress' for the next four years, as I have a multitude of other chores. I start by making covers for the highly-varnished wooden pods for the winches and the tops of the deck hatches. The downside, however, is that we only get to see the beautiful woodwork when we're actually sailing and the covers are off.

Just after we arrive at Governor's Harbour, we notice a couple on a yacht anchored some way off our dock among the few other boats moored there. We've watched them several times, rowing ashore in their dinghy and walking off. One evening we hail them and ask them to join us on board for a drink and snacks. Steve and Susie are from Australia—seasoned sailors in Trochus, an 8-metre Vega. After a few meetings with this delightful and knowledgeable couple, we offer the use of our rented facilities for laundry and showers, but they remain fiercely independent.

A trip to Miami gives us a respite from responsibilities. We visit boat shows, chart shops and boat chandlers; we buy gear, books, charts and storm sails and, my favourite, a hand-held GPS. We never once get near a regular mall—those days are over. In the evenings we visit Jazz Clubs for some cool relaxation.

Back at the dock, when Steve and Susie offer, we gratefully accept their help to reinstall the unwieldy sails—any advice they like to give is thoroughly welcome. We spend several hours working together and enjoying a few beers.

A calm day is needed to install the self-furling genoa which has just been returned from Miami with its new sacrificial Sunbrella edge—a 40-cm wide strip of ultraviolet-resistant material which will, when the sail is furled, prevent exposure to the sun. It rolls up smoothly, without a trace of sail showing anywhere. We also re-install the fully battened mainsail and flake it onto the boom. It is the first and last time the sail flakes in such a beautiful conformation.

One day, Robin arrives home from work with some news.

"There is an article in the newspaper," he says, "Orca's captain, Kevin McNaulty, has had his sentence reduced from 11 to 9 years."

"What? Why would that be?"

"He appealed his sentence, apparently, and because he had fully cooperated with authorities, it was reduced. Judge Harre wants other drug-runners to learn that if they are helpful, they will get lighter sentences."

This opens up an old wound. Any mention of the drug runners induces a visceral response in me.

"It makes me wonder what he wanted with us," I say, "whether it would have had any bearing on the case."

While we are in Governor's Harbour, I have my first boat accident. I trip when stepping aboard and my right leg slips between the dock wall and the concrete hull. It is at this moment that the wind decides to blow, pinning my thigh to the dock. I crawl back onto the dock and inside the house. I haven't broken any bones but it turns out that my thigh muscle has been squashed and the sheath split. It is excruciatingly painful but I recover in a couple of weeks without anything more serious than an odd-shaped thigh muscle.

"You've got to be more careful," Robin warns me, "we can't have you injuring yourself when we're sailing."

Oh, yes, I think, we're supposed to be going sailing.

Robin is attending a course on celestial navigation run by our local yacht club and has booked me on the next course. We must know how to navigate using a sextant and the positions of the heavenly bodies. I borrow numerous library books, to learn the theoretical side of all things sailing. I even read from cover to cover, Adlard Coles' book Heavy Weather Sailing. What a chilling read it is! Little do I realize that I'll be writing Chapter 26 for the fifth Edition.

We've only been a few months in the townhouse at Governor's Harbour when our landlord wants to sell the property. Once again we will have to move and find somewhere to moor Orca and Spirit of Carmanagh. Being the good citizen that I am, I offer to show prospective clients around, to save him employing a real estate agent—who knows, maybe he'll share the commission he would have had to pay.

I should have had it in writing. I do a good selling job to some prospective clients who buy the property but the landlord is not parting with any cash, not even a bit off our rent. I guess that's what one expects from a wealthy old boy.

Skinflint that he is, he cycles from his house to the townhouse to check the hydro meter monthly and gives us a handwritten bill, rather than go to the expense of putting the hydro meter in the name of renters.

We broadcast to friends and colleagues that we are looking for a home. One of our yacht club members owns a lot on a canal in North Sound Estates and we view it, undeveloped and secluded. The lot is full of stately casuarina trees.

"It will be perfect, I love it!" I say.

"Yes, it's great, isn't it? We'll have to hire someone to build a dock and erect a shed for a sail locker and storage area."

I can't imagine what we did with our time before the yacht. This business is taking over the whole of our lives.

We agree with the landlord to cut short our rental to allow the purchasers to move in and will leave in July, 1992.

"But where are we going to stay when we leave here and put Orca on her own dock?" I naively ask Robin.

He gives me a penetrating look. "We'll live on Orca, of course."

"But she's not ready."

"Whether she's ready or not, we're going to live on her in July."

It is at this point that I admit I've only been pretending we're going sailing. I love working on the yacht, restoring her beauty, I love the parties, the attention of our friends and she will make an enchanting miniature home, but are we really going long-distance sailing?

Preparations have suddenly become serious and focussed. I start to plan things like storage of food and clothes and try to imagine waking, showering, breakfasting and leaving for work from Orca. It is more difficult than I like to admit.

~~~~~

MAGGI ANSELL

www.ingramcontent.com/pod-product-compliance
Lightning Source LLC
Chambersburg PA
CBHW061011280326
41935CB00009B/924